MANAGING HUMAN DEVELOPMENT

MANAGING HUMAN DEVELOPMENT

MANU N KULKARNI

GYAN

GYAN PUBLISHING HOUSE

NEW DELHI-110002

Manging Human Development

Rs. 720

ISBN: 81-212-0960-9

Published in 2007 in India by
Gyan Publishing House
5, Ansari Road, Darya Ganj,
New Delhi-110002
Phones : 23282060, 23261060
Fax : 011-23285914
E-mail: books@gyanbooks.com
Website: www.gyanbooks.com

Lasser Type Setting by: Rudra Computer Graphics, Delhi
Printed at : Salasar Imaging System, Delhi

Contents

Foreword

With a long career in research, administration, and training at the international, national and state levels, and in civil society institutions, Dr. M.N. Kulkarni has amassed a wealth of experience and valuable insights in various aspects of economic and social development. In the following essays he has discussed the basic issues which impinge on the welfare of common man: the issues of health, education and governance. His intimate knowledge of the functioning of the development initiatives at various levels has enabled him to give convincing account of what has gone wrong in our delivery systems and how to correct the maladies. The discussion centers round the impact which various measures in these areas have made, and are making, on the lives of the common man; one who works and toils in the dust.

His major concern, and where he has considerable expertise, is the issues related to health. In a number of essays on this theme Dr. Kulkarni has given an account of the sorry state of various health-related programs, and suggested ways to improve upon the existing situation. He highlights three main lessons in this regard. Firstly, in a country like ours health issues have to be treated in a compaign mode, centered around the community's welfare. In the second place, he emphasizes that such campaigns should be made "inclusive," i.e., covering, especially, those sections who are deprived of access to not only the private medical facilities but are also denied the public facilities. The third lesson he draws is that we should respect the field level health workers and empower them to carry on their tasks in effective ways. If they are treated properly there is every reason to hope that several among them - as the case of the Needle and Tea shop suggests - would bypass the hurdles, innovate and deliver the services to really deserving people. A negative view of the ground level health workers is not likely to help.

The writings in the second section of the book are mainly focussed on the Girls and Women. An important message the author gives is to emphasize the role of prospective mothers. According to him our concern should not only be the health of women but also the health of the infant which is impacted by the health of the mother. The second point which he emphasizes is that the poor children, especially girls, can be helped, whether they are victims of child labour or child prostitution, if beginning is made by helping the parents. And this can not be done by legislation alone. The state has greater responsibility for the development of the deprived children - boys and girls - than merely enacting legislation.

On empowerment of girl child he emphasizes two major initiatives. These include a massive program of girls' education, and raising their age of marriage. These measures more than any other program he rightly asserts, will result in the empowerment of women, and will enable them to play a constructive role in the society. To achieve the objective of gender equity he emphasizes both the short term and the long-term measures. With his intimate knowledge of the field conditions his suggestions have a ring of credibility. In order to buttress his propositions he has given several examples from the field.

Next to Health and Women Empowerment his major concern is the state of Education, especially primary and elementary education. Dr. Kulkarni has made an important point in his writings on education that there are several factors responsible in achieving true objective of children's education and each one has to be looked into. The principal elements of the system are: teachers, their qualification and dedications; school and its environment; parents and environment at home; the learning level of the child. None of these can be ignored if the objective is "quality education" to the children. His reference to the approach of Tagore and Gandhi provides another element of the successful education system, namely closeness to nature. By bringing schools closer to nature and making them more attractive place to learn will help in imparting meaningful education at the elementary level. Though emphasizing different elements he ascribes pivotal role to the teacher who, as he graphicaly puts, is more than a “black board operator”.

In the section on Food, Feeding, Water and Hygiene his message is loud and clear. For ensuring universal food security, it is important that the basic responsibility should be entrusted to panchayats. Involvement of panchayat can synergise various efforts to ensure larger production of food and its equitable distribution. Similarly, empowerment of women, more than any other measure, can accelerate the rate of reduction of mal-nutrition.

He rightly emphasizes the importance of water conservation in every part of the country, and underlines involvement of people in such efforts. He cites the example of the peoples movement for rainwater harvesting in Madhya Pradesh as an example. With the rich experience in our country, he maintains, for launching the programs of land and water conservation one need not go to the World Bank for advice, or even for resources. Peoples own wisdom can ensure conservation of natural resources in most economic manner.

It is heartening to note that Dr. Kulkarni does not hesitate to raise issues which for one reason or other are swept under the carpet. An excellent example is the article titled “The Right to Defecate.” Provisions of latrines is not only a sanitary measure, it is also an instrument of women empowerment. Conspicuous absence of latrines, especially in the villages, make the women the main sufferers. In this respect he has followed the plea of late Kamala Choudhary who also made the provision of latrines in villages and towns a key element in any movement of women empowerment. Woman who defecate in public losses her dignity, a fact which need to be understood and appreciated.

An equally important characteristic of his writings is the courageous and bold ways in which he can raise the issues which acquire status of ‘holy cows’ in some influential sections. An excellent example is his treatment of the issue of compulsory iodization of salt, an issue on which many Gandhian workers have registered their dissent. He has given unqualified support to the government measure to make iodization of salt compulsory. However, in order to ensure that it does not add to the financial burden on the poor, he has suggested iodization at the production stage. This is one example of his taking a bold stand on issues of health, education and civil liberty.

Another example is his views on the current practice of involving teachers in mid-day meal preparation. He has given convincing reasons to conclude that such involvement instead of helping the cause of education is likely to be harmful. He takes similar courageous, and unconventional, stand in other areas, for example, while pleading for breast-feeding. What makes his arguments quite convincing is not only the empathy and the "feel" for the people whom he consider his main audience but also a thorough technical knowledge of all aspects of a problem he deals with.

In the section on Governance and the Civil Society, Dr. Kulkarni brings to bear his very intimate and practical knowledge in these areas. This, together with his acquaintance with the literature and practices in other countries has enabled him to raise substantive issues of governance as well as the role of civil society at ideological as well as practical level.

A theme which recurs again and again not only in these two sections but throughout the book is his emphasis on strengthening the Panchayat Raj Institutions. He maintains that only by strengthening these institution we can hope to solve some of the vexatious problems in governance. Being a realist he is equally concerned that unless more resources are devolved to Panchayati Raj Institutions, and they have an access to modem knowledge in the areas they are dealing with, we cannot expect tangible results from these institutions. Strengthening human resources in PRI segment not only involves periodical training of the Panchayat Raj functionaries but a more dependable support by subject matter specialists, by the 'Think Tanks' as he calls them.

While dealing with the public programs he emphasizes the "social marketing" aspect of these programmes, in the absence of such an approach the developmental programs are likely to remain dormant. He finds that strong PRI are necessary for citizens' empowerment as much as for country's development. In one of the papers he posed the question: if in China local bodies could help in accelerating the pace of industrialization, why not local bodies in India?

Coming to the NGO's sector he advocates NGOs role as a bridge between government and local communities. He classifies NGOs in a few major categories, i.e. those whose main function is advocacy, those who act mainly as agents for development, and those who experiment with alternative ways of doing things. He reports several examples of the institutions which are able to carry out all these functions effectively. On the question of the resources for the Panchayats he not only advocates development of higher resources to these bodies, also advocates that PR should use their ingenuity in raising more resources. An interesting suggestion offered by Dr. Kulkarni is that a 'local development fund' may be given to the Panchayat Leaders on lines of the "Local Development Fund" given to MLAs and MPs. He traces the global thinking on the role of NGOs, and documents different steps taken by the United Nations and other international organizations to make use of these agencies for their programmes. If we wish to take the programs closer to the people not only these institutions should be fully involved but their style of functioning should also be people friendly.

His writings in the section on Technology also reflects his deep concerns for the people. It is reflected in the title of this section, "Emerging Technology For Whom?" He fully appreciates developments in modem technology, but is equally concerned about the "technological divide" between haves and have-nots. He has given several examples, especially in the field of pharmaceutical industry and IT industry, to establish the point that merely following the path set by the western countries is not likely to lead us to our destination. The practical way in which he looks into the problems of technology is amply illustrated by his discussion on GM seeds. He discusses issues such as; to what extent we should go in pursuing GM Technologies, how do we regulate these technologies, how do we provide an element of crop insurance to mitigate the risk farmer is likely to take. While discussing modem technologies he pleads for cautions and the takes a pragmatic view and is not going to the extremes, as some NGOs have done, but has taken a realistic stand, based on field level experience.

These writings are truly eye opener in several respects. The author is underestimating his contribution when he mentions that these are reflection of someone working at the "dust level". These are very insightful pieces, full of practical wisdom. It was a pleasure to read Dr. Kulkarni's writings, and equally a pleasure to recommend these to all those who are concerned with the basic problems of human development not only in some macro sense but at the ground level. The book is for the people who are willing to learn from dust as the author has certainly done.

Padma Bhusan Prof. Vijay Sankar Vyas

Jaipur
20 May, 2006

Prologue

These are the thoughts of a pedestrian development worker who worked with the Agents of Development (State and International) in the dust and fields across India and other countries and observed how most ordinary people react and respond, participate and withdraw in human development programmes which directly affect them. They do it all the time either with despondency or jubilation. Over the years 1960 to 1998 I traveled over the length and breadth of the country and the world from Kashmir to Kanyakumari and from Assam to Amritsar and from Ghana to Afghanistan, Copenhagen to Cape Comorin not just as a Job holder of UNICEF and the Government of Karnataka but more in the pursuit of development work. These thoughts have sprung up from the joys and sorrows of the people whom this author went on observing, ruminating over the schemes and Yojanas of the State, why and how projects and programmes fail and succeed, analyzing and articulating through the media and Professional Platforms and expressing them from time to time sometimes breaking protocols and civil service conduct rules.

As I read back and forth these articles published in Economic Political Weekly, Economic Times, Times of India, Indian Express, Deccan Herald, M.P. Chronicle, Tribune, Humanscape, Down to Earth, Mainstream and Manushi the ideas and thoughts come out as topical and current as they were some thirty years ago. In fact they assume more importance as we enter the new global order. Issues of child labour, child and women abuse and poverty and malnutrition and health for the urban and rural poor continue to baffle International Aid Agencies and Soveirgn States in the new

Millennium. So we have Millennium Development Goals reiterating the old Goals and highlighting the unfulfilled promises of the leaders of the World thus reflecting on the poor Development leadership of the Politicians around the World. These issues of human development and well-being keep popping up from time to time and the development Planners and implementers all the time put forward excuses why they could not achieve what they promised. The blame game goes on and on and the people express their anger in the polls the only time when the poor exercise their powers. The sheen and shine of the Government at the time will go away and the new leaders come up to proclaim the same old goals of removing poverty and providing jobs, till they are again thrown out by the voters for non-fulfilling their promises. In India this has been going on since India declared its tryst with destiny in 1947.

These thoughts also reflect the good and the bad times when they were written. The poignant and tense times this author witnessed was in Punjab during the Eighties when he Worked as UNICEF Representative for the States of the Punjab, Haryana and Himachal Pradesh between 1985 to 1991, when Punjab witnessed the worst times. I cannot but recall the emotional poem of Harbhajan Singh when the Deputy. Inspector General of Police Mr. A.S. Atwal was shot dead near the Golden Temple in Amritsar.

"The whole world beholds my agony
Four sides and Four ages echo my
cries Something unthinkable has
happened at thy abode.
Sift religion from irreligion.
Thy deori is besmeared
Pray wash it clean.

Prabhji know thyself
Treat not thy own man as other
To slay him in thy home

On my lips is thy blissful name
In hands rests thy Prashad,
An attack from behind slays thy man
Thy holy and truthful tank stands as witness

So does the doorway where I fall
Who shall go to for appeal?

But I am a refugee seeking succor
At thy Darbar
You are my Anchor and Protector
A Source of all my hopes
Shield thy own man
Snap not the ties of faith"

I was shielded in Punjab no doubt by the Spirit of Prabhji. It was a winter night some where near Ludhiana I was returning to Chandigarh from the field trip and it was almost midnight when four young men with AK 47 stopped my UNICEF white Peugeot and my Sikh driver Jasbir Singh stopped the car and the boys asked about me and I got down to plead with the smart young boys and started uttering in fear "this car belongs to Children, (They did not understand the acronym UNICEF) and we save the lives of kids and mothers by providing them polio drops, measles and tetanus vaccines". One of the boys questioned me whether I am doing Nash Bandhi work I flatly said No. The boys felt that I am doing good work and one of them said. "If you ever do Nash Bandhi we will kill you because we need more Sikhs for Khalistan and advised my driver not to go further as there is danger to us and asked us to return to Ludhiana and halt there.

In every nook and corner of Punjab, I drove in the midst of fear and terror to see how our vaccines and cold chain worked and how the Government Auxiliary Nurse Midwives protected the young mothers and new borns from vaccine preventable diseases. Vaccines and needles saved my life and the lives of many children of Punjab. The Auxiliary Nurse Midwives of the Punjab Health Department and many Rotary friends organized polio days and I termed them as Needle Brigade. In Mandi Gobindgarh near Patiala, in sleek Maruti cars, kids were brought for immunization by the Rotarians and given Jacha-Bacha Cards after the polio drops. Punjab, then was a region of contrast - fear of bullets and the joy of polio drops went together.

These are the thoughts which pay tribute to the most ordinary folks; who run the Sarkari Yojanas, the most ordinary men and women who deliver the services to the people of India. Thousands of Nurse Midwives, thousands of Agricultural Extension workers , thousands of school teachers, thousands of village accountants, across the length and breadth of the Country, keep the wheels of government moving in good times and bad times, in summer and winter, in disasters and peace times, in rainy and dry days. They lack. advanced knowledge and skills but they know how to innovate, if they want, and they also know how not to do it if they do not want to do it. Somewhere in the Shivalik Hills, in a hot summer when the temperature was 40 degree centigrade, I landed in the Government Health Sub Centre and it was housed in a thatched roof and the ANM Nirmala Devi was busy getting the kids to start her immunization session. When I asked her how will she sterilize the needles because without sterilization these are not safe and I did not see any stove. She smiled and took me to a tea shop opposite the Sub Centre and said, "This Bhai sterilizes all the needles in his stove and gives me back and then I use them to prick the kids. When I asked the tea shop owner, will you do it free of charge or you charge for it, he said, Sir, these are my village kids and I am doing this as service to them to save their lives.

This is innovation and customer relationship management and call it by any name the fact remains that Niramala Devi has done her work without stove and without kerosene and she did not give an excuse that Government has not supplied the stove and the kerosene. This is how the story of "Needles and Tea Shops" in this Book, captures the innovative work of the Nurse Midwife Niramala Devi.

There are many Nirmala Devis in India and they are the movers and shakers of India. And if at all India shines it is because of them and not because of our politicians or bureaucrats, planners or policy analysts, aid agency specialists or activists.

Women's issues need not be the concern only of women and feminist groups in the country. One woman activist dubbed me as Male Feminist and the most agonizing moment for me was to see many girls sexually abused, women and mothers suffering from the problems of water, sanitation, privacy for defecation and hunger and malnutrition, safe delivery practices, across the length and breadth of the country. I keep repeating the smart conversation between a young Collector in MP and Prince Charles of UK, who was once visiting Kanha National Park in MP. It was late in the evening, when hordes of women squatting on the road side for defecation got up when the car lights flashed on the road. The Prince asked the young Collector why these women are getting up and the young Collector coolly said, "Sir they were all waiting for your arrival and now they got up to greet you". This is how our smart bureaucracy protects the image of India but does nothing to these unfortunate women. My one piece "Right to Defecate" which appeared in Manushi - the women's journal edited by fire brand Madhu Kishwar, is still relevant and in many parts of the country, women suffer a great deal on this count.

Policies, politicians, people - are the three legs of democratic governance in India.This author over the years, observed very closely, many Chief Ministers and Ministers and interacted with them for advancing the cause of landless in the villages, women, mothers and children in the course of his four decades of development work. Late Jim Grant head of UNICEF under whose inspiration this author worked, kept telling the statesmen and politicians of the World that saving lives of children, mothers and women is good politics and good economics. All politicians are well intentioned but they need to be constantly goaded not just with *ideas* but with *tactics and strategies,* which they understand. Very often development specialists end up not doing that. Once I had arranged a photo session for bringing out a poster on Polio Eradication campaign in Haryana and the then Chief Minister, late Devi Lal ji was to administer a polio drop to a Haryanvi newborn for that photo. When he was given a drop he was not aware where to put it and Whispered to the child, "beta ankh kholo' (child open your eyes). Suddenly I had to tell him Sir, polio has to be dropped in the mouth and not in the eyes. And then he asked the mother of the kid to get the mouth opened. At that time late Devi Lal ji had some eye infection and he was putting lot of drops in his eyes! Perhaps, he thought that polio drops were also to be put in eyes. This is narrated not with the intention of berating Devi Lal ji but highlighting the need for development workers for constant advocacy with the politicians of all ranks with knowledge and tactics for putting them into action. The Chief Minister of H.P.

Mr. Veerabhadra Singh was in tears when he saw the UNICEF film on iodine deficiency disorders in Kangra Valley of Himachal and he moved the Government to fight this biggest micro nutrient disorders affecting the children of Himachal with great vigor. The Chief Minster of M.P. Mr. Digvijay Singh, was a champion of governance through Panchayti Raj and his tenure in M.P. saw the birth of new generation of Panchayat women who were "Learning to Rule" at the grassroots for the first time. The issues of governance at the grassroots are still relevant and all the dreams of empowering the Gram Sabhas and Gram Panchayats have been eluded despite the proud declaration of politicians of all hues and shades. Late Chief Minister Dev Raj Urs, the "Pipe Man" of Karnataka was a champion of the land to the tiller and propounded the theory of "one man one profession". His tenure in Karnataka saw the emergence of land tillers and tenants becoming land owners and brought dignity to the tiller of the land.

Many of the thoughts in this collection, have captured not just the programmes then implemented, but also reflect on the policies of the State, International Development Agencies and Civil Society groups. Civil Society Groups claim that they are nearer to people, where the action is, and in the long run, they can only experiment and show how the programmes can be implemented more efficiently and perhaps honestly, but they cannot scale up. Many Partnership Programmes with Civil Society groups have been experimented but are not brought to "scale". Even the much acclaimed Joint Forest Management has shown many problems of conflict and stress, between the forest dweller, the forest departments and the NGOs. There is love-hate relationship between the State and the Civil Society groups and in this process people become the victims. With more and more Corporates taking up the social responsibility and keep talking about triple bottom lines (Profits, People and the Planet) the boundaries between civil society, the corporates and the State are getting blurred. Triple bottom lines can also mean triple partnership between State, Civil Society and the Corporates. The new Millennium would witness the shifting of roles between all these partners.

We are moving into the digital century and many emerging technologies affecting life and living are emerging fast. But what has been the impact of these technologies and who benefits from these, are the issues that are not only hotly debated but also pushed into the lives of farmers, consumers, patients and the people. Instead of fighting diseases, some drug companies have discovered diseases to fit their drugs. Some thoughts have been shared in this book on these technologies, which would have far reaching effects on the people at large in the coming decades.

In the timeless fellowship of human spirit, these "thoughts from the dust" have emerged over the years and they would continue to bother the policy makers, the politicians and the people at large.

Acknowledgements

It has been said that behind every successful person there is one elemantary truth. Somewhere, someway, someone cared about their growth and development. I am not a successful man but a happy man who got so much love affection and inspiration which has sustainded me to keep talking and understanding the mysteries of the most ordinary human beings. I always took delight in talking to taxi drivers in any part of the world, cruise boys on the high seas, room boys in hotels and so on, because I learnt a lot from them. I have over the years, learnt a great deal from vegetable vendors, fruit and flower sellers. school teachers, forest guards and village accountants, Nurse Midwives, village mothers. I owe them all my deep sense of gratitude to understand the realities of life.

In sixties, the Bombay School of Economics was a center for many young people to make a career in the field of commerce, economics and civil services, I was lucky to get inspired to think analytically in whatever job I did from my guru, Prof Vijay Shankar Vyas, who was not only my teacher but has remained till to date as my mentor and well wisher. Late Editor Sachin Chaudhuri of Economics Weekly and late Krishna Raj, his successor in Economic and Political Weekly, were the ones who shaped me to write with an eye on the "forgotten". Padma Prakash, former Dy Editor of the Economic and Political Weekly and the present Editor, C Rammanohar Reddy, have continued to encourage me to write as the Sepical Correspondent of EPW, the most prestigious Development Journal in the world. I feel not only great but also privileged.

My wife Vijayalaxmi, and my children Sanjay and Pammi who are my colsest link with time, kept on pestering me to bring out these Thoughts in this Book and my thanks to them for their "filial" persistance. When alone, my Pomerarian pet Jimmy, kept my morale high to pen down words from time to time.

I thank Sunita Narain Editor of Down to Earth, K.N. Shanta Kumar Editor and AVS Namboodri, Associate Editor and Janaki Murali Assistant Editor of Deccan Herald who have supported my thoughts from time to time in their edit pages and columns.

I owe a sense of gratitude to B.P. Garg and Amit Garg of Gyan Publishing House who first asked me to write a book on child survival but ended up in bringing out.

Manu N Kulkarni

1

Saving Lives and Promoting Good Health

Public interest advertising, social marketing of health messages to men, women and children are emerging as a profitable business for ad agencies. Although social legislation has not succeeded in banishing social evils like dowry, bride burning, child marriage and prostitution the question now is can marketing of social laws like suppression of immoral traffic, antidowry laws, help to eradicate these evils? Like social *adalats,* can marketing help to hasten the process of improving public health awareness and pave the way for changing health and behaviour of the people? We hear about advertisement warfare to win customer loyalties. Can such social advertisement warfare help to change the behaviour pattern of large number of the poor public to adopt health technologies which are low cost and high value added?

The bulk of the poor (audience) are illiterate, malnourished, without much access to basic services like protected water and sanitation, health and education and organised employment. Their purchasing power is poor. It is they who constitute our reproductive age group who produce more children and also face the worst forms of morbidity, malnutrition and mortality. They cannot 'read', they can only 'hear' and 'see', What they see cannot be purchased (fancy products like shampoo, detergents, pressure cookers, hot foods etc.) These products are beyond their reach. They want clean water, they want to know how not to approach doctors for their ailments, which are generally curable at their own level. They do not need cat scan, ultra voilet rays for their ailing limbs and heart transplant facilities, which are needed mostly for the rich. They need ideas which are doable and not products which are beyond the reach of their purchasing power. Unfortunately ad agencies are good in *product* marketing and not in marketing of *ideas.* How then will we reach our client audience?

We have various media - the print, the folk (inter-personal) audio, video, TV and the most important radio. The folk (traditional) and the radio are *nearest* to these poor households both in the urban slums and rural hutments and the messages are transmitted much faster through radio and folk media. The radio is still considered by the poor in Maharashtra as the Listening Goddess - who cannot be seen but whose voice can be heard.

Information to the poor generally passes through in a zig zag and horizontal fashion. Most of our electronic mass media - like TV, the press/print/ad messages transfer information in a *vertical* fashion. The information to the deprived families (both in rural and urban slums) somewhat moves in the *horizontal* and non-linear fashion.

Complexity of the audience mind does not allow the capturing of the message instantaneously. It takes time to know, to accept, and then to practice. What is known is not accepted and what is accepted is not practiced. Most of our health message marketing is based on the naive assumption that there exists a knowledge gap among the poor and hence just sell the message with an attractive logo and brand name. Then the knowledge (information) will be accepted and practised automatically. But this never happens. Even the most sophisticated and . literate audience, despite the awareness of the statutory warning "Smoking is injurious to health", do not give up smoking easily.

The information transfer among the poor household takes place through indirect mechanisms like gossip among men in tea and bidi shops and gossip sessions of the women when they gather around a village well, pond, bathing ghats, and temples. The health matters affecting poor women like pregnancy, maternity, child spacing, family planning are not talked about openly. When public health advertisement makes such information "open" a sense of shyness and distrust is shown by these poor women and the "closeness" of information is lost.

Unfortunately *glasnost* does not work when it comes to information sharing on private health! Private health is not like DDT spraying for malaria eradication. The chances of private health information sharing are better when it is shared through informal gossip sessions, interpersonal communication, folk media or street theatre. Commercial Ads cannot penetrate the antenna of the poor and the deprived.

Another problem of marketing health information is what is called "relatedness". Unlike product marketing (e.g. shampoo or soap) where related questions are few, the consumer has many related questions to ask when it comes to social marketing. When a message like "pinch of salt and scoop of sugar can save the life of infant with diarrhoea" is thrown open, at one stroke, a series of questions and doubts arise in the mind of the poor mother. What if there is no sugar, can gur or jaggery do, boiled water or any water, how much water, how many times the dose/drink, how long, at what frequency, and so on. All such related questions cannot be answered by commerical or public interest ads or campaign. They can at best be *discussed* face to face with a health worker or interpersonally talked over. Unfortunately our medical fraternity has not been very receptive to pass on minimum health knowledge to their clients, lest they loose them for ever! The ad agencies have a difficult task of capturing the health promoting knowledge from medical establishments and converting that knowledge into *information* in a form and content, which can be easily understood, accepted and practiced by poor people.

Marketing Nirodh is not the same as marketing good health. The former is a product and the latter is an idea. A relative concept. Health is a function of so many ifs and buts. It is not a tool or a technique but an end product by itself. It is easy to position a product, but when it comes to positioning an idea, the traditional marketing agencies, attuned to product marketing, find it difficult

Health among the poor is not a basic felt need. Till they fall sick they are not concerned with disease curing or health" promoting practices. For a poor family the next meal is their concern. In such a situation "messages on malnutrition, blindness, anaemia, are meaningless. Positioning, therefore is out of context. Selling good health is no doubt important but how to do it is the question. Commercial Ads, social marketing theories are simplistic techniques for capturing the complex audience mind of the poor.

Health for all by-2000 A.D. has been accepted as an integral strategy of national development plans in most of the developing countries. The Government of India has adopted a National Health Policy which seeks to usher in health revolution based on health practices which are affordable and workable by a large section of the population. WHO and UNICEF, the two major international agencies, connected with the health of the people of the world, have declared that health revolution is possible if there is political will, particularly in the nations where high death rates and low incomes have contributed to the miseries of the poor. In particular, UNICEF 1984 report on the State of the World's Children has made significant pointers to the need for and the prospects of ushering in Child Health Revolution based on existing affordable health technologies and health practices which are easy to practise even by the poorest of the poor family. Women (mothers) and children constitute nearly half the population in India and their health cuts at the root of the health of the nation (people).

Is this revolution possible in India, and what are lessons of the Green Revolution efforts in the country which could be used to spearhead such a revolution by mothers since children are a part of mother's life and living? Rural women did play a significant role in Indid's Green Revolution. Are there any parallels between agricultural production strategies pursued in the fifties and sixties which culminated in what has been termed Green Revolution in the seventies, and Child Health Revolution which is now being talked about?

The preamble of the charter of WHO says, "Health is a state of complete physical, mental and social well-being and not merely the absence of disease or infirmity". Roots of a successful health revolution have to be traced, therefore, to development strategies which have "enabled" the capturing or attainment of physical, mental and social well-being by a majority of the people, in whatever measure. Green Revolution in India, by all available evidence, did contribute to the attainment, despite its uneven gains, of physical (agricultural) and social well-being of the farming families in the country. Therefore, it is appropriate to search for "clues", if any, in the Green Revolution strategy which our country pioneered through the decades 1960-75, which would help to usher in Child Health Revolution.

India's food crisis, aggravated by the drought of late 50s, led to the initiation of a Community Development Programme for transforming traditional values of people, creating suitable institutional and administrative infrastructure, raising the efficiency of production, generating additional employment and providing social services, amenities and welfare. However, the CD programme did not boost agricultural production to any marked extent. The Government of India's Report on India's Food Crisis and steps to meet it (1959) advocated a target of 110 million tons for 1965-66, the last year of the Third Plan. Such a food crisis could only be met, the Report said, by increasing food production if "an all-out emergency food production programme is undertaken and adequate resources are made available." Recognising that India was a large country and no blanket programme could fit all areas and situations, the team suggested that "improvement programmes" should be tailored to fit the conditions faced by individual cultivators, village by village, block by block and area by area.

Being confident that rapid increase in food production was possible if known improvements were adopted in effective combination, the team recommended that improvement programmes should be designed on the adoption of combination of practices.

Finally, the team drew attention to the need to create a high level authority to allocate resources on a priority basis to co-ordinate various inputs and to enforce decisions giving priority to food production. Food crisis report was accepted by a high-level Inter-Ministry Committee in 1959 and this led to the initiation of pilot projects in selected areas having favourable conditions for maximizing production. This strategy also found its entry in the Third Plan (1961) which concluded that "whatever is physically practicable should be made financially possible and the potential of each area should be developed to the utmost extent possible.

This was the raison d'etre of the Intensive Agricultural District Programme (IADP), which was the precursor of the Green Revolution in India. IADP was initially taken up in seven States, namely, Thanjavur (Tamilnadu). West Godavari (AP), Shahabad (Bihar), Rajpur (MP), Aligarh (UP), Ludhiana (Punjab) and Pali (Rajasthan). Between 1962-64, IADP has expanded to cover ten additional districts and parts of districts. All these districts were known for "potentialities" for quick food production covering paddy and wheat. The major objectives of IADP were:

- To demonstrate, in pilot districts, the most effective ways of expanding national food production;
- To increase the income of the cultivator and his family;
- To increase the economic resources and potential of the villages; and
- To provide an adequate agricultural base for more rapid economic development and social betterment.

In order to achieve these objectives, the strategy was worked out carefully to produce results at the farm/family level. One of the major planks of the IADP was to *evolve* and popularize a "package of practices" and *facilitate* their adoption at the farm level. These practices were based on carefully tested seed variety (seed technology), right combination of inputs at the right time and at right place, and the provision of complementary support services like storage, processing and marketing. This package of practices was tested for cost and productivity through services of on-farm demonstrations which were called Adaptive Research Trials. Constraints on input supplies were totally removed by "saturating" inputs in the selected districts.

Another hallmark of the strategy was the creation of nucleus of functionaries at the district level exclusively meant for this programme, that is, project officers and a few subject-matter specialists under the overall leadership of District Collectors. Unlike the CD structure, where the BDO was the co-ordinator, the IADP structure entrusted the District Collector as the Chief Executive of the programme and this was a crucial innovation for the success of the programme, since the collectors were able to use their power and prestige for ushering in agricultural production revolution by effective coordination of all inputs, logistics and complementary support-systems. At the State and Central levels similar coordinating roles were fixed on Chief Secretaries, Directors of Agriculture and Union Secretary with a Central Ministerial Committee presided over by Union Minister of Agriculture. (It is worth recalling here how former Food Minister C. Subramaniam played a dynamic role in India's food self-sufficiency and food security). The real breakthrough, in yield was possible, not by supplies, but by *seed technology,* particularly the high-yielding variety of paddy (Karuna, Padma IR-8, etc.) and wheat (Sonalika, etc.). Wheat seed research in Punjab Agricultural University at ludhiana and paddy research through Adaptive Research Trials in Thanjavur continuously tried out genetically improved variety of seeds duly tested on farm conditions for wider adoption. There is considerable evidence now that small farmers adopted HYV seeds almost on par with the large farmers, or even better (M. Prahladachar, *Income Distribution Effects of the Green Revolution in India: A Review of Empirical Evidence World Development* (November 1983).

In Ludhiana, Mexican Wheat production (HYV) rose by 78 per cent from 1958-61 to 1961-65. In East Godavari the paddy yields (IR-8, TNI) registered an increase of 17 to 19 per cent as compared with the control plots. In Thanjavur paddy yields on treated plots increased by about one-fourth and in some cases, the gains were well over 40 per cent.

It was estimated that for each additional rupee spent on the package of practices, the return to the cultivator was Rs. 2.62. ADT-27 variety of paddy was acclaimed as the "seed of destiny" and "heavenly god" and it presented the opportunity to convert most of the single-cropped area into double-cropped one. This "mass conversion" was unprecedented. Those small farmers who adopted ADT-27 did so without access to assured water from supplementary minor irrigation works and achieved yields ranging from 50 to 200 per cent over the earlier years.

Thus the Indian small and medium farmers pioneered such a Green Revolution; and in paddy cultivation, role of women, particularly nursery raising and transplanting was crucial. Given the appropriate and affordable technology with right coordination of facilities and services by the development bureaucracy, India's farming people demonstrated that they can respond to the challenge of food self-sufficiency.

CAN SUCH a challenge be accepted by Indian rural mothers to usher in Child Health Revolution? What are the strategic choices involved in such a revolution? Are there any compulsions, like the food famine, which would prompt the rural mothers to pave the way for Child Health Revolution? Is there an affordable and acceptable technology which could be easily adopted by the rural poor-mothers? Are there any package of health practices which could be adopted without much of investments by rural families? What precisely is the role of development bureaucracy of the state in Child Health Revolution? Are there any 'clues' in Green Revolution which could be seen as possible approaches for initiating Child Health Revolution?

The major partners in Child Health Revolution are the rural mothers, particularly those belonging to the landless and assetless categories whose purchasing power is meagre, and they are caught in the vicious circle of poverty, low ihcome, more children, high mortality and morbidities leading to low productivity, low wages, low incomes and thus the vicious circle continues. In Green Revolution (GR) the strategy was maximum production at less cost. In Child Health Revolution (CHR) the strategy is one of low infant mortality, better protection from diseases, better family and environmental support and a good preparation for life.

In GR the state had to provide a massive investment on generation of seed technology (HYV), demonstration of that technology and its profitability through package of practices so that the acceptance of that' technology was made easy. Secondly, the state machinery, particularly the District Collectorate, was given clear clear-cut responsibility, accountability and authority to produce results (increased production); agronomists, credit specialists, water management specialists, extension specialists and seed technologist of the Agriculture Department were to work under the leadership of the District Collector.

In CHR, there is need to identify leadership at the District level, not at the Block level, which can mobilise resources and disseminate the health practices on an emergency basis. District bureaucracy in India is always efficient in handling situations of crisis nature, like floods and famine, law and order, elections and the like. Elections to Parliament and State legislatures are handled with utmost precision and meticulous care. In all these the District Collector is deeply involved. In GR such a responsibility was clearly cast on District Collectors/Commissioners. As someone said that war is too serious a matter to be left to Generals; similarly CHR cannot just be left to Chief Medical Officer of the District. Unlike in GR where agricultural scientists struggled to produce "seed technology" and demonstrate its utility and acceptability, in CHR technology is already available and we have only to demonstrate it.

Two important technologies which influence CHR are oral rehydration therapy (ORT) to control diarrhoeal episodes, and immunization against child killers like DPT, Polio, BCG. ORT technology which is a solution in a glass of good water with three finger pinch salt and four finger scoop of sugar is easy to accept. Recent advances have shown that Rice ORT or various fluids containing cereals or starch from root vegetables with or without added proteins with salt are powerful solutions for controlling body dehydration. ORT is the first remedy available to a mother and despite its scientific value, no efforts have been made by our medical fraternity to "demonstrate" it to our rural mothers. We must remember that principal actors in CHR are mothers and fathers and not children. The former have to initiate CHR on behalf of children and they have to accept the health technologies. Infant deaths due to diarrhoeal episodes and infectious diseases are anywhere in the range of 30-40 per cent of total infant deaths, as revealed by official health statistics of primary health centres all over India. Hence the need of the hour is to "demonstrate" the package of child health practices — the basic components of which are monitoring the growth of the child preferably through weighing, oral rehydration therapy, immunization, food supplementation, family spacing and female education.

Just as package of agricultural practices in GR were demonstrated to farming families, through adaptive research trials and "on-farm" demonstrations, similar "on-family" demonstrations and adaptive research trials for administering ORTs and other package of health practices could be taken up with "families" who have been identified as below-the-poverty-line families in Integrated Rural Development Programme in India which is now covering all the 5000 and odd development Blocks. The District Collectors are already involved in economic programmes but not in health programmes at the District level, although depending on personal interest some Collectors have taken interest in health activities. "On-family" demonstration of ORT has been successfully taken up in Bangladesh by the Bangladesh Rural Advancement Committee (BRAC), a non-governmental organisation. BRAC programme initially started in 1979 for a population of over 300,000 has now plans to take up "on-family" demonstrations among 58,000 families in 662 villages for spreading the efficacy of ORT technology. Their Lobon-gur mixture of ORT is almost a rural household name.

The present immunization coverage of eligible children in rural areas is most inadequate for two reasons: (a) rural mothers are not convinced of the need or efficacy of immunization for protecting the lives of her children; (b) mismanagement of immunisation operations. The former needs behavioural changes and is a slow process, the latter is quick and could be managed. The former again needs demonstration on why and how the latter needs efficient logistics and follow-up. In GR the logistics of input supplies like fertilisers, seeds to reach the farmers in time to catch the sowing season, was carefully planned and executed. Similar seasonal dimensions are also involved in CHR. Diarrhoeal episodes are high in wet season. CHR strategy demands high degree of logistics management. Immunization of course could be done in all twelve months but harvesting period is bad for mothers, since they are tied down to the fields. Scheduling the immunisation shots could be staggered just after sowing season, just before harvest or soon after harvest and in between sowing and harvesting.

In GR farming practices were not only demonstrated but disseminated through all types of media. In Thanjavur, roadside hoardings were put up before sowing season on the type of paddy seeds recommended for the season and the input dosage required. Radio Farm Forums and broadcasts were massively organised.

Farm yields of the small farmers were given wide publicity in the press and radio. A similar media planning in CHR first to popularise the health messages and then to publicise the *outcome* of the adoption would help a great deal. Presently there is emphasis more on the need for package of health practices than on the outcome of the adopted practice, by a cross-section of poverty-stricken families. Whatever outcomes are publicised by professionals engaged in ehancement of child health, are more propagandist type and are not communicated in a language which a rural mother could understand. Stray outcomes of child health interventions would not appeal to rural mothers who have no time to accept the miracles of these interventions; since they are tied down to the field or the kitchen.

In GR technologists, rural sociologists behavioural scientists and international agencies joined hands as a team to help Indian farmers to usher in GR. In CHR, a similar strategy would go a long way. ICMR, Home Science and Medical Colleges, Ministries of Health, Works and Housing, Social Welfare, Rural Development and international agencies have to join hands and go as a *team* to the District leadership. Although to some extent this team approach has been adopted in Integrated Child Development Scheme at the block level, the involvement of the District leadership is not very pronounced. As a result the District leadership feels that child and mother health is the look-out of the child development project officer of the block than his team at the district! Unlike the District Collector the BDO or the CDPO at the block does not carry that power and prestige required for a massive and emergency programme like CHR.

In GR, the farming family had an investment to make, by way of improving his land and paying for the factors of production. In CHR the investment that a rural mother makes is insignificant compared to GR; ORT does not cost even 50 paise but its return is hundred-fold higher in terms of what she could have paid to a doctor had she gone to him/her for hospitalised treatment of her child. Just as in GR, the return to cost incurred on adopting package of practices were publicised in advance and then compared to the yield obtained a similar approach on the *cost* of child health practices have to be publicised in advance and then *compared* to the health of the child that has *emerged* as a result of ORT or immunization.

In GR yields obtained as a result of acceptance of improved package of agricultural practices were widely publicised to induce others to accept them. Similarly in CHR, we could attempt physical weighing of infants regularly, for purposes of growth monitoring, to demonstrate how ORT and food supplementation have helped to increase the weight of the infants. In a way infants are like paddy or wheat plants and their weights have to increase, just as more crop yields mean more prosperity for the family. Whatever investment that a family makes towards CHR is an investment in kind, which would come back to the family several fold.

GR was a precursor for the innovation of many area-based farming programmes in India like Intensive Agricultural Area Programme (IAAP), Drought Prone Area Programme, Command Area Development Programme, Small Farmers/Marginal Farmers Development Programme (Fourth and Fifth Plans) and now the Integrated Rural Development Programme covering all the blocks of the country (Seventh Plan).

In GR Indian farmers proved that their literacy need not come in the way of acceptance of scientific package of agricultural practices. Thanjavur farmers had higher literacy than Ludhiana farmers, but their adoption of practices was lower as compared with Ludhiana farmers whose literacy was lower but they adopted the improved packages faster with startling results. Literacy need not be a deterrent in CHR, because technologies for ushering in CHR could be adopted even by the most illiterate mothers. One need not wait for the literacy of rural mothers to pick up although female education does help a great help for speeding up CHR.

Improved health practices are adopted better and faster by rural families in a situation of rising or stable incomes. IRD is one programme which seeks to lift the rural poverty-stricken family to a threshold income level; CHR has better prospects of success if child health practices and interventions are tagged on to such economic interventions so that economic, physical and social well-being of the rural family is ensured.

How Useful is Pulse Strategy for Polio Eradication?

The Universal Immunisation Programme (UIP), launched in 1985 by the govemment of India has come a long way. After a decade of experience in managing this programme. the GOI launched the Nutional Immunisation Days for Polio (NIDs) in December 1995 to achieve polio eradication in the country by the year 2000. In the words of ministry of health "In India UIP has been able to increase the oral polio vaccine (OPV) coverage levels among infants to over 90 per cent for four successive years, which is a commendable achievement and the number of polio cases have dropped significantly". Hence, the GOI decided to implement NIDs beginning in December 1995 to achieve polio eradication by the year 2000. There can be NIDs for measles also which is another killer disease for children. The last NID for polio which was oficially called pulse polio immunisation (PPI) (December 9, 1995 and January 20, 1996) was the biggest ever operation conducted by the Indian states in recent times for tackling the crippling disease called polio. Generally PPIs are organised during low transmission season of polio viruses between November and February in India. The peak transmission is from May to Septemher. Besides the cold months are preferable because cold chain problems are less intractable in winter months for handling heat sensitive polio vaccine. The pulse polio was in addition to the norma immunisation schedule that has been going on in all parts of the country on fixed days in each month. The term pulse has been used to describe this sudden simultaneous, mass administration of OPV on a single day to all children of 0-3 years age group.

Initial reports from all states in the country have indicated that millions of 0-3 kids have been administered with polio doses on these NIDs. The NIDs were marked by the fervour and enthusiasm of the local community leaders, Rotarians, Lions, politicians in mohallas, villages, towns, district, state and national capitals. The Indian bureaucracy wakes up on two occasions: (1) when disasters strike and (2) when elections are ordered. The NIDs were treated as a polling event, although conducting poll and administering OPV are two different operations with differing results. But the bureaucracy understands the language of a poll more than that of the OPV. Hence whoever invoked the parallels between polling and putting OPV dose in the mouth of crying kids should be complimented. But for this sincerity on the part of workers, the NIDs would not have been so successful and would have remained the lacklustre business of doctors and nurses. If India is to eradicate polio and such NIDs are to be repeated in the coming years at least till the year 2000, then we have to find out what were the lessons learnt from the 1995 NIDs, and how can the coverage levels and surveillance systems be improved to track the last case of polio in the country?

There are at least six major areas of operation in NIDs: (I) administration and organisation, (2) enumeration of the eligible kids, (3) logistics and cold chain, (4) information and communication and (5) evaluation and assessment and (6) continuous surveillance. In a typical poll event all the manpower and transport are pooled by the collectors of the district and polling booths are set up. In many states such OPV booths were set up and manned by a couple of people. Unlike the poll where there is a threat of rigging and false voting, there is no such threat but the danger is that of improper administration of doses and wrong handling of heat sensitive OPV vials. Some collectors had put teachers revenue inspectors/village patwaris for administering doses. They had never done this work and they were scared also. I saw in one OPV booth an industrial inspector trying to mix OPV of two vials in one and then administer. When I asked him why he was doing, he said he had taken two vials from the vaccine carrier without knowing and hence, he wanted to mix in one when both vials were half. In this process of mixing the temperature of the vaccine gets affected. He was not aware that vaccine mixing will lead to temperature distortion and also loss of vaccine efficiency. Hence, the best strategy would be to entrust dosage administration only to male/female health workers and anganwadi workers who have been doing regular immunisation on fixed days in their areas. Luckily, there are no reported vaccine-related disasters. In many areas the large number of private urban clinics, which regularly offered routine immunisation, were not allowed to open their clinics. Some families are attached to certain clinics and they did not quite trust a school teacher giving polio drops. In one city nearly 70 private clinics were denied the facility of providing pulse polio. More polio booths would have served more children without any extra cost to the government. All that was needed was extra doses of polio vaccine which they were getting anyhow in the normal course for their regular imrnunisation from the chief medical officers of the district.

Enumeration of the eligible kids of 0-3 for PPI was attempted by different collectors/CMOs in different ways. Some administrators insisted that there should be wardwise/villagewise enumeration. So school teachers and children were asked to enumerate the eligible kids from house-to-house. Unlike the voters list where voters come forward to register their names, very few mothers take the trouble of informing the PPI booths in advance and get their names registered. Even when the enumeration was done, names of children, were often found to be missing when the actual immunisation was done. Some vaccinators even turned down the child/ mother when this happened, despite instructions not to refuse any child the polio drop. The whole exercise of enumeration was a waste of time, effort and stationery. But then how would we have known the vaccine requirements? There is an established norm for this, 9-10 per cent of the population is in the age group 0-3 years. The CMOs are well aware of this, but enumeration exercise was made compulsory beforc the NIDs due to bureaucratic pressure. Enumeration was also found useless when in bus/railway stations PPI booths were set up and anyone could take the child and get polio drops.

Logistics and the cold chain is the heart and soul of any immunisation programme - whether fixed day schedule or campaign mode like the NIDs. OPV is highly heat sensitive and has to be kept: at +2°C to +8°C, when it is taken out from the main storage where it has to be kept at -20°C. Over the years Indian primary health care system has built a fairly efficient cold chain system to maintain perfect temperature of the vaccine from the manufacturer till it reaches the mouth of the child. The GOI mobilised extra cold boxes and vaccine carriers through the UNICEF and other bilateral agencies for the NIDs. All vehicles were mobilised to carry vaccine from the district store to all the PPI booths (they ranged from 3,000 to 6,000 in a typical district). Some of the vaccine carriers supplied by Blow Kings were of substandard quality - the lids did not close properly. As a result the ice-packs in the vaccine carriers were melting fast affecting the temperature inside the vaccine carriers. Lakhs of ice-packs were to be frozen. Some CMOs/collectors showed their managerial skills by adopting very ingenious ways of making ice-packs. Raw ice melts fast but a ice-packs retain their temperature much longer. Hence,' ice-packs are used in all routine immunisation. One has to be careful in the selection of vaccine carriers. It is unfortunate that India still does not manufacture all the cold chain equipment required for the country's immunisation programme although we boast of manufacturing sophisticated aircraft.

The vaccine itself is more important than the vaccine carriers. In the present NIDs, by and large the OPV was supplied by Redicura Pharma (a private sector unit) and Hafkine Institute (a public sector unit). In the course of my whirlwind visit to many PPI booths, I found the vaccine of Redicura Pharma not only short of declared doses (supposed to be 20-dose vial) but also, the aluminium cup was difficult to open without a sharp knife. How can the vaccinator open it with her/his finger nails? I had to help a vaccinator open the vial with my ball point pen with great difficulty. Many others who observed Redicura Pharma vials had the same story to narrate. Our quick assessment of the quantity of the doses in these Redicura Pharma vial was around 15-17 doses. If we allow for wastage then each vial had just 12 to 14 doses. Manufacturers cannot take the vaccinators who are mostly health workers and anganwadi workers for a ride and blame them for their reckless wastage. We do not know whether lot quality assurance sampling (LQAS) was done or not. Vaccine quality and quantity is a crucial element of such a vast operation like the PPI. Perhaps the GOI may take up the vaccine production and quality issue with the manufacturers.

The high point of the NIDs were the massive publicity and media exposure provided to the event both by the press and the NGOs like the Rotary International. By now Rotary's contribution to the polio eradication programme globally is well known. Their caps and T-shirts were popular. But those mohallas/slum/hamlet level community leader's like an elderly person or a sarpanch or a councillor played remarkable roles by bringing kids on their cycles and on their shoulders. A final concern is that as children grow into adulthood, we keep adding new stock of kids to the pool and we should not neglect the regular imrnunisation programme that is already on the ground. I heard some women saying "Phoren polio drops have corne, better give it before it is finished. You may not get it again". The personnel of our health system have to educate people so that the regular immunisation goes on round the year and the goal of polio eradication is achieved. PPI cannot substitute the regular fixed day immunisation, but can at best supplement it.

Is polio eradication possible with the present trend of high coverage of immunisation in all developed and some developing countries? What are the difficulties in wiping out this disease from the face of the earth? What operational and management strategies are needed in view of the WHO goal of polio eradication by the year 2000? What types of vaccine are needed to combat vaccine-preventible diseases like polio?

These were some of the questions I had the privilege of asking Dr. Henderson in Baltimore. He became the Associate Director of Life Sciences in the President's Office (Science and Technology) in White House, Washington.

Dr. Henderson, a tall man with an obstreperous cowlick", as described by the Johns Hopkins Magazine, proudly feels that a sum of nearly $96 million spent on small-pox eradication has already been recovered and many of the strategies of the small-pox eradication programme are still relevant for the global eradication of polio and other vaccine-preventible diseases affecting millions of children around the world.

However, according to Dr. Henderson, there are some basic differences between the two in matters like vaccine availability, quality and administration. Unlike the small pox vaccine, which is not heat sensitive and does not require an elaborate cold-chain system, the polio vaccine is heat-sensitive and needs to be stored constantly at +2°C to +4°C till it is administered to a child. Moreover, the child has to be brought to a health centres thrice for three doses at an interval of 6, 10 and 14 weeks.

Is it possible to make a single anti-polio dose which ensures easy administration? Dr. Henderson laments that nearly $ 100 million are needed today for vaccine research, testing and development. He says: "Vaccines are a bit of an orphan in our medical armamentarium, because they are not as lucrative as drugs are. They really are every body's business but nobody's business!"

UNICEF thinks that vaccine research is not its priority because it is an action organigsation and not an R & D body. The World Health Organisation (Who) says that it is short of funds.

Dr. Henderson feels that a single-dose polio vaccine for a child, instead of the three-dose one, should be ideal and efforts should be made to make the single dose in such a way that it can be given to a child like a toffee. During early nineties number of the drop-outs from the first dose to the third dose are enormous and even educated mothers cannot bring their infants three times to the health centre because of factors like forgetfulness, transportation difficulties and health centre failures.

According to Dr. Henderson, childhood diseases have no national boundaries and the polio virus in stools travel any where. Therefore, polio virus isolation, identification and intratypic differentiation are extremely important. The processes require an extensive network of laboratories around the world. Our laboratory scientists always disagree with one another and surveillance keeps nagging.

Dr. Henderson was all praise for the Pan-American Health Organisation, which has played a unique role in the Pan-American region in polio eradication campaigns. Brazillians can do certain things extraordinarily well, as they have shown in polio eradication efforts. The credit for this should go to PAHO. WHO and PAHO are like first cousins in the American region and all countries in the region pay their annual subscriptions to both WHO and PAHO. PAHO was established much earlier than WHO. We wish we had in Asia an AHO to motivate Asian communities to participate in health promotion activities.

A remarkable decline in number of confirmed cases has occurred in the Americas in the face of an improving surveillance system. In only a few areas the wild polio virus is found circulating.

Three strategies for immunisation have been successfully used in that region (a) a regular and routine expanded programme for the immunisation delivery system (b) observance of National Immunisation Days which significantly keep raising immunisation coverage levels and (c) mopping up operations through the house-to-house delivery of the oral polio doses in areas where the polio virus may be circulating.

Dr. Henderson says his appointment in the White House is purely political and he will be there as long as President Bush wants him there. But he will use his assignment as the "Bully pulpit" to advocate more funds for vaccine research and greater White House awareness of the child survival programmes. USAID has already committed itself to the global eradication of childhood diseases, including polio. Will the other countries follow suit?

It was a summer month when the temperature was 40°C and somewhere in the Shivalik hills, women with their babies were waiting in a village health sub centre for immunisation. The Health worker had gone to the nearby PHC to bring the vaccine. I was looking around at the used vials, syringes, needles and the stove which was dusty with nonuse. Were the needles and syringes bring sterilised to ensure safe and protected vaccination?

Nirmala Devi, the health worker, returned with a vaccine carrier with a nervous look. She was scared to see the District Health Officer with me. I quietly asked her: "Tell me, how do you sterilise the needles and syringes?" She replied with hesitation: "The stove is under repair and there is no kerosene. I spend my own money on its repair but still it is not in working order."

Then I asked: "How will you sterilise?" She then took me and the District Health Officer to a nearby tea shop. The owner explained that she gets the syringes and needles boiled in his shop. When we asked the shop keeper: "Will this not affect your business?" he promptly replied: "Yes, but the health of the children of my village is important and this is my service to the children."

This is how in hundreds of village health workers are carrying out the Immunisation Mission. There are three partners in this mission: Vaccine manufacturer, vaccinator and the mother/child. Very often, if vaccination caused deaths occur, we find health personnel blaming the vaccine (manufacturer) and not finding out the human error which can occur from the time vaccine leaves the manufacturer until it reaches the child. There is what is called the "cold chain"--which means that at every stage between manufacture and administering, the vaccine must be kept at a temperature between +2°C to +8°C, when the temperature fluctuates the vaccine gets damaged.

Unlike smallpox vaccination where there was only one type of vaccine and needle, in universal child immunisation, there are multiple vaccines to be administered at different periods of time through different routes. (DPT is intramuscular, BCG is intradermal, polio is oral). This creates management problems at every level and the Health Worker at the level of the child and mother can either make or mar the programme.

The needle and the syringe are the vital instruments of immunisation and if they are used in unsterile conditions they may prove fatal. How do we ensure the sterile quality of needle and syringe? High-tech doctors are using disposable needles and syringes but in our vast public health system the disposable needles and syringes are never disposed but reused. Contaminated needles and syringes could play havoc with the lives of infants. The rule of thumb should be "single sterile needle and syringe for single shot for a single mother/child."

The mothers role in immunisation is more important than that of vaccinators. Thanks to TV and mass media, mothers are now aware of the value of lifesaving vaccines. But the problem is how the public health system can attract the mother to come repeatedly to have the child vaccinated before the child reaches her/his first birthday. (Three times polio and DPT with a months interval, one time BCG at birth and one measles on the child's ninth month).

Drop-outs are many and the immunity is lost. Reasons given by mothers are the lack of information on the need to return for second and third doses and the absence of the vaccinator.

This is where the mothers and health workers. "appointment" becomes critical. Will both keep up the "appointment" for the health of the child and herself (mother needs/two doses of tetanus vaccine during pregnancy). This is the challenge of universal child immunisation.

The Needle Brigade

Are there any parallels between polls and mass immunisation camps? Any comparison between polling and vaccination may appear prima facie absurd, but think again. Election process in India is organised efficiently. (Perhaps the only process done, efficiently in india!). Every step is well planned and executed and nothing is left to chance. Before the poll is held, a voters list is published indicating the names' of eligible voters, house number, age sex, mohalla, street etc. They are legally notified, objections called and the list finalised. These voters alone get the right to vote.

Before the polling day many political party candidates go to the voters, woo them with promises,give them a slip indicating place and name of the polling station, serial number of the voter in the voters list so that voter is facilitated to go and vote. The actual poll is conducted meticulously. First a voter goes to get his/her name checked in the voter list, then proceeds to get the ballot paper, then goes to the booth where ballot paper is marked, folded and put into the ballot box. An indelible mark on the finger shows that she or he has voted.

In mass immunisation camps, if camp is to be successfull, one has to adopt the strategy of polling days. First is the enumeration of eligible infants and, pregnant mothers for immunisation. Just as not all members in a family can vote, similarly not all can be immunised. Only infants and pregnant mothers, can be immunised not the older members. Enumeration of infants and pregnant mothers has to be done, like voters list preparation, in all urban and rural areas. Voters enumeration is done once in five years or whenever elections are announced but enumeration of infants and pregnant mothers for vaccination is a continuous daily process, (New borns are to be enumerated all the time). Unlike the voters, who can vote till they die, vaccination can not be done to older people. After the poll the voter if he/she has voted gets an indelible ink mark on his/her index finger which is a proof of casting the vote. Similarly (if the infant is vaccinated soon after birth with BCG, there will be scar on the arm, which is a proof of effective BCG).

To prepare the staff members of the Health Departments of Punjab and Haryana and Rotary Club volunteers for the mass immunisation camps I spoke at several meetings from October to December. These similarities between polling day and immunisation day.

For example on Gandhi Jayanti day I went to Mandi Gobindgarh, the steel town of Patiala district. I reached in the morning along with the Civil Surgeon of Patiala. Young, Rotarian President Gupta and his. Rotary colleagues had worked hard in the previous week to identify all eligible infants and pregnant mothers in Mandi Gobindgarh town. Rtn Gupta had allocated each of the Immunisation centres to rotary members who were asked to mobilise, motivate and publicise the mass camp, provide identify stips, immunisation card, and physically bringing them to the immunisation camp, Earlier my impression of Rotarians was that of armchair social workers but rotarians of Mandi Gobindgarh proved that they can work in the slums. I saw them bringing in their sleek Maruti cars, slum children and women, getting them registered in the immunisation sesssion, giving them the "Jacha-Bacha" card, getting the vaccination done by sophisticated disposable syringes and neeedles, giving the kids chocolates and reminding the mothers to bring the kids for the remaining shots.

The Rotary Wheel in Mandi Gobindgarh was moving on Oct 2 and Rtn Gupta has informed me that the wheel is moving even now! Rotary Polio Plus programme was launched globally but locally Rotarians like Gupta have made it a living activity not just a rhetoric.

Rogi Kalyan Samitis : Whither Patient's Welfare?

Over the years, the MP Government has pioneered several innovative programmes in the field of public health like Jana Swasthya Rakshaks to provide basic healthcare at the doorsteps of rural famlies and establishing Rogi Kalyan Samitis (RKS) in all the district hospitals and community health centres, to mop up resources by way of user charges to provide better services to patients visiting these hospitals.

These are all laudable objectives but what are the lessons learnt particularly in the context of patients?

Well-being and care as a result of increased user charges collected by these RKS is not known. According to a State Government's publication distributed to the participants of UNDP-sponsored seminar in Bhopal on August 25-26, 2001 on decentralisation and governance, RKS collection stood at Rs. 45 crore which is a good example of public-private partnership indeed.

The RKS in Madhya Pradesh, established in Government hospitals of medical colleges, district hospitals and community health centres, are registered societies and the management bodies consist of people's representatives of the area, members of IMA, members of PR bodies and Nagarpalikas and health functionaries of the hospitals.

The oldest RKS is in the MY Hospital, Indore. RKS can utilise all government assets to impose user charges and can determine the quantum of the charges.

The main functions envisaged for the RKS are to raise funds through donations, loans from financial institutions and other donors, utilise land available in the hospital for commercial purposes or construct shops, manage canteens and provide amenities to the rogis and their attendants, manage ambulance vans of hospitals, permit private pathology, MRI, CAT scan, sonography services etc. and set up their units within the hospital premises in return for providing their services at a rate fixed by the RKS.

The user charges collected are not deposited in the Government treasury but are made available for spending on the welfare of patients as per the directions of the RKS executive committee.

The executive committee of the district hospital RKS consists of the minister in-charge of the district as per the Zila Sarkar arrangements. The objectives of the RKS as per the Government order are to improve management of the hospital with community participation, ensure proper maintenance of hospitals and arrange for quality drugs and diet and functioning equipment for care, ensure better service delivery, effect a continual upgrade of facilities and organise training and skill upgrade workshops for hospital staff.

On the lines of the RKS in MY Hospital, Indore, Bhopal Medical College Hospital, Ujjain, Dewas, Mandsaur and Gwalior are now functioning for more than 7-8 years.

In many of these hospitals, RKS have purchased costly equipment like photo-therapy units, ICCD, Elisa readers, ENT microscopes, TMT machine and audiometers and CT scan equip, ment.

Along with these RKS, district Red Cross societies also function in these hospitals and one does not know the overlapping and duplication of services. But it does not matter as long as the patients are served better.

Even after 7-8 years of the RKS functioning in Madhya Pradesh, one does not know how these RKS are serving patients. Hospital management is now a big and complicated business.

Behind all the sophisticated CAT scans and x-ray machines, one should not forget that there is a 'PATIENT' waiting for care, safety and protection in the place, waiting to get out of the hospital as soon as possible after getting cured or fairly satisfied with the care that he/she gets in the hospital.

They should feel happy with their visit to the hospital and perhaps may return only as a last resort! One does not know even in a better-managed MY Hospital, Indore what is the 'Kalyan' level (patient satisfaction or well-being level) of the Rogis (patients) admitted in a typical month or year. There are no scientific patient satisfaction surveys done to know, how good or bad the patient care is.

Today, the health care industry spends more on the equipment and technology and less on the patient satisfaction surveys.

Biomedical waste disposal methods and systems and reducing the hospital infections, which are increasing day by day, also come low on priority lists.

Many big hospitals in the private sector are not bothered about patient satisfaction levels and proper medical waste disposal by installing incinerators and taking care of the life saving equipment by calibrating them from time to time.

As per a notification of the Ministry of Environment of the Government of India, hospitals and nursing homes in towns with population of below 30 lakh and with less than 50 beds and above have to install hospital waste disposal systems before December 2002 and for those above 50 beds, the last date was December 1999. We do not know whether the RKS have established these systems and if not, the office-bearers of RKS will face prosecution!

If the RKS have to sustain and the patients have to be cared for - efficiently and effectively - then all the 600-odd RKS in the State have to be certified under some law or regulation .or standards established for assessing the 'best practices' adopted by these RKS in Madhya Pradesh. The present standards for hospitals are those adopted and practiced under ISO 9001:2000.

These are Europe-based and market driven standards applicable for all service sectors like health care organisations and educational institutions. There is no law in India to compel hospitals to go in for these ISO standards and many are not interested in adopting these. Many think wrongly that these ISO standards are meant only for manufacturing and industrial sectors.

In the US, the Joint Commission for Accreditation of Health Care Organisations (JCAHO) set standards for all types of hospitals failing which the insurance companies will not reimburse the treatment costs to patients who get themselves treated in hospitals which are not certified by JCAHO. In India nobody has bothered to "impose best practices" on either the private hospitals or the Government-owned ones.

The Ministry of Environment notifications on the biomedical waste disposal do not cover the overall functioning of hospitals with a concern for the 'well-being or the patient satisfaction'. Just by applying the Consumer Act to the functioning of the hospitals one does not ensure patient well-being because safety, care and cure and diagnosis are all a continuous process and not just negligence or death which alone is fought as is the case with the majority of provisions under the Consumer Protection Act.

Health care is just not a human rights issue and goes beyond that. The most important objectives of the RKS are to ensure patient satisfaction through the use of hospital resources, both human and technological. RKS have installed sophisticated equipment, which is the easiest thing to do. But they have to be calibrated all the time and certified according to the quality testing and certifying agencies in the country.

In Chennai and other cities, the Government of India has established quality testing labs, which the hospitals have to use. Oxygen cylinders without oxygen have been used in many hospitals in India resulting in fatalities of the patients!

Hence calibration is a must in the RKS managed hospitals in Madhya Pradesh. Similarly, private diagnostic operators have been allowed to operate and charge the patients under the RKS management, which is not only unethical but also dangerous.

The hospital staff can be trained to provide all these diagnostic testing services and the RKS are anyhow collecting the user charges to cover the costs.

I found in Raipur Hospital (now in Chhattisgarh) that user charges collected under the RKS are not used for patient care and are diverted for non-patient activities, which is bad ethics and practice.

If the Government of Madhya Pradesh is serious about the idea, then the 600-odd RKS have to be audited not just for financial discipline but also for patient care and satisfaction.

There is a saying in quality circles - 'you do what you say and say what you do'. If you apply this principle to the RKS in Madhya Pradesh, we do not know how good they are for the well-being of the patients. The Government has to bring out a white paper on the functioning of these RKS. People of the State have a right to know how much is the 'Kalyan of Rogis' as a result of RKS in public hospitals.

Universal Immunisation Programme in India: Issues of Sustainability

The Universal Immunisation Programme (UIP) in India has made an effort to make at least one vital service to the mother and child accessible and affordable. Universalisation of immunisation is the first step towards health for all. Unlike small pox, which was eradicated once for al!, immunisation is a continuous and ongoing process. Anyone concerned with public health must now rhink of the various issues of the sustainability of UIP.

The Universal Immunisation Programme (UIP) was launched in 1985 by the government of India, ministry of health, as a national programme with the objective of immunising 85 per cent of new-borns and 100 per cent of expectant mothers by 1990 against six vaccine preventable diseases, viz, measles, pertusis (whooping cough), neo-natal tetanus, polio, tuberculosis and diphtheria. 'Subsequently targets were revised to achieve 100 per cent coverage levels' so as to make it universal, although technically 85 per cent coverage levels would ensure herd immunity, except for pregnant mothers who need to be covered fully (Communication issued by Ministry of Health, National Immunisation Mission to all

States dated September 11, 1990 to cover 100 per cent of the eligible infants). Available figures on coverage levels achieved reveal that in all states and UTs near 100 per cent coverage levels have been achieved in all antigens except measles.

Some critics have questioned the UIP itself by dubbing it as a selective primary health care intervention, and "an unholy alliance of National and international power brokers [who] could impose their will on hundreds of millions of human beings living in the poor countries of the world and make them forget all that happened at Alma Ata in 1978[2]. Unfortunately primary healthcare has been given many different definitions in different contexts Even in the same country, where contexts change, over time, definitions have also differed. For some primary health care is no more than first contact care. For others it means using primary level health care personnel to carry out basic health care services, and for still others it means a second class of medicine in areas where appropriate medical care cannot be given to the majority of the population. Many of these definitions. including, selective primary health care, are not consistent with the term primary health care as, used at the Alma Ata. The report of the director general of WHO and executive director of UNICEF on Alma Ata Conference of 1978 states:

> Primary Health Care is a practical approach to making essential health care universally accessible to individuals and families in the community in an acceptable and affordable way, and with their full participation. The approach has evolved over the years partly in the light of experience, positive and negative, based on basic health services in a number of countries. But it means much more than the mere extension of basic health services.
>
> It has social and development dimensions, and if properly applied, will influence the way in which the rest of the health system functions. Its shape is determined by social goals, such as improvement of the quality of life and maximum benefits to the greatest number and these goals are attained by social means, such as acceptance of greater responsibility for health

by communities and individuals and their active panicipation in attaining it. The healthier people are, the more likely they are able to contribute to social and economic development and. such development in turn provides the additional resources and social energy that can facilitate health development. So primary health care and community efforts towards social and economic development in general are most likely to succeed when they are mutually supportive. Also just as the health sector functions best in harmony with other social and economic sectors, *so there is a need for harmony within the health sector through support to primary health care by all other levels (emphasis mine)*[3].

UIP in India has made an effort to provide at least one service to the mother and child accessible and affordable and universalisation of immunisation is the first step towards health for all. Unlike smallpox, which was eradicated once for all, immunisation is a continuous and ongoing process of ensuring protection to all the new-borns round the year. Unfortunately overzealous promotion of family planning programme to the neglect of Mother Child Health Programme in the last four decades, has not brought down the birth rates nor the infant mortality rates, which have close relationships.

Among the poor communities simple arithmetic works-more children mean more hands and if some die some remain and child survival assumes a critical issue among the poor. If children born survive there is no need for more children. The critics of UIP therefore have to see this simple logic and assess its strategic importance. to the demographic situation of the country. It is the neglect of mother and child health component of family planning programme in the past which has contributed to the slow pace of fertility reduction. There is global evidence to show that whenever mortality is high fertility is also high.

Fertility and Child Survival are closely linked and no single direction of cause and effect can be completely demonstrated. When a child survives, the chances of leaving good space between births is more easily ensured. Secondly only when the number of children surviving exceeds the parents' desired family size will they consider family planning for purposes of limiting their family size, although the evidence is quite clear that spacing itself is necessary for the survival of children[4].

Any attempt to reduce fertility without reducing mortality would be like putting the cart before the horse. UIP would therefore help in reducing India's exploding population.

This note is an attempt to analyse the sustainability aspects of UIP and not to go into the merits or demerits of UIP as such; because universal child immunisation has been accepted by world public health leaders as both an affordable and cost effective strategy not only for child survival but also for promoting primary health care[5].

The outcome of Bellagio meeting was a plan not only to immunise all the world's, children as an impetus to primary health care, but also to promote other effective means—ranging from oral rehydration to child spacing and family planning, where and when opportunities presented themselves, to reduce morbidity and mortality in this most vulnerable of all groups. UIP has come to stay in India and anyone concerned with public health must now think of its various sustainability issues, than engage in absurd polemical discussions. One knows little about how to sustain UIP nor is one clear about what we mean by sustainability. Therefore any discussion and debate on sustainability of UIP is one step forward in understanding its various dimensions.

UIP was launched in India as a living memorial to the late prime minister Indira Gandhi and as such lot of political commitment was visible since the inception of the programme. A national co-ordination committee for UIP was constituted with the health secretary as chairman and other members from Indian Academy of Paediatrics, Indian Medical Association, Rotary International, etc.

All the 500-and odd districts and union territories were selected in a phased manner, adequate staff was sanctioned at the district to handle this programme. The UIP was given the status of a Technology Mission in 1988 which provided a sense of urgency to the programme. Any assessment of such a vast programme particularly in a country of India's size, dimension and complexity, has to be based on certain managerial tests. Is it possible for one programme like UIP with high coverage, attained quickly, to be less vigorous than another with lower coverage but pulling for a long? Can an Indian UIP be an ideal one which has achieved high coverage, but will also sustain it? An ideal UIP might be judged on what is called ACLIVE principle[6].

Administration and Organisation of UIP

UIP was well-designed at the central level with joint secretary of health as mission director and at the state-level a full time state (EPI) officer was mission director. But at the district level, although the post of district immunisation officer (DIO) was created and the majority of states did appoint them, they were a dejected lot in terms of their powers for drawing and disbursing funds, control of staff under them and their equation with powerful district family planning officers (DFPOs).

In some states both DIOs and DFPOs came into conflicts even for spending small amounts for repair of immunisation vehicles and for getting electrical wirings done for cold room, the DIOs had to depend on DFPOs. Wherever the district civil surgeons chief medical officers (CMOs) were managerially effective there were no conflicts between DIOs and DFPOs. The attitude of some CMOs were no different. We still hear the CMOs saying that immunisation programmes are affecting the family planning work, without realising that both are supportive to the health of mother and child. In the long run at the district level the dichotomy of providing two officers one for immunisation and another for family planning could be done away with so that child survival and child spacing is considered as a continuum.

At the level of primary health centre, the medical officers (MOs) and at the sub centre, the multipurpose health workers (MHWs) really matter in the provision of immunisation services. At this level immunisation cannot be done under the 'camp' style of the family planning programme. However, given a choice MHWs' and MOs would like to do family planning rather than provide immunisation because of the incentive money involved in family planning. Sustainability of UIP demands that workers provide immunisation on a fixed day and time once a month. Although fixed day strategy has been accepted by the GOI at the sub-centre level, this strategy is still to be institutionalised in many states. Disruption of vaccination session is still common. One study revealed that out of 383 workers at sub-centres 54.2 per cent stated that they experienced disruption in immunisation services.

The proportion of workers stating reasons for disruption were 50.6 per cent due to shortage of vaccine/diluent, 37.3 per cent called for other duties, 28.8 per cent absence of workers, 23.2 per cent due to lack of transport, 7.4 per cent due to shortage of syringes and 6.8 per cent due to shortage of needles[7]. A successful fixed day strategy presupposes that the frequency, timing, place and name of vaccinators are made known to the villagers and urban dwellers and that the supervisors are free to visit any of the fixed day cen tres for inspection without prior notice. Haryana state EPI mission has designed micro-plans for each of their PHCs in the state. Vaccination services are provided in all the sub-centres of the PHCs every week in such a way that all the villages attached to the sub-centres are covered once a month for immunisation services.

UIP cannot sustain unless in thousands of PHCs, sub-centres, and urban health centres, immunisation services are provided as a routine service. In urban slums, small towns and large cities because of inadequate health infrastructure and floating migrant population, immunisation services remain sporadic. A large number of private medical practitioners (PMPs) are still not tapped for immunisation, because the system of indenting and supplying vaccines to them, feed back from them has not yet been perfected. A large number of infants and mothers still miss vaccinations, involuntarily.

In one of the surveys on missed opportunities for immunisation done by Christian Medical College in Ludhiana it was revealed that out of 120, 0-23 months children who visited the CMC OPD for sickness treatment, nearly 80 children missed getting vaccinated because of lack of vaccination[8].

TABLE 1
COLD, CHAIN EQUIPMENT SUPPLIED BY UNICEF

(Rs. Millions)

Recurring 1985-90		*Non-Recurring 1985-90*	*Total (Numbers)*	*Total (Expenditure)*
Vaccines	820.25	Walk in coolers	275	47.72
Syringes and needles	328.50	Deep freezers	2125	19.20
Immunisation cards	102.50	ILRs	28000	287.20
POL vans vehicles	34.20	Vaccine Carriers	300000	69.85
Maintenance allowance mopeds (as per state rules	43.80	Transportation-van vehicles	800	65.40
		Moped	30000	226.20
Maintenance repairs cold chain (5 per cent)	40.67	Refrigerated trucks	4	2.10
		Total		717.67
Health education material (3.5 per cent)	49.75			
Monitoring and				

(Contd.)

(Contd.Table. 1)

(Rs. Millions)

Recurring 1985-90		*Non-Recurring 1985-90*	
		Total (Numbers)	*Total (Expenditure)*
Monitoring and evaluation (2 per cent)	27.35		
Contingency (2 per cent)	27.35		
Incentive (2 per cent)	27.35		
Salaries (5 per cent)	69.75		
Total	1571.47		

Daily vaccination in major urban hospitals would reduce missed opportunities and increase the sustainability. Routine recording of immunisation status of all eligible children, who attend OPDs would increase coverage levels as well as sustain them.

One of the reasons for not providing daily immunisation is the fear of vaccine wastage, absence of cold chain facility, etc. But with the availability of 1- or 5-dose vaccines, vaccine wastage need not be a deterrent for daily vaccination.

Although the ministry of health has clarified that even if one child comes for vaccination, a vial has to be opened, the fear of audit haunts the health workers, who want to make sure that cost of wastage is not deducted from their salaries.

Mass immunisation camps are no substitute for fixed-day strategy.

> Where infrastructure and managerial skills are weak, efforts may falter earlier, and even initial efforts, if not properly planned and executed, may exact an exorbitant cost in terms of other health activities, suspended in order to carry out these immunisation activities. In such camps older children who are able to walk on their own, receive most of the vaccines[9].

In nationwide mass immunisation camps held in October, November and December of 1990, in collaboration with state health departments, the Rotary International and the Indian Medical Association, many such older children got vaccinated. Experience in other countries is no different. In Senegal the average monthly coverage rate during the six months following the campaign was only 29.8 per cent as opposed to 40 per cent during the five months before the campaign. The greatest share of immunisations (53.3 per cent of the total) was achieved by the social centres which were already carrying out immunisations before the campaign. Fixed and/or mobile, strategies resulting combinations have different costs and different results.

No one has proven which combination results in the highest coverage sustained over the long term. It seems probable that the most robust approach is the flexible one, to combine strategies according to local needs, resources and opportunities, yielding the most, for the least for the longest[11].

Census or Enumeration of Pregnant Mothers and New-borns

Identifying the pregnant mothers and new-borns in rural and urban areas and bringing them for vaccination is a difficult process for the health workers. Enumeration is a continuous process and there are no perfect systems for identifying the target group.

Present problems of delayed vaccination or non-vaccination of infants and pregnant mothers, are attributed partly to the 'missed' pregnant mothers and infants from the 'enumeration register' of these eligibles. Successful identification and registration of new-borns for vaccination depends on the success achieved in identifying the pregnant women/mothers for vaccination (including anti-natal care). Unfortunately among poor communifies pregnancy is never revealed early and anti-natal care is almost non-existent, because these women do not interact with formal health systems. Informal health systems like Traditional Birth Attendants, with whom pregnant women of poor communities interact, do not always insist on TT vaccination. Once these pregnant mothers are missed from anti-natal care and TT vaccination, their new-borns are also missed from being vaccinated.

Inter-village and inter-town migrations of pregnant women compound the problems of their identification. New-borns are presently identified through birth registration system. Birth and death registration is compulsory under the law. But birth registration is done for several purposes like admitting a child for school, for claiming consumer benefits like getting a ration card, etc. The person who registers the birth is different from the person who vaccinates and if there is no co-ordination, the child is likely to miss or delay the vaccination. The mother might have registered herself for anti-natal care in one village/town, but she delivers in another village/town. (Generally for first deliveries women go to their parents' village/town.) If she has an anti-natal card it helps the health worker to track her vaccination status despite migrations. Women who are worried about their next meal never bother about anti-natal care or card.

As part of UIP the government of India/ states have evolved village enumeration (census) registers for pregnant mothers and infants, to track them for vaccination. For this system of enumeration to work, the health worker has to be smart enough to know the village families intimately so that she/he does not miss any eligible mother or infant. In urban areas problems are compounded because of the poor health infrastructure and humanpower shortage for MCH care. Perfect enumeration needs horizontal co-ordination with several groups which interact with women, like women's clubs, women's co-operatives, well-baby clinics, etc. In Himachal Pradesh the EPI mission urged all mahila mandals in the state to identify first and foremost a newly married girl in their respective villages and track her to know when she gets pregnant, when she delivers a child, so that at every stage mahila mandal members keep the health worker informed. Accurate census or enumeration to capture all eligible mothers and infants is therefore critical to the sustainability of UIP.

Logistics and Cold Chain

Although oral polio vaccine became available as early as in 1968, the incidence of poliomyelitis did not show a sustained decline until proper attention was given to the managerial aspects of the programme including the cold chain. In UIP logistics entail two principal activities-timely provision of vaccines, needles and syringes and maintenance of a reliable cold chain to keep vaccines viable. Without a working cold chain provision of correct amounts of vaccine and other necessary equipment is useless. Cold chain is a system that ensures the potency of a vaccine from the time of manufacture to the time it is given to a child or a pregnant woman.

All vaccines are sensitive to heat and BCG and measles vaccines are also sensitive to ultraviolet light. A lot of heat at one time (e.g. in a closed vehicle in the Sun) or a little amount of heat over many exposures (constant openings of refrigerator door) can damage vaccines to the same extent. Furthermore some vaccines should be frozen at some points along the chain, while other vaccines must never be frozen which increases the complexity of the cold chain (see chart 1). Two critical issues assume importance (a) How many scheduled immunisation sessions had to be cancelled or postponed because of lack of logistics support, including lack of vaccines, injection and sterilisation materials, transport, fuel, kerosene, etc, (b) Are all injections being given with a sterile syringe and a sterile needle?[12]

UIP has brought in its wake for the first time in India a massive cold chain structure from the manufacturer right up to the districts, PHCs and sub-centres. Table 1 reveals the cold chain equipment supplied by UNICEF as part of the UIP in India during 1985-90 worth Rs. 717.67 million. The recurrent costs during 1985-90 were estimated at Rs. 1,571.47 million. The start up costs of providing cold chain equipment, vaccines, injection equipment for a population of 10 million are estimated to be almost two million dollars. The recurrent costs of the cold chain like spare parts, tools, account for the largest proportion of operating costs (44 per cent), whereas capital costs include 23 per cent for purchase, 6 per cent for delivery, 25 per cent for energy. According to UNICEF the overall share of total programme expenditure utilised for recurrent inputs is in the order of 40 per cent, with variations between 15 and 54 per cent, depending upon the type of country and programme sector (Table 2).

Sustainability of UIP means the recurrent costs are absorbed by the UIP host country, so that external funding support is gradually phased out and self-sustaining health care services are adopted over a period of time. At present UIP is a centrally-sponsored programme and the states would continue the programme as long as the centre keeps it going. If UIP is just the beginning for building the edifice of primary health care, then the UIP infrastructure has to be strengthened. Under the family welfare (planning) programme, which is also a centrally-sponsored programme. contingency funds for repair of vehicles, consumables like kerosene, are mostly adequate and these are at the disposal of DFPOs and in some states DIOs are not even allowed access to these contingency funds.

In a typical state for a fiscal year, the family planning (welfare) budget is roughly Rs. 89 lakh. Whereas UIP budget is around Rs. 36.41 lakh. A large chunk of the family planning budget goes towards incentive money for motivators, acceptors and other intermediaries. In contrast UIP has demonstrated that without cash incentive mothers do get their infants vaccinated if quality vaccination services are provided. If both programmes are combined there would be economies of scale in expenditure and

Chart-1

Vaccine Level Maximum Storage Time	Central Store up to 8 months	Regional up to 3 months	Health Care up to 1 month	Transport up to 1 week
Measles Yellow Fever Oral Polio	-15°C to -25°C			
DPT Tetanus Toxoid IPV DT BCG			2°C to 8°C	

Note: - Never freeze DPT, IPV or Tetanus (all of which freeze at temperatures below 3 C)

- Storage times are recommended maximum figures.

Remember to check expiry dates.

(Adapted from 'Manage the Cold Chain', WHO, February 1985.)

more MCH and family planning services could be provided at less cost-the same worker providing family planning and immunisation services more efficiently and effectively.

At present depending on the mercy of DFPOs the DIOs get some contingency funds. Some states have made a provision of Rs. 2,000 per year per PHC as contingency for purchase of kerosene, etc. In many sub-centres it is usual to find stoves without kerosene, there is kerosene but no stove, sometimes the stove is not working, if both are there, there is no drum steriliser! But there are also smart health workers in these sub-centres, who mobilise community help to carry out safe vaccination, despite kerosene shortage and other handicaps. This author came across a health worker in the Shivalik hills of Himachal, who befriended a tea-shop keeper to get her needles and syringes sterilised, when her stove and kerosene failed[13]. This worker was found adopting a primary health care strategy in the real sense by involving the communities.

There are far-reaching implications of sterilising needles and syringes. in the context of primary health care. It is now well-established that human immunodeficiency virus (HIV) causes acquired immuno deficiency syndrome (AIDS). HIV spreads among others, through the use of unsterile needles and other skin-piercing practices. Women of reproductive age are more likely to have contact with health care providers than men because of their need for prenatal care and family planning services and their children's need for immunisation[14]. Hence health workers need to be constantly oriented on the dangers of using unsterile needles and syringes and promoting, what is called, sterile needle and sterile syringe for every child that comes in contact.

Reusable syringes and needles are cost-effective and safer than disposable ones. In a vast public health infrastructure that is prevailing in a country of India's size, disposable syringes are less likely to be disposed of, because of the temptation of the workers to recycle them or sell them back. Hence the danger of HIV. In the past in the early days of family planning, condoms supplied by the family planning clinics were freely used by children as balloons. Disposable syringes/needles in PHCs and sub-centres, if not properly destroyed, would have the dangerous consequences of being recycled back in the health system. Hence UIP managers have to budget for, reusable syringes and needles for long-term sustainability of UIP, till such time 'auto-destruct' syringes are commercially made available.

India has still not achieved self-reliance in its manufacturing capacity of cold chain equipment and the efforts of the technology mission on immunisation have not borne fruit. Even simple cold chain equipment like vaccine carriers or drum sterilisers are not taken up by manufacturers on a large scale, because there is not much demand either from state health directorates or from PMPs. An effective cold chain system at the state, district, PHCs and sub-centres presupposes that (a) there is no breakdown of the cold chain, due to failure of electricity, (b) contingency grants are adequate to carry out minor repairs involving small expenditures, (c) health workers have sufficient stocks of consumables like kerosene, cotton, etc. (d) workers carry vaccines to their sub-centres and out-reach sessions in vaccine carriers with full frozen ice packs and not water filled packs, (e) if there is breakdown of the cold chain at any level, the repair is done within 24 hours and the damaged vaccines are destroyed, and (f) ensure honest checking of temperature of each link in the chain everyday. If UIP is to be sustained, then sustainability, of cold chain is an important desideratum. UIP cold chain can also be used for distributing essential drugs, family planning supplies, blood collection and distribution, etc.

At present the centre, states and districts do forecast vaccine requirements fairly well, but forecasting of other UIP supply needs, such as equipment and spare parts is not developed as yet. "Improved inventory and stock control systems are needed urgently in order to provide (a) cost data for forecasting budgets, (b) utilisation data for forecasting requirement for vaccines, supplies and spareparts, (c) equipment and transport replacements However, in many states Health and Equipment Repair Organisations (HERO) are still not established and in the absence of such HEROs, cold chain equipment maintenance would pose problems. Transport expenditures account for approximately 20 per cent of UNICEF and other bilateral agencies assisting UIP. Although transport is a major UIP logistics concern, it has been sadly neglected. It is a familiar site in majority of civil hospitals in

TABLE 2
Percentage of Recurrent Costs in Total UNICEF Assistance

Type of Programmes	*Least Developed Countries (UN Designation)*	*Non-LDC Lower/Lower-Middle Income Countries like India*	*Upper, Middle and Highier Income Countries*
EPI	54	44	46
Diarrhoeal disease control	52	50	47
Water and sanitation	37	15	39
Education	35	30	43
Nutrition	34	40	26
Other basic health	40	27	26

the country to see grounded jeeps, station-wagons-an appearance of graveyard of four-wheelers!

Information, Education and Communication

When the Indian family planning programme was launched in the early 60s, the Information, Education and Communication (IEC) component was basically directed towards motivating eligible couples in the reproductive age group to adopt family planning practices and the media used was basically the print media and the radio (TV was not available then). The providers of family planning services, mostly the doctors were not subjected to rigorous training and orientation in IEC. Family planning was treated more medical technique than a social action, involving mothers and fathers who were the prime actors. There were few attempts to learn about people's beliefs, acceptance and practices on family planning nor were there conscious decisions to link family planning to maternal and child health or to the well-being of the family. However UIP was launched in 1985 with better media endowment, good training of health workers and doctors and with attempts to build a people's programme so that maternal and child health was viewed as a first step towards a healthy family. "Efforts to augment demand generation and community participation for immunisation must focus on the consumers of the programme with due regard to their problems, needs, biases and aspirations. Highest level of political commitment to the programme can have a maximal translation into action by appropriate health education and dissemination of information in a language people can understand and with a cultural bias familiar to them"[16].

UIP managers both at the centre and states have tackled IEC efforts in the following ways during 1985-90:

(a) Training and communication of UIP for government sector medical officers, health workers, ICDS workers, teachers, etc. (b) Communication of UIP related messages to mothers and fathers, through radio, TV, print and folk media. (c) Motivating NGO sectors like Rotary, Lions, Indian Medical Association members, medical college faculty to take up social mobilisation activities for UIP. All these were attempted in different states in varying degrees of success and disappointment. Three-tier training for UIP was attempted, the first tier for the district-level programme officers, the second tier for the PHC level doctors who supervise UIP and the third tier for the sub-centre level health workers/ANMs who actually did the vaccination work. The central ministry of health adapted sections from the WHO's four-volume Training Manual on National Immunisation Programme, viz, 'Conducting the Immunisation Session', 'Manage the Cold Chain System', 'Evaluate Vaccination and Coverage' and 'Conduct Disease Surveillance'. In addition 'manuals for health workers' on UIP in regional languages were brought out in large number. While there was no dearth of manuals, teaching aids like video cassettes on different facets of UIP, the actual training and orientation left much to be desired.

For instance the ministry of health has allowed vaccine wastage up to 50 per cent for heat-sensitive vaccine like polio, measles, but these instructions, in some states, have not been passed on to health workers, who actually do the vaccinations. Training and supervision particularly in a person-intensive programme like immunisation, go together, because the PHC medical officer, who superviser an immunisation session conducted by a health worker, whether in a clinic or an outreach session, can observe the mistakes that take place in actual vaccination (e.g. problems like the health worker doing subcutaneous vaccination where it should have been intramuscular, or refusing to vaccinate a child with minor fever, etc. could all be corrected on the spot).

In one of the KAP studies done by National Review of Immunisation in 1989, the answers given by auxiliary nurse midwives (ANMs), to a dominant question "If a mother brings a child having one of the following six conditions, would you accept, child for vaccination or refuse?", were revealing (see Table 3).

This means training and orientation of ANMs leaves much to be desired. Unfortunately, wherever this author has visited PHCs in some states, medical officers feel that "it is too small a job for them to look into". Doctors' own knowledge not only on MCH practices but also on many other public health issues depends on how much they keep updating their knowledge. There are no periodic regional language public health news letters to reach the health workers across the country. (Recently the Post Graduate

Institute of Medical Education and Research, Chandigarh, has launched out a quarterly English newsletter, *Paediatric Primary Care,* for distribution to all the PHCs in the country. The ministry of health (GOI) brings out in English a monthly *National Immunisation Mission Feedback Information and Technical Update.* If this is brought out also in regional languages health workers would benefit, and this would contribute to some extent to the sustainability of UIP. Already 30 districts have been selected for acute respiratory infection disease reduction and many districts are implementing plans for control of diarrhoeal diseases. Hence instead of just calling it National Immunisation Update, it could be called *National Mother and Child Health Mission Update* and include all operational experiences of MCH programmes across the country.

Mass communication for UIP has been tremendous and the media penetration particularly TV messages on immunisation has been exciting. This has no doubt helped to generate demand for immunisation services, in those areas which have high per capita endowment of TV sets. In some states notably in Punjab the song and drama division of the ministry of information and broadcasting has trained folk artists to spread messages on immunisation and child health. Both the electronic and folk media can supplement the KAP of mothers and fathers towards family health.

Sustainability of IEC presupposes that all the facts for life are spread in unison so that primary health care strategies are understood both by service providers and consumers. Nobody has calculated the cost of replenishing and improving IEC materials supplied country-wide during 1985-90. Already a large number of tin-plated posters on vaccine preventable diseases distributed in 1985 all over the country have been disfigured and lie rusted. States which have reached high coverage levels in UIP have to concentrate on disease reduction and accordingly IEC materials have to be different from those for states which have not reached high coverage levels. After all the objective of UIP is not vaccination but disease reduction. What is the role of villagers and town dwellers in reporting outbreak of vaccine preventable diseases? A plethora of IEC materials designed for different segments of the con-sumers like school teachers, village elders, opinion makers, mothers, doctors, health workers at different periods of time have to be continuously updated and discarded, so that messages are not out of tune with changing epidemiological situation.

Efforts to motivate NGO sectors like Rotary, medical colleges and the Indian Medical Association fraternity during 1985-90 have been a mixed experience. Some say that if two doctors disagree on a diagnosis, the patient dies! Several doctors in medical colleges and in the Indian Medical Association, the Indian Academy of Paediatricians, expressed differences on a range of UIP matters like different schedule of immunisation, storage, transport of vaccines and special instituations in which various vaccines and use of immunoglobulins may be used. This resulted in confusion among the lay public and the clinicians alike. In one medical college this author had seen three types of immunisation schedules that were adopted, one in the paediatric department, another type in the gynaecology/obstetrics department and a third in the department of social and preventive medicine! The national schedule of immunisation adopted by the ministry of health (GOI) was distorted, creating confusion in the minds of mothers. The Indian Academy of Paediatrics had to bring out an update on immunisation in practice to help to clear the conflicting opinions of different PMPs[17].

Universal child/mother immunisation means both private and public sector doctors vaccinate at every opportunity. At present in urban areas not all PMPs are doing immunisation in their clinics, despite willingness of district civil surgeons/chief medical officers to provide cost-free vaccines, but with a stipulation that PMPs furnish data on vaccinations done, every time they obtain fresh stock of vaccines. PMPs are allowed to levy what are called 'service charges' but not the price of the vaccine. But this author's experience in some of the urban areas is that the PMPs do not have cold chain facilities, they do not have a thorough knowledge of vaccine preservation methods, and do not have adequate logistics to bring vaccines from the district stores. Some PMPs treat the vaccines as drugs which can be stored on shelves! Hence IEC for PMPs has to be designed selectively and followed up with

TABLE 3: ANMs' RESPONSES ON IMMUNISATION

Conditions from which the child is Suffering	*Percentage of ANMs Giving Response*	
	Refuse	Accept
1. Cough/cold	53.2	46.8
2. Diarrhoea vomitting	82.4	17.6
3. Fever below 101°F	59.7	40.3
4. Fever above 101°F	93.7	6.3
5. Malnutrition	56.7	43.0
6. Skin disease/boils	69.0	30.9

constant orientation, feedback and back-up system for proper reporting of vaccinations done as well as surveillance of vaccine preventible diseases to the district/PHC medical officers/municipal authorities, etc. At present reporting of vaccinations done by PMPs is either weak or non-existent.

The Rotary 'polio-plus' programme in India has been contributing both money and voluntary humanpower for social mobilisation towards UIP. Voluntary humanpower of the Rotary came forward in different places in different ways, some contributed IEC materials like banners, posters and some went from house-to-house and brought the eligible infants and mothers for vaccination to the special camps. Some Rotarians served at mass immunisation camps and went about systematically first identifying eligibles in their towns (as we do voter identification), giving them vaccination cards (voter identification slips), bringing them *to* vaccination sites (casting the vote) and following them for subsequent doses. The Rotary Club of Mandi' Gobindgarh in Patiala district of Punjab conducted the programme like this[18]. How do we sustain the enthusiasm of Rotary and other voluntary groups in UIP and other health promotion activities? This needs continuous and selective IEC support to these groups from the health sector managers.

Vaccines and Vaccination Strategies

We have already analysed the trade-offs between fixed-day strategies and mobile/outreach immunisation camps. A 'best' VIP strategy is one in which immunisation services are piggybacked with other primary health care interventions like vitamin A prophylaxis, ORT, ARI and family planning services, so that it is both cost effective and impact generating. India has already established a countrywide network of primary health centre and sub-centres. We have now to ensure that this system works and we do not need new structures and systems. UIP in India has already used this structure and available evidence suggests that it has worked.

Table 4
Some Reported Incident of Deaths Following Vaccinations

Year	*Incidents Total*	*Measles Vaccine*	*Other Vaccines*	*Other Drugs*	*Temporal*
1985	1	0	0	1	0
1986	9	4	2	1	2
1987	4	4	0	0	0
1988	11	9	1	0	1
Total	25	17	3	2	3

Source: National Immunisation Mission, Ministry of Health, GOI, 1989.

Among the problems faced during 1985-90, particularly in the early stages, the one concerning adverse reactions was crucial. Some of the adverse reactions associated with measles vaccination led to the death of some children, which surcharged public anger, media outrage, and fear among the mothers and vaccinators alike.

Several investigations done soon after adverse reactions, by the states, revealed that they were mostly related to human errors, like faulty sterilisation practices, faulty cold chain, bad diluents, etc. and not due to sub-standard vaccines. There are three partners in an immunisation process, viz, mother (child), vaccinator and vaccines (vaccine manufacturer). Whenever adverse reactions take place the tendency is to blame the vaccine manufacturer, who is never present in the vaccination session. It is expedient to pass on the responsibility to the manufacturer to save the situation. In one district a measles vial was reconstituted one month prior to the administration of the vaccine, syringes and needles were not sterilised, and 12 children were vaccinated from a ten-dose vial. In another district semiused measles vaccine vial was to be contaminated with pseudomonas and candida species, but unused vaccine vial of the same batch was found to be of standard quality. In another mishap of another district the health worker was issued 40 doses (four vials) of measles vaccine and he was reported to have kept these vials at room temperature.

However, such incidents are now on the decline, thanks to improved training and supervision. One report of vaccination-induced mishap is sufficient to reverse the progress of UIP. With new vaccines coming in the wake of new advances, vaccination strategies at the PHCs/sub-centres, have to be improved constantly, so that it is possible to sustain all health care strategies.

Evaluation and Results of Immunisation Programme

Evaluation of UIP consists of the following four interrelated aspects, which determine its sustainability (a) monitoring of vaccines, coverage, cold chain integrity and supervision of vaccinators performance to measure their efficiency and effectiveness; (b) surveillance of target diseases to determine their extent and distribution; (c) review of strategies and operations for' improved implementation; and (d) analysis of data to determine the value of immunisation in terms of costs and benefits. At present in most of the districts civil surgeons/chief medical officers do have a system of monthly meetings to review all health programmes in the district. Similarly monthly meetings are held by medical officers of PHCs to review all health programmes at the PHC level, in which all health workers and supervisors attend. In a majority of these meetings administrative matters like staff not getting salary arrears, constraints in achieving physical targets (like family planning targets), malaria cases detected, immunisation targets achieved, etc. are discussed. Little time is left to discuss managerial and programmatic problems like why certain categories of women (e.g. slum women) are not bringing their children, why dropouts for certain antigens are not coning down, why in certain pockets disease trends are not coming down despite high coverage levels of immunisation, etc. These programmatic stock-taking of immunisation has implications for sustaining UIP since it serves the purposes of management audit of the programme, and thus helps improved implementation.

In some PHCs smart medical officers have used these monthly meetings to retrain, motivate and recharge the managerial capabilities of health workers. In those PHCs having reached high coverage levels of immunisation, the efforts of health workers have to be directed towards, what the experts in smallpox eradication programme call, a surveillance containment strategy[19].

Surveillance means 'watch with suspicion attention and authority'. Wherever consistently high coverage levels are reported, even a single case of polio or measles is to be treated as an outbreak and as such investigated. If this happens then we can conclude that surveillance is taking place and both attention and authority are supposed to have been applied. Due to its high mortality measles is the most important disease to monitor. It is also a good indicator of immunisation effectiveness as measles vaccine is normally the last antigen to be given. Line listing of cases in hospitals is now attempted in the country as part of a country-wide surveillance system for vaccine preventable diseases. But hospital data are biased because a change in peoples' use of the hospital can affect the number of admissions without a real change in the community incidence. Still a good surveillance system including line listing will help document reductions in morbidity and mortality that occur when high coverage levels are achieved.

In addition to several monitoring and evaluation tools a programme like the UIP needs constant quality improvement in its day-to-day management so that mothers are assured of the quality service and the programme thus sustains. Several computer and management-based programmes are now developed by WHO and other donor agencies, like coverage survey analysis system (COSAS), EPI information system (EPIIS), lot quality assurance sampling (LQAS), 75 house survey, rapid assessments, to help the managers of UIP to improve the effectiveness of the programme[20]. But these cannot substitute the local gut knowledge of medical officers, who can manage UIP at their level, with hindsight and foresight.

References

1. Ministry of Health, GOI, *Universal Immunisation* by 1990, New Delhi, 1985.
2. D. Banerjee, 'Politics of Immunisation Programme', *Economic and Political Weekly,* April 7, 1990, and 'Crash of Immunisation Programme: Consequences of a Totalitarian Approach', *International Journal of Health Services* Vol. 20, No. 3, pp. 501-510, 1990.
3. See *Primary Health Care: A Joint Report* by director general of WHO and executive director UNICEF, Geneva, WHO, 1978.
4 Fred Sai,Senior Population Adviser, World Bank, *Protecting the World's Children-An Agenda for the 1990s,* The Task Force for Child Survival, Tufts University European Centre, Talloires, France, March 10-12, 1988.
5. See Task Force for Child Survival, *Protecting the World's Children,* Bellagio II, Colombia, October 1985. The Task Force was formed by the five of the Bellagio Con-ference participants, viz, WHO, UNICEF, World Bank, UNDP and Rockefeller Foundation. This task force still continues to oversee immunisation programme globally and brings out *World Immunisation News* from Atlanta, USA.
6. ALIVE was used by Donald A Henderson, chief medical officer of WHO's Smallpox Eradication Unit from 1966 to 1977 and former dean of Johns Hopkins School of Hygiene and Public Health, Baltimore. ALIVE stands for A for administration and organisation, L for logistics, and cold chain, I for information, education and communication, V for vaccines and vaccination strategies and E for evaluation. But this author has added C after A and made it ACLIVE. This C refers to census or enumeration of new-borns.
7. National Institute of Health and Family Welfare, *National Review of Immunisation Programme in India,* New Delhi, 1989, p. 9.
8 Christian Medical College, Department of Community Medicine, *Survey of Missed Opportunities in Ludhiana City,* June 1989.

9. *WHO Planning Principles for Accelerated Immunisation Activities,* a joint WHO/UNICEF Statement, Geneva, 1985, p. 17.
10. J P Unger, 'Can Intensive Campaigns Dynamise Front-Line Health Services? Evaluation of an Immunisation Campaign in Thies Health District Senegal', *Social Science and Medicine,* Vol. 32, No. 3, pp. 249-59, 1991.
11. *EPI Essentials-A Guide for Programme Officers,* REACH, Arlington (USA), 1989, p. 49.
12. *Evaluation and Monitoring of National Immunisation Programme,* WHO, Geneva, 1986, p. 20.
13. Manu N Kulkarni, 'Of Needles and Tea Shops', *Tribune,* Spectrum column devoted for development news and views, Chandigarh, December 1, 1988.
14. *AIDS Prevention: Guidelines for MCH/FP Programme Managers,* WHO Geneva, 1990, p. 37.
15. *EPI Logistics and Cold Chain-Improving Quality,* WHO, Geneva, 1990, p. 9.
16. Ministry of Health, GOI, *Towards Universal Immunisation by 1990,* New Delhi, 1985, p. 40.
17. See S K Mittal and S Kukreja, *Immunisation in Practice.* Indian Academy of Paediatrics, Delhi Branch, 1989.
18. See Manu N Kulkarni, 'Needle Brigade', *Tribune,* Spectrum Column, Chandigarh, January 10, 1991.
19. Donald A Henderson, *Victory over Smallpox: An Interview on Population Information Programme,* Johns Hopkins University, March-April, Baltimore, 1986.
20. *EPI Essential - A Guide for Programme Officers, Resources for Child Health (REACH),* Arlington, USA, 1989, pp. 130-32.

Child Survival Programmes Revisited

The very evident flaws in India's polio eradication programme launched in the 1980s are indicative of the fact that bodies at the international (UNICEF) and the national level (i.e. the Indian government) have failed in their primary task of controlling child mortality rates. Similar experiences have been reported from other countries. The UNICEF needs to rededicate itself anew to the health-related goals that form a vital part of the millennium development goals, by reaching out to groups and organisations operating at the grass root level.

Child survival programmes (CSPs) launched by UNICEF in the 1980s in cooperation with many developing countries focused primarily on ensuring the survival of children by protecting them against what were called vaccine preventable diseases (VPDs) like diphtheria, tetanus, polio and measles. In these programmes, initially mothers were not assigned any significance. But then suddenly WHO and other donor agencies discovered the "forgotten mothers" and launched what was then called reproductive child health (RCH) programmes focusing on the reproductive problems of mothers particularly promoting safe delivery practices and maternal care along with child care. The World Summit for Children in 1990 called for a worldwide reduction in child mortality to below 70 deaths per 1000 live births by the year 2000. This "call" has still not been met. The *Lancet* - a British medical journal has criticised the UNICEF's handling of these goals in several issues. It is unfortunate that UNICEF/WHO have not taken these critical global analytical reflections by a premier medical journal like the *Lancet* seriously. The situation has been further compounded by the explosive spread of HIV / AIDS killing millions of infants through what has been known as mother to child transmission of the HIV virus. In Africa child mortality rates are soaring. Then came the millennium development goals (MDGs). Out of the eight goals three goals are directly related to CSPs and they are unlikely to be achieved even by the deadline of 2015 according to all present indications. "Apart from three of the eight goals, eight of the 18 targets and eighteen of the 48 indicators relate to health - so no one can say that development is just about economic growth[2]. Health-related goals, however, are crucial to the overall attainment of MDGs.

The scathing attack of the editor of the *Lancet* on the leadership of the world's leading agency - UNICEF- responsible for protecting the lives of mothers and children needs to be examined carefully to know where things have gone wrong: "UNICEF has lost its way during Carol Bellamy's long term of office. A corporate lawyer and financier for many years, Bellamy went on to become a New York politician who was thrust into a position that demanded deep experience of children's issues - and especially child health - worldwide. It was a role that she, was ill equipped for the job despite her evident enthusiasm for UNICEF's ideals. While Bellamy has focused on girls' education, early childhood development, immunisation, HIV/AIDS and protecting children from violence, abuse exploitation, she has failed to address the essential health needs of children. In contrast, Carol Bellamy's predecessor, (the) late James Grant during his 15-year tenure, showed an unflagging commitment, vision and dedication to improving the lives of the world's least advantaged - the mothers and children of the developing world."[3]

Many have raised doubts even on the well established polio eradication programme in India: "According to the National Polio Surveillance Project data 60 per cent of those who developed polio in 2001 were administered four or more doses of oral polio vaccine (OPV), 44 per cent in 2002 of those who contracted the disease were administered the vaccine and in 2003 this figure went up to 51 per cent[4]. It is therefore essential that we examine how these CSPs have been managed and what has been the impact of these CSPs on infant mortality, maternal mortality and morbidities even before we talk of child rights. First, mother and child have to survive and their "right to life" has to be ensured before we think of their rights for education and upbringing. The Bellagio Child Survival Study Group in Italy under the auspices of the Rockefeller Foundation in February 2003 critically examined the global scenario of child survival and the *Lancet* brought out a special issue on matters affecting child survival in the world[5].

Why and How Children Die?

The CSPs are basically aimed at reducing infant mortality rate and are closely linked to this, is the maternal mortality rate as indicators in many developing countries have shown in the past. When the infant mortality is higher, it usually leads to multiple pregnancies and that leads to maternal depletion and subsequent mortality of mothers. More than 10 million children die each year, largely because of preventable causes and mostly in poor countries. Six countries account for 50 per cent of worldwide deaths among children younger than five years and 42 countries for 90 per cent. The causes of death differ substantially from one country to another as does the epidemiology. The key factors are undernutrition coupled with infectious diseases and pneumonia and diarrhoea also remain the main causes everywhere. Hence, the universal immunisation of both mother and the child was the weapon used to fight IMR and MMR. Now HIV/AIDS is responsible for more than 10 per cent of deaths in just three of the 42 countries. According to the UNICEF report on meeting the promises of the World Summit for Children, polio is still endemic in 20 countries, less than 50 per cent of children under one year of age in sub-Saharan Africa receive DPT3, in 14 countries measles vaccination coverage is less than 50 per cent, 27 countries account for 90 per cent of all remaining neo-natal tetanus and vertical single focus acute respiratory infection (ARI) programmes seem to have had little impact[6]. Similarly, there is no world-wide evidence that MMR has declined over the last decade. 5,15,000 women still die every year as a result of pregnancy and child birth. The reach of delivery care is only 36 per cent in south Asia and 42 per cent in sub-Saharan Africa and available evidence shows little change during 1990s in the prevalence of anaemia among pregnant women.

Who is responsible for this dismal situation? National/local governments across the world who plan and monitor the CSP programmes or is it the lead agency for overseeing the lot of the world's children - UNICEF? Has vaccine technology failed or has the management of VPDs failed? What is the role of WHO in rendering technical advice on controversial vaccines like oral polio vaccine or injectible vaccines? What has been the leadership role of bodies like UNICEF/WHO in mobilising global resources and global leadership for tackling these CSPs? These questions come to the fore when we attempt to analyse the causes and consequences and look for remedial strategies and actions for better outcomes and results.

Impact of Immunisation

Universal Immunisation Programme (UIP) the world over was the sheet anchor of CSPs and its coverage and impact is still not visible on children across the world although it has contributed significantly to the reduction of VPDs. UIP has to be judged on what is called ACLIVE principle[7]. A stands for administration and organisation, C for continuous enumeration (census) of newborns to catch them for vaccination, L for logistics and cold chain for vaccine storage and movement, I for information education and communication, V for vaccines and vaccination strategies and E for evaluation of coverage and impact. The father of small pox eradication programme Donald Henderson used the administration, logistics, information, vaccine, evaluation (ALIVE) principle. Unlike small pox vaccine which was just one dose, in CSR, a range of vaccines are used and their proper storage is very crucial to maintain their potency. Hence as a part of UIP, cold chain and tracking of newborns (census) becomes critical. Unlike small pox which was a one shot affair. UIP is long term and continuous. However, despite the massive coverage of polio immunisation programme its complete eradication remains elusive even in developed countries. The Government launched the national immunisation days which were also termed as Pulse Polio Immunisation (PPIs) in 1995 and over the last 10 years no one knows how effectively these PPIs have been conducted and what have been the gains and losses in the entire campaign[8]. The most serious problem not just in PPIs but in the entire UIP is the way in which the cold chain has been maintained to keep the vaccine potent by maintaining the required temperature (see Chart on temperature requirement in vaccine storage).

Basically there are four partners in the UIP programme - the mother, the child (mother has to bring the child for immunisation), the vaccine administrator and the vaccine itself (how potent is it and how is it preserved). Unless all the four are synchronised the impact of the UIP is not felt. It was February 23, 2003 in a Bangalore suburb when the national immunisation day and the pulse polio drive was inaugurated with fanfare. It was noon when interviewed the mother, the vaccine administrator and saw the vaccine carrier to see how well it was kept. I discovered that there was no ice in the ice pack, and the vaccine vial was half-empty; the vaccine administrator was not sure for how long the vial had been open. Such pulse polio centres immediately raise doubts on matters of vaccine efficiency and the potency of the polio vaccine.

Bangalore proud of a flagship public-private partnership called Bangalore Agenda Task Force (BATF).The Karnataka health department should have joined hands with them to conduct lot quality assurance sampling (LQAS) as per the WHO mandate to see how effectively the polio vaccine is stored.

How Cold is the Cold Chain?

Besides, the vaccine technology itself is changing fast since the launch of PPIs. There is now a section of scientists advo-cating the use of inactivated polio vaccine (IPV) than the OPV. The OPV in some areas has led to what is termed as vaccine associated paralytic polio (V APP) "Jacob John leading virologist in CMC Vellore is a strong advocate of IPV and according to him IPV evokes a strong immune response and also generates immunity in the inner lining of the digestive tract (which was supposed to be one of OPV's advantages) and creates a herd effect by reducing transmission of the virus to others. These were all the qualities of a good vaccine according to Jacob John[9]. WHO - the global health leader - is still not able to decide on the future of polio vaccine technology, whether to switch to IPV or continue with the OPV. The global certification of polio eradication would be confined only to the elimination of wild polio virus and this is an important difference between small pox and polio eradication. OPV has created uncertainty whether the polio virus will ever be eliminated. After more than ten years of being polio-free, the Carribbean island of Hispaniola reported outbreak of the disease in the summer of 2000.

UNICEF Leadership Failure

Next in significance to vaccine and its storage, the vital partner is the mother-child partnership for getting the vaccine inserted/injected. Dropout rates in UIP are a bad sign and according to UNICEF, health systems in countries where the dropout rate is more than 10 per cent are considered flawed[10]. Drop outs could reflect lower motivation among mothers to bring back their kids for completing the shots or unresponsive vaccine administrators that do not augur well for the health of the young children and present a challenge for local health delivery system. The Bellagio Child Survival Study Group makes "a distinction between intervention and delivery strategies. Reducing child mortality and achieving the millennium development goals for child survival depend on whether effective and sustainable interventions can be delivered to high proportion of children and mothers. The distinction between interventions and delivery strategies is essential. The knowledge base for designing implementing and Sustaining effective delivery strategies is scattered and in most cases, context specific. A major research priority is how to effectively scale up the successful experience of many local projects, this area of research has unfortunately received much less attention than the development or small-scale implementation of new interventions."[11] The WHO's choosing interventions that are cost effective (CHOICE) project is examining various combinations of interventions and their cost effectiveness. But UNICEF has better knowledge on this than WHO because of UNICEF's vast network of field offices and its grassroot experience in and around 165 countries of the world with a rich knowledge pool. It is here where the global leadership of UNICEF during Carol Bellamy for a decade failed miserably. This poor leadership of UNICEF stands out in sharp contrast to the towering personality and leadership of late Jim Grant who touched the conscience of world leaders when he organised the first ever World Summit of Leaders on Children in 1990. Jim Grant's strategy of setting specific, measurable goals, lobbying tirelessly for their achievements, monitoring and publicising progress towards them was remarkable in the history of world development. In the decade and half he spent as head of UNICEF, he personally met more than 100 heads of state to enlist their personal and political support for the achievement of specific goals for children. He would meet them carrying iodised salt and an ORS packet in his coat to demonstrate to the heads of states how simple and powerful techniques can prevent childhood deaths.

The present millennium development goals were actually conceived by Jim Grant when he organised the First World Summit Storage on Children in 1990. The world leaders need to be reminded of their broken promises now, not just by UN bodies but by private foundations like the Bill Gates Foundation, Bellagio Child Survival. Group, drug companies, civil society groups, professional societies ministries of health, education and finance of developing countries who have to steer their ministries into action. These alliances for child survival are in bad shape now and they must be forged at global, regional, national and local levels. HIV/AIDS is now a big

Chart-2

Vaccine Level Maximum Storage Time	*Central Store up to 8 months*	*Regional up to 3 months*	*Health Care up to 1 month*	*Transport up to 1 week*
Measles Yellow Fever Oral Polio	-15 °C to -25 °C			
DPT Tetanus Toxoid IPV DT BCG			2 °C to 8 °C	

Note: - Never freeze DPT, IPV or Tetanus (all of which freeze at temperatures below 3 °C)

- Storage times are recommended maximum figures.

Remember to check expiry dates.

(Adapted from 'Manage the Cold Chain', WHO, February 1985.)

threat and we need to think of new vaccines, new infant feeding practices to save both mothers and newborns suffering from HIV / AIDS. UNICEF estimated that 7,20,000 infants were born with HIV worldwide in 2001 and till the HIV vaccine is found, we have to save these infants with costly anti-retrovirals which have to be subsidised if we care for the infants.

Misplaced emphasis on child rights by the present leadership of UNICEF is not only unfortunate but tragic. Preoccupation with rights ignores the fact that children will have no opportunity for development at all unless they survive. The most fundamental right of all is the right to survive and in the words of *Lancet* "child survival must sit at the core of UNICEF's advocacy and country work. Currently and shamefully it does not."

Notes

1. 'Informed Choices for Attaining the MDGs', *Lancet,* September 11, 2004.
2. Andy Haines and Andrew Cassels, 'Can Millenium Development Goals Be Attained' *British Medical Journal.* August 14, 2004.
3. *Lancet,* December 11, 2004.
4. Yash Paul, 'Check the Vaccine: Why Are Children Developing Polio even after Inoculation'? *Down to Earth.* February 15, 2005.
5. *Lancet,* Vol. 361, 2003, www.thelancet.com.
6. UNICEF, *'We the Children'* New York, 2001,p. 20.
7. Manu N Kulkarni, 'UIP in India - Issues of Sustainability'. *Economic and Political Weekly.* July 4, 1992.
8. Manu N Kulkarni, How Useful is Pulse Strategy for Polio Eradication'. *Economic and Political Weekly,* March 15. 1997.
9. N Gopal Raj. 'Eradicating Polio'. *The Hindu,* Chennai, November 23, 2004.
10. UNICEF, 'The Progress of Nations', 2000, New York, p. 22.
11. The *Lancet,* Vol. 362, July 12, 2003.

2

Girls, Women and Mothers: Missing Links

It is very unfortunate that NGO leaders like Shankar Singh et al defend child marriages in Rajasthan, when they assert: "The internal logic of child marriage is fairly sound. Child weddings take place primarily amongst OBCs and dalits and therefore most often poorer families." According to them "the 'muklava' or 'gohna' is delayed and the married girl does not go to the in-laws' place till the age of 18 which is the legal age of consent. There is sufficient internal pressure within rural communities to support any effort to delay the ceremony of mukhlava."

Will Singh and his friends provide family-level evidence: regarding the delay in mukhlava among the married adolescent girls in Rajasthan? If one does a survey, girl-by-girl and ascertain when they got married and when they were sent to in-laws' house for mukhlava we would really come to know the time gap between marriage and mukhlava.In the absence of such evidence it is all a social hunch not supported by facts. In fact the pressures are different. The in-laws of the girls do not want the girls to go to school because she is 'married'. In one of my field visits in a village of Gwalior district of MP, I asked the mother of the girl who was married at 13, why the girl was not going to school, the mother replied that the in-laws and particularly the husband of the girl (age 20) does not want his 'girl-wife' to go to school lest, she becomes more literate than him. Girls when 'sold' in marriage get a price (called natra in these districts of MP). Hence there are economic pressures for marrying girls early. These parents put forward the excuse of not getting bridegrooms later when girls grow. But the hidden agenda is to get the price for the girl!. The NGOs, the parents of both the girl and the boy and the caste leaders shall join hands in this campaign against child marriage. The incident in Rajasthan where Banwari was gang raped because she campaigned against child marriage, is unfortunate, but that incident instead of slowing down the campaign should intensify it, and NGOs instead of defending child marriage should vehemently intensify their fight against early marriage of girls.

The districts of Mandsaur, Ratlam, Rajgarh and Guna in MP which are bordering Rajasthan have similar problems of child marriage and on akshaya tritiya (akha teej), in these districts thousands of girls are married in group marriages.The collectors of these districts in MP have launched campaigns against child marriages and have successfully averted and postponed such marriages using persuasive, coercive and other social mobilisation techniques. In Mandsaur district a dynamic collector successfully used his government functionaries, the press, the NGOs and caste leaders to avert and postpone hundreds of child marriages among the OBCs like lohars, dhobis. kumavat, gujars, mali, chamar and patidar. He mobilised everybody in the district for this campaign.

The success of his work may be estimated from the following cases: In Narsinghpur Block Galyakhodi village the parent Madanlal cancelled the engagement of the girl child Manju just before the group marriage, when Koumi Ekta Committee and Nari Hitchintak volunteers approached him and explained him the consequences of girl child marriage.Nehru Yuvak Kendra and Mahila Balvikas Adhikari in Umaheda village in Mandsaur district approached a family where girl child was to be married. The pandit, Shankarlal who was ready to solemnise the marriage turned around and said that he will never solemnise such a marriage which affects the life of the child and folded his book and 'pethi' and also pledged to tell other panditjis not to solemnise girl child marriages.

The jatha in Sitamahu village filed a complaint with the police against four parents trying to marry their girls (12 years old) under the Child Marriage Restraint Act.

Four school-going boys of Narasinghpur in Mandsaur pledged not to marry, despite the pressure of their parents, before reaching the age 20 and would complete their study. Kharvahi village resident Phulsinha Dangi got his 12-year-old daughter Anita married to a 30-year-old man and on the muklava (gohna) day she fainted with vaginal ruptures and was admitted to district hospital and was treated by Manju Jain *(Sandhya Prakash,* Indore, May 16). Police complaint was filed and a case was registered.

In Sitamahu block, Meriakhedi village, child-bridegroom Shankar Gurjar, learnt when he was ready to go in 'barat', that the marriage ceremony was cancelled, he threw his 'pagdi' and jumped from the cart and ran away to play with his friends. 'Barat lauti' is a story in which six girls were stopped from wedlock when volunteers of Kaumi Ekta Parishad and government functionaries landed in the house of Ramnarayan Kumavat in Lodha village of Mandsaur district and stopped his four small daughters from facing the barat.

In Ratana village the lady drum beater in the festivals, Geeta Devi, when approached by volunteers of campaign against child marriage, agreed not to beat the drum in the marriage of girls of her village and took a pledge before the goddess Durga of the village, that she would never do such things again.

Such small acts initiated by a cross section of village communities can alone bring awareness and build social pressures against child marriage. Campaigns are one time activities but the collectors have kept a vigil on such families who have cancelled the marriages so they do not perform the marriages of girls secretly. The girls of these families have to be put into school, which alone can empower these girls and schooling alone is the best weapon against child marriage.

Silver Lining

For many girls in the Morena and Sagar districts of M.P., adolescene meant the begining of a lifetime of exploitation. Till Rama Sanhei and Champaben showed them it could be different.

The Bedia community has long been associated with the flesh trade. With a population of more than 10 lakhs it is spread over Madhya Pradesh (M.P.), Rajasthan, and parts of Uttar Pradesh (U.P.). Traditionally a farming community, the feudal *zamindari* system and falling land productivity gradually combined to draw this tribe down into prostitution.

Eventually, the birth of the girl child became a cause for celebration for the Bedias because she meant a steady source of income for the family by her service to the *zamindars.* There was no female infanticide in the community as a girl child meant luck. In fact the boy child came to be considered a liability.

Although the Bedia community is singled out in connection with the flesh trade, the practice is also prevalent among other backward communities. Parts of Gwalior, Morena, Bhind, Sagar, Rajgarh, Ratlam are known for their flourishing flesh trade, the constitutional provisions against child prostitutition notwithstanding. This is also the child marriage belt where many teenage girls are married off in the *Akshaya Tritiya* every year despite laws against it.

For years, Bedia girls were taken into custody under some pretext by the police and sexually abused. These girls were eventually sent to Delhi or Bombay by their parents with the connivance of the police. However two individuals had taken up battle with, the M.P. police. They are Champaben of Satyashodhan Ashram at Patharia and Ram Sanhei.

Considered the Mahatma Gandhi of the Bedia community, Ram Sanhei, founder of the Abhudaya Ashram of Morena, has relentlessly fought his own community on the issue of child prostitution. On December 15,1988, he filed a public interest petition in the M.P. High Court asserting that 1,631 women and 126 children were illegally lodged at the women's short stay home, Gwalior: He claimed that those involved were let off without a trial when they falsely alleged that the women and girls were loitering and thus had to be detained in the short stay home indefinitely. The High Court observed that the state government and the district magistrate had not taken any action under section 13 of the Suppression of Immoral Traffic Act, 1956. The court further pointed out that special police officers had been appointed in areas where prostitution had not been declared as prohibited. On the other hand, the special police had not been appointed in areas where prostitution had been prohibited. Finally the court concluded that the State, other than discharging routine functions, had not taken any action to curb the evil of immoral traffic.

This forced the government to initiate reformist programmes like the Jawali Yojana to tackle the issue of girl child prostitution and begin the "social overhauling" of the Bedias. Under Jawali Yojana, a two-stage protection and promotion is envisaged. The first stage would comprise the enrolment of girls at age six in primary schools. The second stage would be to admit the girls in middle schools or provide vocational education or training so they do not fall prey to the flesh trade.

Ram Sanhei began his Abhudaya Ashram in a rented building with local donations. Girls, mostly of the Bedia community, study there both at the primary and secondary levels, in a residential setting. Jawali Yojana envisages a payment of Rs.200 per girl per month to meet the cost of boarding and lodging. Sanhei's biggest concern is providing a decent future for the girls when they pass out.

Like Sanhei, Champa Ben is waging a one-person crusade against the coercing of girls into the flesh trade. Champa Ben is a Sarvodayite who has worked with Acharya Vinoba Bhave and got her first lessons in non-violent struggle from Wardha. She looks at the problem of child prostitution from the perspective of the Bedia family. The adult male members in the family never worked and depended solely on the forced earnings of the girl who lost her childhood to prostitution. Through education, she has convinced the male members of the family to do intensive farming and with better production of cash crops like soyabean, they are earning more. They have also been persuaded to send their daughters to school. For the last ten years, Champa Ben has performed the marriages of hundreds of Bedia girls in the age-group of 14-16 and some much younger. However, this has opened her to the charge of encouraging child marriage.

Her argument that she is protecting the girls from being forced into the flesh trade is perhaps too simplistic. That child marriage is being used to counter the social evil of prostitution is hardly a solution.

What is required is a deeper and more circumspect handling of the situation. To begin with, social empowerment of the girls through education and the provision of means of earning a livelihood is extremely important. For that, the state has to shed its lackadaisical attitude and address the problem seriously. First and foremost is the compulsory primary schooling of all girls - Bedia and non-Bedia up to the age of 14. For girls between 14 and 18, many villages do not have middle schools and this particularly is the age when girls are forced into the flesh trade or married off.

What is needed are some sort of vocational schools on the lines of the one established in Denmark which does not provide any school certificate but trains adolescent boys and girls to acquire skills which can be used for self-employment later on. Vocational education is needed in many non-tribal areas of M.P., particularly the early child marriage belts like Ratlam, Mandsaur, Rajgarh, Morena, Bhind and Sagar. In these areas, communities like Sahus, Chaurasias, Dangis, etc. practice early child marriage. Another pernicious practice prevalent in this area is that of *Natra* where one married girl is traded between many men. This is a sort of personalised prostitution which is extremely demeaning. In these districts; vocational or folk schools could be started on the model of Bahai vocational school at Indore. It provides a three-month programme of literacy, handicraft skills, production skills, communication skills and legal literacy (for example how to file a police complaint if harassed), conceived specially for tribal girls. This training helps the girls to become, if not salaried workers, then at least responsible mothers.

Adolescent girls in the rural areas need to be exposed to basic skills of home management, livestock and farm management, agro-processing and horticulture skills, so that they can also earn and manage their homes better.

Many more like Champa Ben and Ram Sanhei are required in M.P. to provide hope of a better future for these girls.

Whose Health - Women's or Mothers'?

Padma Prakash questions the safe motherhood initiatives when she says, "Largest proportion of maternal deaths was due to anaemia which cannot be tackled at the point of pregnancy and is a reflection of the social status of women. Among the desperate programmes of the late 80s was the safe motherhood initiative, launched through the initiative of the World Bank and WHO which continued to short-sightedly address the problem of motherhood and not of women. All mothers are women but not all women are mothers, and it looks as though Prakash is more concerned with the health of non-mothers than mothers.

Maternal mortality, next to infant mortality, is more acute in India and other developing countries (see the table). For an Indian vidual woman, the risk of maternal death is influenced both by the risk associated with pregnancy and by the number of times she becomes pregnant. Each time a woman becomes pregnant, she runs the risk of maternal death again and this adds up over her life time. The WHO estimates that there are 5,00,000 maternal deaths worldwide every year. This is almost one every minute. A maternal death is defined by WHO as the death of a woman while pregnant or within 42 days of termination of pregnancy, irrespective of the duration or site of the pregnancy, from any cause related to or aggravated by the pregnancy or its management, but not from accidental causes. Thus a death from complications of induced abortion is maternal death, since it is considered to be due to the management of the pregnancy. By the definition, pregnancy is a necessary precondition for maternal death. Thus,anything that reduces fertility (all other things being equal) will reduce maternal deaths in the population. As we can see from the table, maternal mortality is higher than the mortality among the women of reproductive age. Hence we have to address maternal mortality issues more urgently than the reproductive health issues of women in general, as is made out by Prakash.

Maternal mortality is notoriously difficult to measure accurately. Even in developed countries where virtually all deaths are recorded, there is often no record of the fact that a woman was pregnant at or shortly before her death. The figures in the table should not be interpreted as showing that the maternal mortality rate in Bangladesh is lower than in India. Rather the purpose is to show the disparity between south-east Asia and the US.

The child survival and safe motherhood programme (CSSM)[1] launched by the centre in India to cover all districts in a

Table : Maternal Deaths Per 1,00,000 Live Births-Substantial and National Studies, 1976-1985

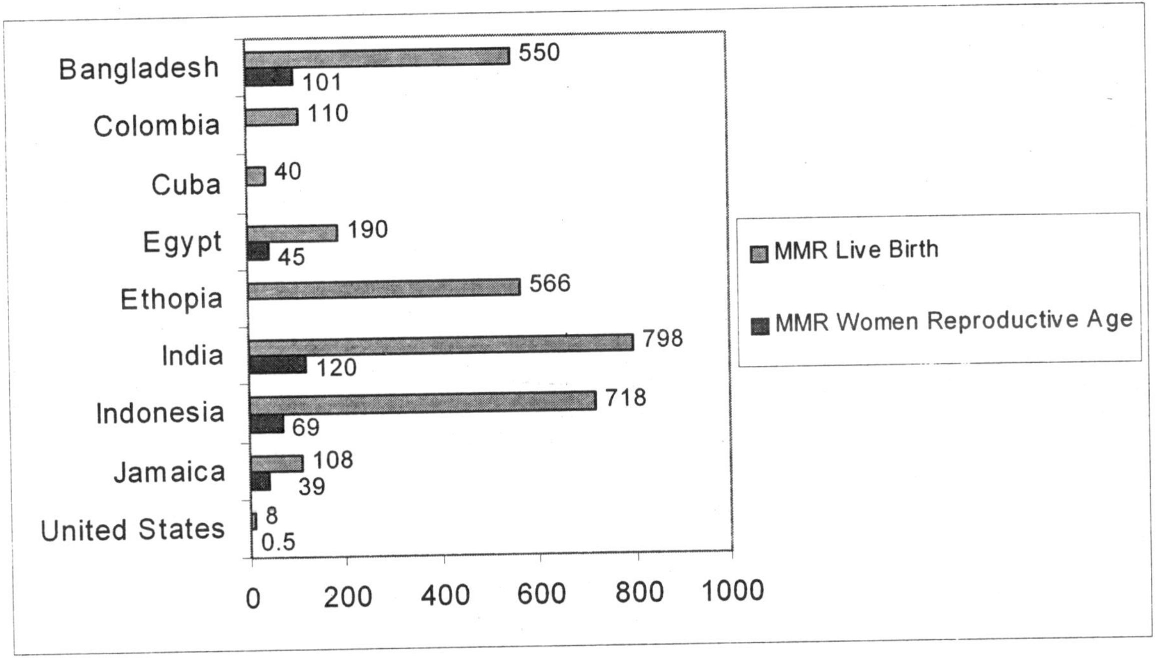

Source : School of public Health, Columbia University, p. 7.

phased manner is therefore a welcome step to tackle the maternal mortality problems. In fact, the government discovered the mother much later than the child! It should have been first Safe Motherhood and then Child Survival Programme. However, better late than never. Having built the sound infrastructure for Universal Immunisation Programme in India in the 1980s, the safe motherhood programme was structured on the edifice of the Universal Immunisation Programme to capture all women and mothers for managing their health. It is not true to say, as Prakash implies, that reproductive health issues are neglected in the safe motherhood programme. There cannot be any other better strategy to tackle reproductive health problems of women under the overall strategy of MCH and its related interventions. Visit any sub-centres or primary health centres the ANM or the block medical officer will not differentiate between a woman and a mother and they are all one in terms of care to be given or examinations to be done. No health functionary fails to integrate the reproductive health problems of women with those of MCH. In fact in the training imparted to the functionaries at all levels under the CSSM programme issues of both reproductive and maternal and non-maternal health are discussed.

It is not true as Prakash says: "The problem has always been that the MCH programmes are not taken seriously but are simply taken as entry points for the family planning programme. If anyone observes the urban or rural health centres no one finds any differentiation being done by the health staff to women and mothers - all are treated equally for their ailments. The CSSM is not a one-point programme as is asserted by Prakash. Various factors affect the well-being of women, mothers and children - socio-economic, environmental, family and, societal. It takes time to tackle socio-economic and societal problems and we cannot sit back and wait for the socio-economic climate to change or miracles to happen. A few obstetric complications are responsible for the great majority of maternal deaths-haemorrhage, infection; hypertension, obstructed labour and complications of induced abortion.The means to prevent deaths from these complications have been available for decades and do not require very sophisticated medical technologies. Under the safe motherhood programme[2] that is, being implemented at present in some districts of the country a three-tier referral structure is built the lowest being he village level traditional birth attendant (TBA or the dai) who is the primary care provider to the mother delivering the child. At present the technical competence of these dais is not adequate. If she can observe the five 'cleans' she can prevent many maternal deaths. These are clean place of the delivery, clean hands, clean cutting of the umbilical cord, clean thread and clean cord free from dirty ash or oil, etc. TBAs must know when to refer the mother to the next referral point like the health sub-centre where the ANM can handle the complications. If the ANM cannot diagnose or handle the complications she has to refer the mother to the next referral unit where complications can be tackled by a trained doctor.

Unfortunately the training of TBAs has not received the required urgent attention. In some cases TBAs cause maternal morbidity and even mortality through unsafe delivery practices such as vaginal examinations, pushing on the abdomen to hasten delivery. Under the safe motherhood programme in the country nearly 5,80,000 TBAs have to be trained. With some supplies and a bit of good training they will be able to handle the majority of deliveries at the village level without hurdles. The estimated average interval from onset to death for major obstetric complications is two hours to two days. Time is the essence in preventing delivery deaths. Unfortunately our referral systems are not geared to handle such timely interventions. Attempts are being made to strengthen first the referral units under the safe motherhood programme. It is too early to assess this programme in the country. But the programme is well-designed and should prove beneficial to the Indian mothers.

References

1. National Child Survival and Safe Motherhood Progmmme, Department of Family Welfare, Government of India, New Delhi.
2. Safe Motherhood Programmes: Options and Issues, Centre for Population and Family Health, School of Public Health, Faculty of Medicine. Columbia University, New York.

Evolving a Women's Policy

Why should we have a policy on women at all, when so many schedules and programmes for women are functioning in MP? Instead of wasting the time and energy of the government why not vigorously implement the ongoing programmes benefiting women? Can we ensure a fair deal for women just by making a policy document on women? Is it not possible to ensure gender Justice in the existing schemes and programmes designed by the government? Can a policy on women bring in gender sensitiveness among government functionaries? How can women themselves have a say in the programms affecting them not only in their designing but also in their implementation and monitoring?

These were some of the questions raised in a brainstorming workshop held in Bhopal (August 17-18, 1995) chaired by chief minister Digvijay Singh, who has personally mooted the idea of evolving a state policy on women after getting it thoroughly discussed with a wide section of women representatives of zilla, janpad, village panchayats and nagarpalikas of the state. The draft policy placed before the state assembly before it finalized for implementation in the state. Hundreds of newly elected women in the panchayats of MP vied with each other to express their happiness and criticisms on the draft policy on women in MP at the Bhopal workshop. The draft policy covers a whole range of issues affecting women in the state. Broadly, the policy goals have been ensuring survival and protection of female life, rullest participalion of women in civil society strengthening their role in decision-making, empowering women to enable them to take fullest advantage of developmental efforts in all fields, affirmative action to ensure women's full participation in economic activity, bringing about sensitisation and attitudinal change in the larger society on the women's question, prevention of atrocities and acts of violence. against women. To achieve these the draft policy has set out several innovative strategies like recognising women as major stake holders in the development of common property resources and ensuring their participation in decision making, reserving a minimum of 30 per cent job reservation for women in all sectors, removing age restrictions for widows, handicapped women in seeking employment. In all sectors, ensuring gender-based data gathering in all governmenl-initiated programmes in the state setting up an expert group in the planning department of the state, to constantly assess the impact of all developmental investments *vis-a-vis* women, and setting up all review mechanism to oversee sectoral implementation of the policy on women by different agencies in the state.

The draft policy has laid special stress on the survival, protection and development of girls' right from conception to delivery and upbringing. Economic empowerment of women has also received special emphasis, not just the flow of credit but also the legal title to land and other assets like housing. Whether ownership of land should be jointly held, not exclusively in the name of wife provoked lot of discussion in the workshop. The chief minister felt that title to land should he jointly held, not exclusively by the wife because it may create reverse exploitation and family disharmony. Bina Agarwal, who is championing the cause of land rights to women, vehemently argued that land titles and asset-entitlement not only provide security but also ensure better productivity of land and other assets, Small sized farms managed by women have shown, both in the green revolution and post-green revolution phases, increased levels of farm productivity.

Sarla Gopalan, however felt, based on Kerala's land reforms experience that as a result of exemption of land ceiling laws on plantations and imposition of ceiling laws on dry lands, many women have ended up with low productivity lands, which have not benefited women, despite their titles to land. Bina Agarwal asserted that all future village wasteland and other land grants in MP should make grants to women's groups for joint management as has been done in West Bengal. One woman panchayat member from Rewa pointed out that getting land rights was hardly any use when illiterate women could not even read and know the actual name in the land records. She and many other women panchayat members felt that it was education and literacy to women which was the basic need of women and the draft policy should put stress on the education and empowerment of women rather than land rights.

The draft policy has lot more to say on women in agriculture, dairy, sericulture, fisheries, horticulture and floriculture. The interesting aspect is giving fishing rights to women's groups in ponds and tanks (tank pattas) and despite 10 years of DWCRA in

MP very few women groups have ever been given fishing rights in village ponds/tanks. Similarly in the Narmada river bed in the summer months many women's groups could have been given lease rights to grow summer cucumbers/kharbooj and fetch cash income. The middlemen lend money to local farmers before the season and collect the harvest at distressingly low price and make a fast buck by selling the produce in cities like Bhopal and Indore. Even if the draft policy makes policy directives, in the absence of grass roots organisation, women cannot get better incomes and economic empowerment remains a dislant dream.

Women's role in forestry in MP has been recognised but the forestry sector has to evolve procedures/practices which help tribal women in better collection of minor forest produce, and effective marketing arrangements. Making a policy is one thing and making things to happen is another. At present tendu patta collection is the biggest operation in MP under which lakhs of women and children participate in the months of March-May and nearly Rs.100 crore are pumped into the tribal economy of MP. The policy stipulates that "wage in tendu leaf collection is handed over to the women of the household" and "at least 20 per cent of the posts of phad munshis in every range are filled up by women in the first two years and the proportion to go up to 50 per cent by the turn of the century". The tendu leaf collection centres in MP are the centres of money and patronage. Head munshis are actual overlords during the collection season and many illiterate women do not always get the right treatment by these male munshis. Hence the need to have some women head munshis. Similarly there was a strong demand by the participants to have at least 50 per cent representation for women in the joint forest management groups in MP. At present we do not know where and how these JFM groups are functioning in the state.

Madhya Pradesh has a Mahila Arthik Nigham and is being converted as MP Mahila Finance and Development Corporation to provide better teeth to its operations. MP has no strong thrift and credit movement because of lack of grass roots organisation. Mobilisation at the village level requires lot of organisational skills. Then only can women come forward and save. It is not just credit but most importantly the marketing of all produce by women. Credit and marketing should go hand in hand. Under DWCRA hundreds of women groups are producing consumer products like masala powder, pickles, mushrooms, papads, leather goods and so many products which have poor quality standards and packaging, which do not fetch good price. There is no umbrella organisation in MP to monitor the production, processing, packaging of such diverse products made by hundreds of women all over the state under several programmes. The urgent need is to bring all such disparate production groups of women under some sort of umbrella organisation to provide technology, capital and market support. In Jabalpur the Lijjat papad group has enabled hundreds of women to obtain sustained incomes by providing umbrella support. One landless woman of this group earned nearly Rs 36,000 by way of bonus alone in a year.

Women's reproductive health issues have been talked over everywhere. But in MP the health of women depends on what they eat and how they care for themselves during pregnancy, what feeding practices they adopt for bringing up their children and finally how they space their families. Given the level of education of women, girls' reproductive health issues are the most difficult ones to tackle. The policy initiatives in the draft policy have tackled the ones which are visible like sex determination tests which are carried on in the state without any compunction by the so-called sex determination clinics in cities like Indore, Raipur, Gwalior. Bhopal, strengthening maternity services in rural and urban PHCs and ensuring the safe motherhood in MP. This is laudable. But the more invisible health issues like maternal anaemia, low birth weight babies born to many mothers in MP, and mothers' nutritional upbringing to improve not only their health but also the health of their children, have not been recognised. These 'invisible' health concerns of women have to receive topmost attention if MP has to have healthy and productive human resources. According to National Family Health Surveys of 1992-93 of the ministry of health, nearly 57.4 per cent of children below the age of 4 are underweights; 21 per cent of children of 0-6 monlhs are underweights, but when they grow to 12-23 months the percentage goes up to 65. That means the stunting which sets in when they are about two years will remain there forever. As compared with

Rajasthan and UP the percentage of mothers doing exclusive breastfeeding in the first six months to one year in MP is just around 31.4 per cent; whereas in UP it is 60.3 per cent and in Rajasthan it is 65.9 per cent. It is this in aspect of malnutrition of both mothers and children that needs targeted attention by those who monitor the implementation of women's Policy in MP in the days to come.

Violence against women is another area where the draft policy has taken some bold initiatives. MP state government wanted to recommend to the center to suitably amend IPC to make rape a capital offence. Any person who has been convicted of an offence against women or against whom charge has been framed by the court will be debarred from holding any office in Panchayati Raj institutions and local bodies or contesting elections to them. But what about the ministers and MLAs? They should also be brought under the purview of this policy.

Another interesting feature of the draft policy is the formation of what are called media courts with women juries to decide the 'obscenity' of newspaper ads in the state, which of late have become ultra-obscene. These media courts would have judicial powers on the lines of consumer courts and will cover both print and electronics media. There is also the problem of 'invisible violence' against women in MP, which is reflected in female infanticide, early child marriages, and pushing girls in flesh trade all contributing to the adverse sex ratio in MP. In Bastar and Chhatisgarh belt, the sex ratio is not adverse but in the more prosperous cash rich districts like Gwalior, Bhind, Morena, Guna, Shivpuri of MP as a result of early child marriages prevalence of girls being pushed into flesh trade in the Bedia community, the districts are witnessing adverse sex, ratios (ranging from 908-806 females per 1000 men). This is an interesting paradox. More household or family wealth does not necessarily mean happiness for girls or women. In contrast, in tribal areas of MP, women are better treated although girls/women's education is still poor in tribal areas. This shows that factors affecting women's status are complicated and do not lend themselves to easy solutions.

Women are the best people to tackle violence against women since no one knows their agony except themselves. Vasudha Digamwar of M ARG, New Delhi. who participated in the workshop said by providing legal literacy to women one can fight against the atrocities against them. Simple legal literacy covering the provisions of law on dowry, wrongful confinement. how to file FIRs, how to face the police and the courts - all would help even the illiterate women to face violent situations. There is a mistaken notion that all-women police stations would help to reduce violence against women. A woman in distress in the police station can at best be heard by a woman police constable but that would not reduce the agony already inflicted. At present there are no organisations, except some NGOs, which provide such legal literacy to illiterate women in the state in a sustained manner. One cannot fight atrocities against women by shouting slogans. We have to fight them with the weapons of law of the land. Hence this legal literacy and knowledge of local laws protecting women is an important cornerstone of the draft policy.

Justice for Delinquents

There are all types of children in India a beggar child (one who customarily indulges in begging, whether on his own or at the behest of someone), a street child (one who spends considerable time living and eking a livelihood on the streets), a destitute child (who does not have any means of livelihood, an uncontrollable child (whose parents complain that the child cannot be controlled), a maltreated child (who is beaten up and battered generally for no reason or rhyme), an exploited child (whose labour is exploited by parents or guardians or others for money and causing damage to the child), an abused child (who is sexually assaulted or utilised for immoral and illegal purposes); a working child (who works or is made to work for money and is thus deprived of school and play), a depressed child (who suffers from emotional insecurity), a traumatised child (who has suffered a psychological trauma), an alienated child (who is unable to relate emotionally with his/her parents) and finally, a delinquent child who has been found to have committed an offence under the law. All these types of children can be clubbed under one sad category, viz, neglected children. What can be done about them? How can all the laws, which are supposed to help them, can be made child-friendly? Who is responsible for their neglect the parents, the family, the state, or the community? We have to address these questions if we have a concern for neglected children.

The National NGO Forum for Street and Working Children convened a workshop in Bangalore on Juvenile Justice Act, 1986, in the context of street and working children (March 28-29, 1994). A number of NGO representatives working for street children, eminent lawyers, jurists, police officers, state welfare agencies and UNICEF professionals debated the various policy and legislative flaws and how to go about improving the lot of the neglected children. Poverty is the root cause of child neglect and the degree to which the state can improve the lot of neglected children by legislation is debatable. We have many laws to control child marriage, child labour, immoral traffic and other social evils. The legislators pass the law and leave the headache of implementing the several bits and pieces of it to bureaucracies, which mess up the whole process. Finally, laws are amended in piecemeal fashion to add to legislative confusion and resultant social disharmony. This has happened to the Juvenile Justice Act of 1986 (JJA), which was passed in a hurry to provide speedy justice to the delinquent children all over the country, replacing many state-level statutes like the State Children Act in Bombay, Madras, etc. The JJA has become outmoded in just a few years thanks to the operation of its provisions by the police and state welfare agencies! According to Ved Kumari of the Faculty of Law of Delhi University : "The JJA divides the children covered by it into delinquent and neglected. However the distinction between delinquent and neglected is slight and subtle. The division is contrary to the philosophy behind the JJA, viz,children are innocent and incapable of realising the consequences of their acts, requiring care and protection and not penalisation. The delinquent actions by the children are more often forced by their circumstances rather than being the result of a hardened deviant strain in their character. The act divides children into two categories on the basis of commission of an offence *per se* rather than their characteristics. The presumption behind this division is that the mere commission of an offence means that these children are a contamination risk and are harder to deal with."

For a police constable any child wandering or sleeping at night in a bus stand or a railway station or in any public shelter is enough to raise his 'suspicion' on the child. Anandan, former IGP of Karnataka and then director of youth in Karnataka, said that the police are fond of booking children under JJA for unseen offences and the police in Karnataka call them as 'towel cases'! (Children are fond of hanging their towels on their shoulder or head and sleep on pavements). It is said that the suspicion of a police constable, discretion of an executive magistrate and estimates of a PWD engineer cannot be questioned! Children are suffering the consequences of this belief under JJA. Police haul up the kids on suspicion and book them for unseen thefts and then the process of 'justice' starts. The trial begins Juvenile Boards, observation homes, judicial magistrates all of them culprits. Endless hearings. Children are harassed and instead of reuniting with their families, they drift even further away. The first interface of the problem is the police. How can we humanise the police? In Bangalore, the Don Bosco group is training the police to make them child-friendly. But a few police officers by their very nature are nice to children. In the words of Reita Panickar of the group, Butterfly in Delhi, the need is for reforming the entire police system and not making a few policemen child-friendly.

The police system treats children on par with adult criminals and the age-old Criminal Procedure Code is applied to them. Delinquent children are mixed with criminal offenders in prisons. Under the JJA, neglected children come to these institutions through juvenile boards and criminal children through juvenile courts. Not all the states have juvenile boards and no magistrates are appointed under JJA to try juvenile offences. In the words of Justice Krishna Iyer, we have delinquent courts but the magistrates do not have any knowledge of child psychology or child development. He feels that we need to evolve juvenile justice jurisprudence in India for the benefit of children.

According to Mitra of the Indian Law Institute, we confuse, the needs of children and their rights. India has signed the Convention on the Rights of the Child in 1992 and in view of these rights, the whole range of laws affecting children have to be re-examined. Every right of the child creates corresponding obligation on the part of the parents, the community and the state. Article 28. of the Convention on the Rights of the Child stipulates that "States recognise, the right of the child to education and with a view to achieve this right progressively and on the basis of equal opportunity, the state shall in particular make primary education available and free to all". Education is both a need and a right. Although there is a need for primary education, the family does not find it useful in the short run. The child is put to-work and the state keeps silent and virtually conspires to keep the child away from school. The situation is just the opposite in China as can be seen from these statements. "If the parents or guardians of school age children fail to send their children to school, they shall be fined in accordance with concrete conditions and other necessary measures shall be adopted to order them to send children to school. In cases where organisations or individuals employ school age children or adolescents for work, business or other labour, such organisations or individuals shall be punished in accordance with the relevant state regulations on banning employment of child labour" (Law of the Peoples Republic of China on Compulsory Education, Degree of the State Education Commission of the Peoples Republic of China, April 12, 1986).

The final issue which received a good deal of attention was the non-institutionalisation of services for children. In the words of Gerry Pinto of UNICEF, "Institutionalisation should be the last resort. JJA, however, presents institutionalisation as the first and almost the only resort. Children are born as children. Children live in situations and circumstances that cause neglect, abandonment and even delinquency." However, the question that continued to linger in the minds of the participants was: How do we do that?

Match-Making Children in Sivakasi

In his analysis of the situation of children in match industry of Sivakasi, Smithu Kothari has extensively quoted the UNICEF Area Development Report and has remarked that most studies on child labour have focused on the economic factors leading to employment of children and that their recommendations have stopped at stressing the need for improvement of working conditions, payment of better wages, provision of facilities for schooling, and stricter enforcement of applicable laws. Kothari claims that his analysis goes beyond the surface reality and investigates the basic socio-economic reasons for the perpetuation of child labour in Sivakasi, the extent to which local and central governments have been negligent and apathetic to the plight of working children., the extent of violation of laws binding employers of children and laws relating to child labour in general. After analysing the whole scenario of child labour exploitation in Sivakasi, Kothari, also like others, stops at the need to improve working conditions, payment of better wages, stricter enforcement of applicable laws, etc.

As one who was involved in the preparation of UNICEF report. I feel that there is need to understand the wider implications of child labour - its employment, exploitation and its impact on child survival and health, not only in the match industry but also in other industries such as carpet-making, embroidery, explosives, mining and various others.

Guarded, secretive, sentimental and emotional approaches to the problem of child labour have precluded state and development agencies from designing strategies and interventions not only to stop children entering the labour market but also to increase their productivity (health and output levels) after their unfortunate entry in the labour market and to make them bargain better for higher incomes for themselves and their parents.

There are several dimensions and manifestations of child labour exploitation which stem from the situation of the poverty of the households. Poverty and the exploitation of child labour go hand in hand.

Several global studies have shown that there is a vicious relationship between nutrition, health and child labour - all go together.

It is a major paradox: it is the poorest population, at the lowest levels of human existence, who are obliged to work the most prematurely. Far from resolving nutritional and health problems, this accentuates them. An average height difference of 4 cm has been noted between girls who began work under the age of 14 and those who did so after 18.[1]

A South African doctor stated that he has seen young children who spent whole days in large sacks trampling down asbestos droppings on their heads. Most of these children died within two years. None were alive 10 years later.[2] The girls who weave the magnificent carpets from Iran, which are a source of admiration to all and of wealth to some, spend the entire day on narrow planks. They are unable to move and their work makes them adopt squatting posture invariably doubled up. A large number of these girls subsequently become sterile or have very difficult pregnancies because of the fixed posture that they have had to adopt. The combined effects of anaemia, malnutrition and overwork are often irreversible. It has been scientifically proved that, in the conditions in which it is usually carried out, the employment of children (not to mention the frequent risks of occupational accidents and diseases as such) is both directly and indirectly harmful for the child and its results will be carried over into adult life.

Another global trend that is observed is that "the countries that have the highest illiteracy rates and the greatest backwardness in school enrolment are in general those which suffer from malnutrition and have the greatest child labour problems. This is obviously not a cause and effect relationship, the correlation is not a mechanical one and therefore not strict. Some countries, such as Mexico, Colombia and Thailand, not to mention Spain and Italy, have largely succeeded in eradicating illiteracy and improving their nutritional situation but remain confronted by the child labour problem."

A child not in school is drawn towards some kind of occupation and the more profitable it is, the more it will please both the child and the family. More than by legislation, it is above all by compulsory free schooling that the employment of children is gradually being reduced in the non-industrial sphere and in agriculture. "Schooling will always be an indispensable adjunct in the struggle against child labour."[3]

The situation of working children in Sivakasi has to be viewed in the context of the above trends. No amount of denunciation of the match industries will help minimise or eliminate the employment of children. In the course of my discussion with the working mothers in the match factories, it was revealed that it was the sheer poverty of the families which has driven everybody in the family, including children, to the match industries. One woman told me that the child in the 'womb' is pledged to the factory and consumption and maternity loans are obtained on the undertaking that the child born, girl or boy, would work for the factory! Over the years the exploitation of children has been going on; and suddenly one fine day we cannot declare a war on this problem and say that the exploitation has to be banned.

There has been no dearth of laws to abolish this practice. Like any other law, the law in Sivakasi banning employment of children, is observed in breach than in practice. Both the factories and the parents of the working children have to be blamed for the present situation of the children. Parents are poor and they want working hands-mostly young than old - to earn more income. Our message of child education will not cut much ice with the factories. Hence education of the child has to be through the parents. Education, formal and non-formal, alone can initiate a break in the present exploitation. Instead of a free and compulsory education as in the other areas, in Sivakasi there is need for stipendary education for the children.

Children and more so the parents have to be lured by making the schools attractive enough, by paying attractive stipends to those who attend the schools. This would work as an incentive for the parents to send their children to schools. At present there is no time for the children to attend schools because they are out for work from 6.00 am to 6.00 pm. In the factory, it is just unthinkable for the factory owner to start a school for the children, since children have to work and not learn, although some factories have put up boards like 'Balwadi' just to declare their faith in the welfare of children. The only place, therefore, for the children to learn would be in their own village. Once the learning process is initiated, other interventions like health, nutrition, and environmental hygiene, including protected water supply would be converged. This also leads to improvement of the village life and living and there would be less attraction for the children to have the so called joyride in the early hour of each day to the match factory in Sivakasi.

The recent press outbursts on child labour in Sivakasi appear to be one of those "occasional sentimental attacks" on the exploitation of children. When some questions are raised in the press and in parliament or when some children die in cracker factories of Sivakasi, there would be some 'enquiry' by the state and the public would be 'told' on the 'steps' taken to 'end' the 'child labour exploitation'. These platitudes would not end the practice nor improve the condition of working children. We need to think of long-term and short-term measures simultaneously. If radical measures are taken, like the closure of match factories or banning the entry of children, we will end up by doing nothing. By providing good schooling, health, nutritional protection, we are not supporting the system of child labour, but trying to win the parents and children and make them to be productive and self-dependant, so that they can look for alternative productive employment in the labour market where knowledge skills and health count.

It is with this background UNICEF report seeks to initiate a process of enabling the parents-children to understand the profitability of early childhood education, health protection and nutritional interventions. This action-proeess needs the will and support of the state and Central governments, parents and factory owners, voluntary agencies in the area. Will this be forthcoming?

Notes

1. E Mendelierich. 'Child Labour'. ILO Review, Geneva. 1979, September/October.
2. James Challies and David Elliman. "Child Workers Today", Quartermaine House, 1979.
3. Abdelwahab Bouhdiba. "Exploitation of Child Labour" Final report submitted by the Special Rapporteur, UN Economic and Social Council, July 1981.

It's Better for the Bhils

Jhabua district in MP is a barren region with little rainfall, and Bhils and Bhilalas have always been at the Centre Stage of development whether in terms of sharing benefits or fighting for benefits. Water and fodder scarcity, degraded soil, poor agriculture and animal husbandry and shrinking forests are the main development problems. In the past and in the present, some Collectors have galvanised the Bhils into working for better living standards. Bhils are not home-bound, but love wandering. They are fun-loving and love sipping toddy and eloping with girls in haats the traditional market place for all kinds of goods. Outsiders feel as though Bhils do not know farming or pasture development, and are fond of cutting forests and practicing shifting cultivation. Or that, they are illiterate and their ideas are therefore backward.

All these assumptions proved wrong in Jhabua. Land is the main resource of these tribals, and their lifestyle is linked to it. One can see examples of - land being managed for better productivity, resulting in a better quality of life. Water conservation has always remained a daunting problem. Under the Rajiv Gandhi Watershed Mission, Jhabua has developed, with the peoples' participation, nearly 70 watersheds with different results. Hathi Pawa is all dry hills, and over the years the rainwater has drained the hillsoil into the nallahs downstream. In an area of 150 hectares, trenches have been dug and the run off water is captured to increase moisture on the hill slopes. In one rainy season, the value of Dinanath and stylo grass grown was nearly Rs.4 lakh, almost equivalent to the wages given to the tribals for digging the trenches. Nagu, the Bhil who is chairman of the Joint forest Management Committee of this hill slope, says, "we will not allow anybody to cut the grass or graze the hills without our permission". There is a sense of pride on Nagu's face.

"All Grass is Flesh" goes the signboard in the Kanha National Park in the Mandla district of MP. But for Bhils, all grass is milk, because with better grass availability, milch cattle yield more milk to feed their children. In the tribal village, there are hamlets around the main central village. The children who cannot walk to the main anganwadi centre remain outside the purview of the health and nutrition care programmes.

The Collector devised a poriyawadi scheme for such children. Nearly 2,000 Bhil girls were recruited as Poriyawadi workers, whose salary of Rs. 200 was met by the Gram Panchayat Vikas Sahayog Nidhi. This fund was created by setting aside 5 per cent from the Jawahar Rozgar Yojana and other funds going to village panchayats for construction work. A massive training programme was organised for the Poriyawadi girls, some of whom were not fully literate but had the native wisdom to understand mother and child health. They were provided cycles to reach remote residences of mothers and children. The cycle is a symbols of empowerment and many unmarried Bhil girls felt liberated, riding these cycles.

But married non-Bhil Poriyawadi Workers felt a little constrained when the villagers reacted strongly to a *bahu* of their village riding a cycle with her *ghunghat* removed.

There are a number of women-oriented schemes both for tribal and non-tribal areas, like Vatsalya Yojana, Mahila Samriddhi Yojana and Ayushmathi Yojana, but the tribal culture and illiteracy come in the way of their full implementation and some distortions creep in as well. For example, the Development of Women and Children in Rural Areas (DWCRA) scheme is hampered by lack of skills, credit and marketing difficulties. Evaluation studies on DWCRA show that all the revolving funds were not revolved, but ended up as initial capital expenditure and very little money was left for production purposes. So the government encourages thrift and savings among women. In Jhabua nearly 500 women's groups have been formed, popularly known as *"Bairanj Kuladi"* called 'women banks' by the local bureaucracy. Badli Bai, President of Bhavan Piplia village savings group, has already collected Rs. 20,000 as savings from 50 women. Badli was sent to see the water-shed project in Ralegaon Siddhi in Maharashra and was thrilled to observe that no males drink alcohol there Badli Bai had never gone outside of her village before. She is now mobilising her group members to influence their husbands to stop drinking and it is already happening. Many members of her group also send their children to school and keeping a watch on the Nurse Bai of the health department, so she does not miss any of the children during the immunisation.

Alirajpur is notorious for murders and theft and the Bhills take pride in such activities. Toddy tapping and dry farming are the main source of livelihood. Nearly 700 girls from 120 villages have been covered by the "Kokila" programme of the Bahai International Vocational Education for Women, Indore, in the last decade.

Janak and Jim McGillian of the Bahais were once detained in the police station, because of their "suspected" movement in these tribal villages. They were released once their bonafides were established. The ethos of the Bahais is to help people to help themselves. The McGillians taught these Bhil girls basic literacy, home management, health and hygiene and most importantly "empowerment values". Soyali, a 19 year old girl from Kulwait village, who attended the Bahai Training Centre, and her father, the sarpanch of the villiage - invited us to stay at their house on one night. Soyali's father said that Soyali lectured to him on the ill effects of drinking, and he felt so ashamed, that in a few days he stopped drinking a rare thing for a Bhil. Another girl from Ozha villiage, Leela, is affected by polio. After she was trained by the Bahais, she ensured that every child get polio drops, and now almost talks like a health worker. Kamy and Ramesh Chauhan from Umrali village are a happy couple. Kamy has learnt to stitch shirts and blouses, and Ramesh helps her iron the clothes. He has stopped drinking and beating her ever since she started earning through her tailoring.

It is common among the Bhils to pay a bride price at a marriage. All these empowered Bhil girls are now fetching high bride prices while the grooms feel inferior to the girls who dress well and talk boldly.

With the right support from the bureaucracy, the Bhils are willing to change for the better. In the words of Mr. Manoj Jhalani, the dream is to realise a Sakshara, Swastha and Kushahal Jhabua. It is not difficult if this participatory development strategy is pursued relentlessly in the years to come.

Tackling Child Abuse

Child abuse manifests itself in several forms and dimensions- physical exploitation (child labour), emotional trauma (child prostitution) and marital harassment (child marriage). In MP the last two abuses are more rampant than the first one although in effect it is debilitating the child worse than the latter two. Passing through the national highway from Mandsaur to Neemuch in MP, we see in the months of January-February lush poppy crop and young Bachada girls smiling and gesturing at you and welcoming you at their dhabas. Poppy crop brings wealth to the district of Mandsaur and the smuggling of opium is a big business in the district. The official price of opium is one third of the black-market price.

While I sat sipping a glass of tea in a dhaba, I saw a small staircase going down to the basement. I asked the middle aged lady-cashier where it went. She smiled and said it was not for me. Then I asked for whom? For truckers. Then I was more curious and I ordered another round of tea and samosas. I continued the conversation. Then she said I could go down. As I stepped down the stairs. I was astonished to see nice cabins laid with cots and a music system. I saw a placard that 'Sola Number' was available that was the code word for a 16-year-old girl. I continued my road journey towards Neemuch and my trooper Isuzu was an attraction for the lady managers of dhabas. Another dhaba girl called me, "Seth, is this a phroen gadi" I said yes. Can you take me in this, she asked and I said yes. Then she hesitated to get into the Isuzu. My next stop was near a shanty house and the women folk gathered I was told, "Doctor log tang karte hai". I said "I am not a doctor". then I asked them why they are against doctors. Then thay said "they come and test us for HIV/AIDS and we are rounded up by the police". Once they found I was a non-medical person they felt at ease and permitted me to talk to young girls. manju (a fictitious name) 15 years and already a mother of a girl child. I asked her whether her client who visit her use condoms and whether she is aware of HIV/AIDS 'bemari'. She said yes and " I make them pay advance before they sleep with me and I make sure that they are using condoms". "If they are not using condoms then they go back without getting refund". Do you store condoms, I ask. Yes, she says but the ANM charges Rs.15 per packet. She asked me whether I could supply condoms (subsequently I sent her a packet of condoms through the sarpanch of the village).I asked her whether she liked this work. She started crying. After a while, she replied pointing to her small baby "Sab, this boy belongs to a doctor in Ujjain'. I asked her how she could tell that. She looked at me and continued "I have put his name in the birth register of this village as the father of this child. Let him deny".

I could see the agony of Manju and several such girls all along the Mandsaur-Neemuch road. Smart innocent and simple-forced by their parents to get into this flesh trade. These Bachada girls are also involved in opium smuggling and the truckers are the conduit for these operations. But the girls are caught for several offences - sex offence, smuggling offence, offence under Prevention of Immoral Traffic Act (PITA) and all the offences that any criminal can think of. Bachada, Bedia and Sansi are the three communities in MP who, through their wretched tradition (parampara), are abusing their young daughters by two expedient processes - child marriage and child prostitution - former one to get rid of the girl child quite early and the latter to earn sustained income till the girl dies of reproductive health ailments.

Why do these and other communities abouse their young daughters? What is the role of the police in apprehending the culprits? What can the judiciary do in tackling these child abuses? What is the role of the government agencies, media, the panchayats, NGOs and the civil society in prevention and elimination of child abuse in MP? What are the institutional and non-institutional mechanisms for tackling child abuse in the state? These were some of the issues which came up for heated debate in the two-day joint workshop that the women and child development department of MP and UNICEF organised on May 12-13, 1997 in Bhopal. The chief minister Digvijay Singh set the tone of the debate by urging all those who have 'conscience' to stop the abuse of girl child in the state and came forward to do anything to stop this abuse. Admitting that some communities in the state have resorted to flesh trade perhaps due to economic compulsion, there is need to provide them alternative 'honourable' occupations so that they lead a dignified life and their daughters are out of such business. Home minister Charandas Mahant said that the police come after the event and the preventive part, which is more important for tackling child abuse, has to precede and should form part of the civil society's work. Yes the police come afterwards but even that follow-up work by the police is not done in MP because the necessary notification for authorising the station house officer or the police inspector to take up investigations under PITA has not been done. PITA was passed in 1956 and till then no cases have been filed under PITA in MP. These are routine notifications and the home department should have looked into this simple administrative matter. As the SP of bilaspur Srivastav confessed when he was the ASP in Mandsaur in 1980 he moved the home department to authorise the inspector under PITA for investigation. This shows that the state was not serious about laws like PITA. The biggest tragedy of these soft laws like the Child Marriage Restraint Act, PITA or any other act affecting women and girls is that they are treated with casualness if not with contempt.

The victim, i.e., the girl or a young woman is never given any benefits under the laws and the culprit always gets the benefit of doubt.

The science of victimology, as the jurisprudence now recognises, is never seriously applied to the juvenile victims. Girls and young women as rape victims are further harassed in court when they are subject to cross examinations and medical records after the rape are value loaded (based on how the doctor feels). All administrative and legal loopholes suits the bureaucracy and the police. The courts are the court of records and not of equity and in the absence of any written complaints, prosecution proceedings and witnesses, medical evidence courts are helpless and ineffective according to Renu Sharma, a district judge in MP. She amplified how under Sections 363,367 of IPC, child abuse in the form of sexual harassment are cognisable offenses and IPC provides enough space for the police to take up these cases if they are really interested. Section 22 of PITA provides for summary proceedings of the child-related offence and if there is will on the part of the police they can still file cases. The police are busy with VIPs, with habitual offenders and law and order. How can they find time for children was the lament of one police officer in the workshop. At present, the complaints are in the form of press stories and the police cannot file cases in courts on the basis of these. The NGOs in MP have not as yet shown their mettle in public interest litigation and their capacities to do so are still not clear. What then is the way out? Allow these girls to graduate to full blown prostitution and everybody then is happy with rehabilitation work. There is money, there is grant for setting up homes for these 'fallen women'. Nari niketans are a hell and no girl or woman wants to stay there. At present, two very good NGOs are doing excellent work in MP, for the empowerment of Bedia girls, Ram Sanhei of Abudhaya Ashram in Morena and Kum Champa behn of Satya Shodan Ashram in Sagar are running 'ashrams shalas'. But the irony is that these ashrams are only upto VII and VIII standards and when girls reach the age of 16 they have nowhere to go except back to their homes and fall into the traps of prostitution. The best option is to extend the entire education stream to cover up to 12th standard so that they cross the critical age of 18 and are capable of self-management. These girls are anyhow smart and what they need is not pity but what is called SMART training - self-management and recognition training. Vocational education has to be combined with such leadership training so that they catch up with the turbulent times of the modern world. The idea of Bedia, Bachada, Sansi Community Development Board was mooted by the participants. But the trouble with such boards is that they become bureaucratic and over a period of time they become white elephants. Instead, small grass roots NGOs should be funded to take up small and SMART ashram shalas so that more such community girls get good education and leadership training at the grass roots without uprooting them from their rural moorings but at the same time making them look beyond their huts and roadside dhabas.

Abused Children - Some Ethical Issues

Ranu Roy has raised some important policy and ethical issues on child labour. We have all types of children-working, missing, ,joyful, sorrowful, playful and generally those who have not missed their childhood in a broad sense of the term. No some person (parents included) wants children to miss their childhood. But society is full of wicked elements and children are made to pay for their comforts, their profits and for their pleasures. Roy has raised basically the following issues: the ethical basis for deciding the rights of child labourers and who decides these rights? How child labourers make known their own inclinations in this matter and who decides the right of a child to be in school, the present, laws on child labour, which are more to do with regulation than- on prohibition and finally; and the issue of rights which cannot be resolved as long as wrongs continue to be the basis for the production and reproduction of human life and a predatory capitalist system is at the roots of the debate rather than the potential of the illusory rights it offers.

In the entire debate on child labour, Roy has missed what is now legally defined as the best interest of the child Both the Indian Constitution and the International Convention on the Rights of Children 1989, which India has signed defines the best interest of the child very clearly. Article 3 of the Convention says "In all actions concerning children, whether undertaken by public or private social welfare institutions, courts of law, administrative authorities or legislative bodies, the best interest of the child be primary consideration". Many courts and activists have for many years argued on what constitutes public interest and we need not enter into hair-splitting discussions on what constitutes the 'best interest' of the child. Ethics like truth is very easy to understand but difficult to follow. The trouble with children under difficult situations as in working/labouring, prostitution, abuse, victimisation, ethnic strife,etc, is that they are harassed not just by parents but by the state as well and it is not difficult to see what is ethical and unethical in this. Everything is unethical, wicked, pernicious and one need not ask the kids about this. We all can see it, feel it and even touch it! Child labour is just one dimension of child abuse.

Unfortunately Roy has only talked about child labour. What about child prostitution which is worst than child labour - whether hazardous or not. Does Roy want some superior or divine authority to decide the ethical basis of child prostitution? I have worked for nearly 20 years for an organisation which deals only with children and I must have talked to thousands of kids in the south Asian sub-continent and I have not come across one kid telling me that she is happy with working or doing physically harmful work. It is just a matter of humanness which tells us what is ethical and unethical for a child to do. In MP some NGOs have organised what are called bal panchayats - an assembly of kids trying to ask questions to the adult panchayat members why their school buildings are leaking, why their parents beat them when they do not want to graze cattle and avoid physically harmful work. Every child on earth wants to play and enjoy his/her childhood and if that is missed s/he feels angry and emotionally tragic. We, as parents come to know this very easily but still we persist in our own biases. Let Roy ask through the Internet how many kids around the world want to get into physically harmful work at the cost of their joy of playing during childhood. Right to play is one of the rights of any child anywhere in the world. Linked with this right is the right to engage in joyful learning and not working in hazardous or not so hazardous work. We have to make a distinction between child work and child labour. All kids in all cultures do help their moms in cutting vegetables, a bit of sibling care accompanying their parents to fields and farms, tending occasionally household animals. That is not harmful and the right of the child in joyful work is not curtailed. It is in this context that we have to understand the needs of child education between the ages of 6-14. Roy doubts the needs of all children for schooling and they are happy to work and primary schooling is an approach of the urban biased elitists. He also blames the supply side of primary education that anyhow is not helpful to the child. But the state cannot shirk its constitutional responsibility of providing schooling to the child. Here again poverty is not the problem. Ask any taxi drivers and 'riksha' pullers in any part of India. They proudly tell that they want to send their kids to Angrezi medium schools. To the question raised by Roy who decides the right of a child in school, the answer is, the child decides and the parents approve the decision and the state provides the learning space. This is how the right of a child to be in school is not only protected but also promoted.

The question of labouring children in farms and factories is a complex one and is further made complex by the factory inspectors, the employers and the parents and all the three are the offenders. Here the state has to be ruthless and it is not difficult to see the kids in factories but still we shed crocodile tears on kids in dangerous/hazardous occupations and show our helplessness. Just as politics is criminalised so also child labour process is criminalised. Just as the law should take its own course, the laws on children passed so far in India, should take their own course. Only if they are implemented ruthlessly, we can see the rights of kids being enjoyed by them. The historical judgment of the Supreme Court of India of December 10, 1996 on child labour if honestly implemented by the state, the employers and the parents then half the working kids in factories would get back their rights for schooling, good health and well being. But as in all other fields of public action, we have failed to protect our kids - our human resources. It is not true as Roy alleges that only under capitalist system of production child labour is rampant and child rights remain illusory. Child abuse and exploitation are transnational and multilayered and endemic to all systems of governance. Warring groups in Somalia to Algeria are using kids. They are used to promote tourism (child pornography and pedophilia) and drug trafficking. Hence, the conscience of world leaders has to be provoked and so that the issues of 'children are at the top of their political, economic and cultural agenda. Then only can we hope to give a better deal to our kids in the 21st century.

Girls and the States

Why are sex determination tests done in nursing homes of Punjab and Haryana, the two wealthiest states of India? Can parents in these prosperous states not afford to have girl babies? Are the girls more a liability than an assest? In the food surplus states of Punjab and Haryana, how come girls are more malnourished than boys? Why are the girls in Punjab, Haryana and HP married before they are adults (mean age of marriage is 16-17).

These are some of the issues on which thought and action is needed if we are serious about improving the status of girls. Action is needed in at least two main areas: (1) Education of girls (2) Increasing the age of marriage.

Gross school enrolment of girls in this region is not even 50 per cent (i.e. out of 100 girls, just 50 enter schools) and the reasons for poor enrolment are the usual ones, like girls are made to bring water and attend to cattle, absence of female teachers in schools, and total apathy of parents. In Jind district of Haryana, local Panchayat leaders once took padyatra in villages to motivate the parents to send girls to schools, without waiting for the government to appoint lady teachers. What is wrong with the male teachers? Why are parents afraid of sending their daughters to male-teacher managed schools? This is where village communities can exert influence on schools and make schools attractive enough for girls. Girls drop out faster than boys, but retention of girls in schools helps the parents to delay early marriages. Fathers in poor communities want to pass on the burden of maintaining daughters to husbands by marrying them off early.

Despite the Child Marriage Restraint Act 1929, a large number of girls are married early. This Act has remained only on paper because there is no way to find out at what age girls are married in villages. Marriages of even the most educated people in India are never registered, and among the poor communities marriages are a childhood affair. When the law is ineffective, social sanctions become important.

Here is a case from the Sangdha block of Sirmour district in HP "Kanta is a Schedule Caste girl who was married off four years ago at the tender age of 11. Her husband was already married and living with his first wife. He married Kanta only to beget a child as he had none from his first wife. Two years ago, Kanta gave birth to a son. In the meantime Kanta's husband's elder brother passed away leaving behind his widow. Six months ago Kanta's husband divorced her through the village panchayat and threw her out. He kept back Kanta's child, which is all that he really wanted from her and married his dead brother's widow. Where should Kanta go now at the young age of 15 is not only her question but,the question of several Kantas in the area. "Somu in Andheri village of Sirmour district was married off by her parents when she was 10 years old. Within a short time her first marriage was dissolved and she was remarried to a man in Rajana village. This also did not last long. She was married a third time and all this, when she was just 13 years old. By the time she understands the implications of married life, she will find herself encircled in the vicious cycle of marriage, divorce, remarriage ad infinitum".

These are not isolated cases. Many such Kantas and Somus are found all over the country and they all struggle to get out of their girlhood agonies. Girlhood and motherhood have to be separated and if they are combined, serious biological and health problems accrue to both the mother and the child. Early marriage is almost universally accompanied by early child bearing contributing to maternal mortality. As long as bearing children is seen as the main or even the only contribution of women to society, there is little prospect of changing the average age at "marriage and first child birth.

Who and how in the government sector and among the communities will these two important facets of the girl child, viz her education and her marriage, be monitored? There are no separate departments for women and children in many states. They are supposed to be looked after by social welfare directorates, but in reality nobody is concerned with monitoring of the girl child status.

We have umpteen laws for improving the wellbeing of girls and women, "but there is no one focal point or enforcing machinery to oversee them".

We have yet to see any public interest litigation against child marriages, although many NGOs have approached courts against child labour exploitation. In villages of Haryana, Punjab and HP, there are village mahila mandals, who should be able to know which parents are getting their daughters married before 18. They should complain such cases either to courts or socially boycott such marriages. In Punjab, roti and beti are sacred, but why in case of beti indifference is seen regarding her schooling and marriage? The mahila mandals are getting grants-in-aid from the state, but most of them carry on not-so-productive activities. If they can take up the enrolment of all girls in their village, see that they are not dropped from school and finally ensure that they are married after 18 years of age, there would be a social miracle. Keeping girls in schools up to their age of 18 than in fields or kitchen is the best way to ensure their improved physical and intellectual health. Tamil Nadu has a scheme of awarding Rs.5,000 as marriage grant to those girls who attend school upto sixth standard and marry after 18.

If these two indicators are monitored by mahila mandals, they would be doing the greatest service to their daughters.

3

Schooling the Children

Between Imagination and Discipline

The debate on making primary education compulsory has been reopened with the possible introduction of the 83rd Constitutional amendment Bill to make the right to education a fundamental right. Many activists in education and adult literacy movements want a public discussion on the Bill.

In the last 50 years primary education is one area where all the best brains in the country have failed to come to grips with the situation in the field of universalising primary education (UPE). Enough is written by the NGOs and GOS on every conceivable issue affecting the schooling of children but still there are millions of children either out of school or dropped out from the school due to multiplicity of reasons. If making the right to education a fundamental right in the Constitution is going to bring back the children to school then we should welcome it. If not, there is no sense in adding one more constitutional provision and make a constitutional mockery of the whole field of elementary education.

UPE is a matter of managing the five disparate elements in a convergent and synergistic manner:

The teacher who should come to school and teach in an interesting and joyful manner so that kids are attracted both to the school and the teacher. Associated with the teacher is the whole UPE bureaucracy, from the Director of Public Instruction to the government regulatory systems and processes which demoralizes teachers;

The learning space or the school building that does not leak during rains and provides cool shelter in summer making the child feel at home in the school. Linked to the space is the whole business of books, curriculum, pedagogical materials, blackboards, chalk pieces etc.

The child without whom there is no UPE. Connected to this are issues like midday meals, cash incentives, freeships and uniforms. It is more difficult for girls to reach schools and remain there although school enrollment figures keep showing full enrollment for both girls and boys!

The parents always influence school enrollment of a child (especially the girl child) and the learning levels of the child — whether the child is learning slow or fast or learning at all. Our UPE pundits and think tanks in research bodies like NCERT and SCERTs and NGO activists should come to the school and sit with the child and observe the levels of learning. Today there is more of research and polemics on minimum levels of learning than actual view of the process of basic education in parts like preschool education as a split component from primary school and adult literacy. The whole stream of early childhood education, primary education and adult literacy have to be viewed as a 'continuum'. A child born in a village or an urban slum should get early child education and elementary education so that we do not have any illiterates anywhere in the country.

In the wake of District Primary Education Programme (DPEP) of the World Bank and externally funded UPE many States have tried to accelerate the process. NGOs and others have started asking questions on why we need external aid for UPE if the State can provide 6% of GDP for pre and primary education. DPEP has now spread in 240 districts across 16 States and there are already questions and criticism on its reach, impact and teacher morale.

The primary task of any long range planning for UPE is to look at the System of Primary Education in a typical State and build a grand vision or a strategy based on the system. At present salary, perks and pension are controlled by Director of Public Instruction (DPI), infrastructure like school buildings are built by State PWD or the local Panchayats, curriculum and training of teachers is decided by the State Center for Educational Research and Training (SCERTs) and the actual training is conducted by District Institute Education and Training (DIET) and the learning levels of school kids is done by the headmasters of schools.

In some States there are automatic promotions. In this process the vision and strategy for UPE gets distorted. The sheet anchor of primary education is the teacher who has been treated as a functionary of the State at the village level and so we find that a typical teacher is doing more non-teaching tasks than teaching. There are criticisms that in the wake of DPEP, States have resorted to appointing para-teachers and demoralising the teaching fraternity. I hold no brief for any State or any Government but why should the NGOs decry Para teachers in a programme like EGS in M.P. These teachers are selected by Panchayats and are paid by them and not by a remote controller like the DPI. The EGS in M.P. was in response to the immediate needs of a school where there was none. Why should the kids be waiting for work being done for simplifying methods of testing kids learning capabilities.

The debate on UPE is carried out by two sets of experts—one the NGO activists who think they alone have the answers on UPE and second the State Educational experts and policy makers in primary education both at the Centre and the States. Even if the constitutional amendments are brought forward what is the guarantee that all kids will be in schools and that their parents would be afraid of keeping them out of school as they are doing at present. The NGOs pride themselves on their small scale projects which they project as the models for replication. In the words of one NGO activist, "Conceived by a few administrators and controlled directly through government fiats such populist programmes like Education Guarantee Schemes tend to trivialise the concept of community participation and undermining genuine grassroots mobilisation. There is an urgent need to desist from such low cost ventures implemented hurriedly with a lot of fanfare but without adequate attention to priory issues of long term sustainability. These are aimed at creating second track education facilities. The priority should be to ensure that every village in the country has a free, functioning, well staffed and well attended regular primary school."

The NGOs pride themselves in primary education success stories across the country like Lok Jumbish, Eklavy Science

Education, National Literacy Movement by Bharata Gyan Vigyan Samiti, MV Foundation schools for tackling Child labor in AP and others. Many of the NGO initiated programmes whether in education or health or sanitation are stand alone programme — once the NGO activists withdraw they all collapse because the people systems like Panchayats in Villages and Nagarpalikas in Urban areas are not involved.

NGOs have a tendency to work away from the organized structures that are already in place like Village Panchayats. NGO-driven pilot projects are just pilots - they remain as pilots and die as pilots. 'Scalability' is the true test of any human development interventions like education, health or water supply so that within a reasonable period of time all habitations and people are covered. NGOs have a vested interest in keeping these small scale projects as islands of excellence so that they can keep their image as 'saviors' and 'martyrs' forever and forever. NGO experts likewise have a tendency to suggest all sorts of pilot experiments in pedagogy, in curriculum design, irrelevant teacher training, outdated value based text books etc.

The tragedy of basic education in India has been to just get a policy of the State to start a school in the Five year plan period and the kids have waited for 50 years to see any school of any type. These schools have responded well to the learning needs of kids in tribal and far flung areas. Just as the 'cohorts' keep moving to the next grade the para teachers can be made permanent as he or she moves in experience and tenure. This is not a cheap teacher provided by the DPEP but a Guruji who is part of the same community of the kids.

The bottom line in UPE is that the child should attend, the parents should send the kids, the teacher teaches and the learning takes place. In the context of 83rd Constitutional amendment the onus of sending the child to school is on parents who can be jailed for not sending the child! But can the State be compelled to provide free and quality education and the answer is why not?

The great apostle of individual liberty John Stuart Mill said almost thousand years back, "that State shall compel the education of every human being who is born as its citizen and that it ought not leave the choice to accept or not to accept education in the hands of parents." But the State has also its duty to provide not just space but also make school and the teacher an attraction to attend and learn. NSS data have confirmed time and again that lack of attraction and the lackluster teaching is the main reason for both drop outs and low enrollments in primary schools.

The Prof. Yash Pal Committee Report on reducing the burden of learning on school children in India published in 1993 did well to highlight the pernicious effect of present 1day learning which saddles a child with 4 kgs of textbooks and distances knowledge from life. By burdening the child in pre and primary schools with "meaningless syllabus and fast paced pedagogy, the child's natural abilities are being smothered at a scale so vast that it cannot be correctly estimated". The report further notes that "a curriculum policy that takes away the elements of joy and enquiry from learning, obviously contributes to the rate at which children leave school, in the early years, undoubtedly under the force of economic and social circumstances.

Prof.Yash Pal and his team were only reminding and reiterating what Rabindranath Tagore and Mahatma Gandhi preached decades ago on right primary education strategies. Tagore worked out a new form of schooling and teaching for village children called Siksha-Satra based on immediate contact with nature, the world outside, and examining the beauty and problems of the countryside. Mahatma Gandhi's experiment with basic education was inspired by the concept of Siksha-Satra.

Creative Possibilities

Tagore invited people like L.K. Elmirhst to work with him. In the words of Elmirhst, "the aim of Siksha-Satra is, through experience in dealing with the over-flowing abundance of child life, its charm and its simplicity, to provide the utmost liberty within surroundings that are filled with creative possibilities .... that field for self-expansion in which all young life finds both training and happiness."

It is between the ages of six and twelve that the growing child is most impressionable and is absorbed with the exploration of sight, smell, hearing, taste and particularly of touch using his/her hands. Existing scientific evidence suggests that learning is more effective if it is linked to the movement of hands and eyes, of touch and of colour. The teacher in such a situation becomes an innovator, a sculptor, an artist, a musician and not just a blackboard operator. He/she will have to write with pebbles, stones, on sand and on the floor; explain different colours, demonstrate through actions such as singing and dancing. Alphabets need to be created from objects, not written. A crow is first shown before the word is written. All this is important because we learn one per cent through taste, two per cent through touch, four per cent through smell, eleven per cent through hearing and eighty two per cent through sight.

From the start therefore the child enters the Siksha-Satra as an apprentice in handicraft as well as in housecraft. This is because unless the child has acquired intimate knowledge of the realities it encounters in day-to-day life it would be unfair to demand long hours of concentrated attention on second hand facts and figures (textbook information) which are divorced from its experience. Of all the learning spaces, the one provided by nature herself is the most commodious and helpful. Under skilled stimulation and guidance there is an unlimited field outside the door for experiencing and experimenting with life. Here textbooks are an anachronism. Nature herself is the best textbook. The teacher rewards the child according his/her powers of observation.

There is no room in the Siksha-Satra for nature study as an abstract subject and one moulded to suit examinations of the Directorate of Public Instruction and School Boards. In real life the child has to face the mosquito at night, perhaps the bug or the flea, the typhoid bacteria, or diarrhoea infections as well as other pests which attack his trees, plants and live-stock. The girl-child has to confront biological and social problems which make greater demands on learning.

Elmirhst sees the conflict between imagination and discipline as one of the most fundamental in the field of education. "On the one side stands the child craving for the freedom to satisfy the fertile imagination of his brain and on the other side the parent and the school teacher, so called practical people, lovers of discipline and routine, their imagination crushed long ago, determined to save the child and all trouble of experiencing for himself or herself". The problem of finding the minimum discipline that is necessary for preservation of maximum liberty is the most difficult task.

Assembly-line Product

We insist that the child shall not start out in life until he/she has learned by heart the facts that we have processed for him/her out of our own experience. This type of instruction which is conventional, artificial and unimaginative, stifles the initiative of the child to make his/her own discoveries and is, to say the least, useless. Unfortunately at present primary schooling is treated as a factory process in which the chid is the raw material to be moulded into an assembly-line product. Freedom to achieve through experience is denied to the child and in the process we deny the child the right to be free.

The Siksha-Satra concept has been transformed into the Sikshak Samkhya in Madhya Pradesh where a silent revolution in primary education is taking place. First and second standard teachers in primary school no longer rely on textbooks for teaching alphabets and numbers. Stories on the thirsty crow, the tortoise and rabbit race and songs on parrots and plants have been used by nearly 30,000 teachers under the Rajiv Gandhi Prathmik Shiksha Mission. The primary school teachers have composed nearly 5000 songs which are being tested to judge the learning milestones and how they help to achieve minimum levels of learning by children (the process of unburdening the child's learning) in first and second standards.

More than 30,000 primary schools spread over 25 Districts of M.P. are now creating history in universalising Primary Education in India. But there are as many critics of Shikshak Samakhya in M.P. and outside as there are primary school children!

If we are concerned with universalising Primary Education in India then we have to have new approaches/techniques of teaching primary school children. Shikshak Samakhya has shown that kids are interested in attending schools if learning is interesting. And learning can be made interesting by teachers only if they are allowed to teach innovatively without the rigidity of textbooks and the "expert" advice of those who sit in Sarkari Bhavans.

In my opinion textbooks are the main cause of high drop outs in 2nd and 3rd standards of primary schools and the sooner we discard them the better it will be for the child and the teacher. Prof. Yash Pal Committee has unfortunately not gone into the unholy alliance built over decades between designer of syllabi, textbook writers and textbook corporations in spinning money and extending mutual kickbacks. The logistics of textbook distribution is still worse. They never reach the children in time and are recycled as waste paper once they fail to reach the hands of the children before the academic year is over.

We have enormous talent among our school teachers to make learning effective and enjoyable for children. Nature itself can provide the best syllabi and the best textbook. It is high time that pundits of primary education in India take the recommendations of the Prof. Yash Pal Committee seriously and not lightly (because the report itself is light with just 30 pages!) and facilitate the universalisation of primary education by adopting child-friendly teaching strategies.

The Tyranny of the Blackboard

Just as there are four factors of farm production like land, labour, credit and enterprise, there are also four essential factors for successful learning by a child at the primary school. Teacher, child, learning materials like books, blackboards, etc: and the parents because the child by itself cannot go to school unless encouraged by the parents. A successful Universal Primary Education System must ensure that all the four factors synchronise successfully in any given school. At present, wherever this synchronisation has taken place, results have been fascinating and revealing. But how do we get these synchronised? If there is a teacher there is no child because the child does not feel attracted towards the teacher, if there is a willing child the teacher is unwilling, if both are there then there are no teaching material and if all the three are there the parents do not encourage the kids to go to school.

But the most important factor is the teacher. She/he can revolutionise the primary school if the teaching is made interesting and can first inspire the child to come to school and hold the child for five years. In the first standard, books are never an attraction for the child. At present, blackboards in some schools in Madhya Pradesh are neither black nor do they appear like a board! In many schools, the blackboards have been whitewashed along with the walls.

Under Operation Blackboard, maps, toys, wisdom blocks, science kit, tool kit, musical instrument, etc: were distributed all over the country, but they were either not used or misused. In many instances teachers could have been scared of such toys getting lost and preferred not to use them.

Existing scientific evidence suggests that learning is more effective if it is linked to the movement of hands, eyes, senses touch and colour.

There is nothing for the child in our schools to see. The blackboard is a lifeless dumb block and the child is not interested in it. The teachers have to operationalise it and in this process if it has to be dismantled, they should be encouraged to do so. Such a process of operationalising the blackboard is silently taking place in five districts of 'MP as part of the Shiksha Samakhya Programme. Teachers have been liberated from their blackboards in these schools and have created their own different blackboards. Some are white, some are black, they are not dumb. The crow made of cycle tube rubber, the sand and stones, tree leaves, vegetable seeds, are now teaching alphabets and mathematics in some of these districts.

Stories of the blind man, singing slates are innovative, materials, which are all used to teach language. Children are enacting plays and communicating themselves. Kids are not statistics or numbers; they are humans with emotions, anger, laughter. They should not be crippled.

A People's Movement in MP

It was December 7 - a winter night - when I landed without any preplan in Devagaon village in Raisen district of Madhya Pradesh to observe how the year-long adult literacy campaign called Padna-Badna was finally evaluated across the State. The Padna-Badna programme was launched in September 1999 by the Rajiv Gandhi Shiksha Mission of Madhya Pradesh to make nearly 25 lakh adult men and women achieve basic literacy skills in a year.

On reaching the village *chaupal* along with a former ZP member of Raisen district, Kalyan Singh the Guruji welcomed us and he was eager to show his worth as a guruji of the Padna-Badna Samiti which is a group of 22 men and women who have formed themselves as the Padna-Badna Samiti (PBS) (village group to read and progress) and get their basic reading and writing skills in place. I asked him to get the members of the PBS and a few women gathered with their veils on. I gave my note pad and ballpoint to Phulbai, one of the PBS members, and requested her to write a few words about the problems of her village. Prompt came her written reply to me *Hamara gaon me ek pakki sadak aur school hona chahiye. Ek he mera mang hai.* - Phulbai." (My village needs a pucca road and a school that is all my demand - Phulbai). Like Phulbai I talked to many other PBS members like Munnilal, Rekhabai and got several written "tests" and got to know how they have learnt to write and also read what they wrote.

On the next day I continued my random journey in different villages of Raisen district which enlisted nearly 60,000 illiterates who expressed themselves to form groups of 3,000 Padna-Badna Samitis and selected 3,000 gurujis to team them to read and write. Pratapgarh is a remote difficult to reach tribal block headquarters a distance of 20 km which I covered in two-and-a-half hours only to see the disappointment of women who complained that they have been left out of the Padna-Badna Samitis. They want to learn but they have been denied the opportunity.

I witnessed another village where a test was being conducted by the evaluators team who administered the test on writing and reading. A jubilant PBS member was struggling to add up 30 to 55. When I asked him how much it is he said 85. I asked him to write it for me. He first wrote 30 and then 55 (one after the other like 30 and then 55 but not 30 and below that 55) but he could write 85 with some mental calculation without proper format/method. In another village, the inhabitants, mostly blacksmiths were complaining that their guruji was not good and he was not regularly coming to teach and they wanted to have a new guruji but could not get another, and as a result they lost the whole year and they are where they were a year back - continue to be illiterate.

Empowering people

In another village, adults complained that they do not have a education guarantee school and their kids are not going to school. Such was the refrain and the voice of people who want to learn.

The test of any adult literacy programme is not just knowing how to write and read but "knowing" what they "write" so that they also "think" on how to achieve what they "feel and want."Madhya Pradesh is showing the way for other BIMARU States on how to empower people (make them fight for their rights) by making them read and write. Padna-Badna is a movement for not just to learn read and write by the illiterate men and women but also to assert their rights as villagers and worthy citizens who can control their own destinies without depending on *Ma Bap Sarkar* headed by Mr. Digvijay Singh - a popular Chief Minister of the State.

The Total Literacy Campaign (TLC) was a flop not just in M.P. but in many other States. The Rajiv Gandhi Shiksha Mission in M.P. revamped the TLC from a Collector-driven one to a demand-driven and people-centred one. All those who want to learn to read and write were encouraged to form PBS and select their own guruji to impart them reading and writing skills in a year. The Shiksha Mission also told these PBS that if they were able to achieve 80 per cent of the reading and writing skills at the end of the evaluation, the guruji would be paid a *gurudakshina* of Rs. 100 per member of the PBS. These gurujis were selected from the village and by the PBS members of the village. Each PBS averaged about 20 members and a *gurudakshina* of Rs. 2,000 at the end of the year was an attraction and also a recognition indeed."

This is in sharp contrast to the earlier TLC strategy where literacy volunteers were selected by the district bureaucracy called the Zilla Sakshrata Committees (ZSCs) and hurried district plans were made and sent directly to the National literacy Mission (NLM) in New Delhi to get funds without the knowledge of even the State Government. The ZSCs, although created to ensure participation of different sections of society, got reduced to a body consisting mainly of government officials and many ZSCs were saddled with misappropriation of funds and what not. The TLC became routinised and it became a programme like any other Centrally sponsored programme in the country.

Novel and Innovative

The average literacy in M.P. is 40 per cent and in some districts like Bastar (which is now in Chattisgarh) women's literacy is just 2 per cent. This new campaign for enhancing literacy through PBS is supposed to kick off the literacy level to 70 per cent in the forthcoming census of February 2001. Even if it achieves 60 per cent literacy levels of both men and women. Madhya Pradesh would have achieved a remarkable breakthrough in the millennium. The State is in the forefront of human development imitiatives. It is the first State in India to have brought out its Human Development Report in 1996 outbeating the forward looking States like Kerala and other southern States. What is also novel and innovative about the PBS campaign is the content of the primers which have been brought in this campaign. The fourth primer of the campaign is titled "Your handbook on your rights".

The Human Rights Commission in M.P. is a body of tired and retired judges who are engaged in running battle with the State Government on what are called in judicial parlance "executive excesses." Human rights education and practice does not come by holding seminars on human rights on U.N. Human Rights Days or by establishing Human Rights Commissions.

The rights perspective has to percolate among the critical mass of people by providing them information and facts about their entitlements, their rights and responsibilities in their own village and beyond. The primers in these campaigns can turn the tables against the government of the day as well. We can recall how the lessons on the ills of liquor in literacy campaigns in Andhra Pradesh brought down the then Government of N.T. Rama Rao. Mr. Digvijay Singh is a shrewd politician and knows equally well how the value of human rights can be used to enhance his own image as well. He is the first Congress Chief Minister in Madhya Pradesh who has completed seven years of governance with the agenda of "people first" without the collapse of his leadership. He is unlike Mr. S.M. Krishna of Karnataka who believes in the agenda of "information technology first."

Enormous Enthusiasm

The PBS campaign in Madhya Pradesh is known for its novelty on several counts. Unlike the TLC and NLM it is an organic programme linked with the villagers' unmet demand for learning, schooling and empowering men and women, the young and the old alike. It is also linked with the gram sabha and the village panchayats which approve the selection of the guruji who is given his *guru dakshina* in the presence of the gram sabha and not behind the Collector's office! Second, it is demand-driven. If you want to learn read and write, then form a group of Padna-Badna and select your own guruji to give you lessons. The TLC was a supply-driven programme where Collectors supplied the volunteers, the primers and the money to the literacy volunteers, and the learners were passive recipients of the wisdom of the literacy volunteers. The third is the enormous enthusiasm of women with veils and without, to come forward to write, read and to empower themselves in the information age.

In all the PBS at least half are women which augurs well for the well-being of the family particularly the growing children. The fourth and most important is one's ability to think beyond writing and reading - what is called the Badna part - growing and developing yourself and your group. Padna-Badna and "then Ladna" should be the watchword of people in Madhya Pradesh in the days to come. Madhya Pradesh is now finalising its right to Information Bill in the State Assembly and this PBS movement would bring strength to the Bill. Ladna (fighting) for one's rights is the biggest virtue of democracy, governance and responsible citizenship.

Universalising Primary Education

In the last 50 years, primary education is one area where all the best brains in the country have failed to come to grips with the situation. UPE basically involves managing following five elements synergistically and not in a piecemeal fashion: (a) The teacher, who should come to school and teaches in an 'attractive, interesting and joyful manner' so that kids are attracted both to the school and the teacher. Associated with the teacher is the whole UPE bureaucracy - from the director of public instruction to the governmental regulatory systems and processes-which demoralises teachers. (b) The learning space or the school building which does not leak during the rains and provides a cool shelter in summer making the child feel at home in the school. Linked to the space is the whole business of books, curriculum, pedagogic materials, black-boards, chalk, etc. (c) The 'child', without whom there is no UPE. Connected with this are issues like mid-day meals, cash incentives, freeships and uniforms. It is more difficult for girls to reach schools and remain there although school enrolment figures keep showing full enrolment for both boys and girls. (d) The parents who always influence school enrolment of a child (especially the girl child). (e) Last but not the least is the learning levels of the child, whether the child is learning slow or fast or learning at all. Our UPE 'pundits' and think-tanks in apex research bodies in cities should come down to the school and sit with the child and see what the levels of learning are. Today there is more of research and polemics on minimum levels of learning than actual work being done for simplifying methods of testing the kids' learning capabilities at the school level. In my list of priorities for achieving success in UPE, tackling the problem of improving teachers' skills, motivation and their empowerment should be the first task. The primary school teacher feels that s/he is not consulted in any of the UPE strategies designed by educational experts and textbook writers. In the primary school system of the state, the teacher has no voice and the state director of public instruction who manages the UPE system does not know the profile and skills of the teachers. Even the service records of the teachers are not available in many states. As a result the pay and pensions systems are in shambles. How do we build the lost morale of the teachers? In some states they are called as 'shiksha karmis' - a designation which many of them find demoralising. In MP the UNICEF started what was popularly called the teacher empowerment programme in 1995 through which more than 40,000 primary school teachers were sensitised and empowered to teach as they liked by ensuring competency based learning. The trainers were drawn from among primary school teachers of government schools and a small amount of Rs.500 were given to each school teacher to make the classroom attractive for the child. The training was short, ranging from one to four days. Nearly 5,000 songs were written by the teachers to teach numbers and alphahets.

The kids were attracted to the schools since the teacher and the kids together danced and sang and learnt alphabets and numbers thus making the learning process a joyful event. The teachers designed what was called pocket board made of cloth. Alphabet and number cards were all used to drill the kids to quickly understand numbers, additions, subtraction, alphabets and words. Teacher-handbooks were written by the same group of teachers and were widely distributed to the teachers who owned as their own unlike the textbooks, which were never liked by them. Then came the World Bank and its DPEP with the large inflows of funds. The rivalry between old and new projects and new money killed this teacher empowerment programme. The rich pedagogical materials produced by the teachers were taken over by the DPEP programme managers and they were quietly put in what is now called the 'sheekana-shikana' package without even acknowledging the teacher empowerment programme efforts. This is nothing but daylight robbery of the teacher's ideas and killing the enthusiasm of teachers. This is one example of how UPE system and its bureaucracy can kill the initiatives of the teachers and scuttle the UPE efforts. Why do we need World Bank finance and bilateral aid for UPE? The Rajiv Gandhi Shiksha Mission in MP proudly declares that under its Education Guarantee Scheme more schools have been opened in a single year than before and have provided 100 per cent access to kids in all parts of the state. If this is so, then what has the government been doing since seventies. The state should stop all World Bank and other bilateral aid for UPE. The state resources are enough to open not only new schools but also ensure the enrolment, retention and learning levels. Now that primary education is being handed over to the panchayats, there is need to the careful about the teachers' placement, pay and perks and, other non-teaching tasks which are increasing day-by-day. One has to be clear about the role of the DPI under the new dispensation. The DPEP has killed the primary education system in MP by creating parallel autonomous UPE management structure, just to enable the use of World Bank/ ECE funds. Teacher's pay and placement is controlled by the DPI, infrastructures like school buildings are created by DPLP, curriculum and training is decided by NSCERT, actual training of teachers is given by the moribund DIETS. In this process the primary school teacher is made to run around from pillar to post. How can we expect teachers to teach? It is wrong to conclude as Rashmi Sharma has done, "teacher quality is tied to area type. The same teacher may adopt a different teaching style when unhappy about being posted in a less developed area. School quality is a part of or function of area type and it is difficult to ensure well functioning schools in less developed regions even with the best intentions. In fact, the best of songs and teaching materials were developed in Halbi by teachers posted in remote villages of Bastar district in MP under the teacher empowerment programme. This is how at the field level in the name of hastening UPE it is actually being killed by not involving the teacher.

The next factor is the learning space such as school buildings. Most of our school buildings look like jail buildings. They have no ventilation, they have leaking roofs, floors with potholes, uninspiring walls and faded black boards. Here again the teacher is not consulted on anything. Look at the Operation Blackboards Programmmes. Equipment and instruments like harmoniums, footballs, tablas, were all procured centrally and sent to all the schools. The teachers were not aware of their use. Many teachers kept them safely under lock and key. Give the teacher a small amount of money to decorate the 'wailing walls' of the schools. They will decorate and draw pictures, write songs and make the space interesting. Why do we need World Bank money to create such colourful school spaces? The Education Guarantee Schools in MP have been started in temples, verandas of panchayat buildings and vacant buildings of village landlords. Once they start a school, the panchayat can build its own school buildings. Community participation can start like this. Similarly all textbooks written by experts never reach in time and the teachers never feel involved in designing learning activities which lead to competencies of the kids. The Textbook Corporation of MP, hired ORG to find out the effectiveness of their textbooks Kushi Kushi and Prashika in Class I to 5 of the schools where these were developed by an NGO on behalf of the government in MP in increasing learning levels. ORG team conducted the tests at the end of the academic year. They observed, "The overall performance of the students was found to be quite disappointing as in none of the classes was the MLL standard of 80 per cent marks accomplished. In all classes the percentage of students who got scores above 60 per cent was considerably higher in non-project schools. From a general look at the scores it would seem that no particular skills were developed by classes 4 and 5 in project or non-project schools. Although Prashika places a great importance on encouraging the students to speak freely, most of them were not able to do so by the end of class I, nor were they able to recognise the written words. The analysis showed that most of the students were unable to understand what was read to them nor were they able to enunciate answers, half of which were to be answered yes or no. Nor were they able to read simple words on flash cards. Some times/ without a blackboard the teacher writes even with pebbles, stones, on sand and on the floor".

Centrally designed textbooks are killing the child's imagination and the teachers are blamed for that. In the words of L K Elmhirst, an associate of Tagore. "All conflict in the field of education is that between imagination and discipline. On one side stands the child craving for the freedom to satisfy the fertile imagination of his brain and on the other side the parent and the school teacher (the textbook writer) (parentnesis mine), the so-called practical people, lovers of discipline and routine their imagination crushed long ago, determined to save the child all trouble of experiencing for himself or herself. Kiran Bhatty's analysis shows that "the interconnections between poverty, child labour and schooling are more complex than has been acknowledged so far in literature. Child labour is relatively unimportant at young ages (6-10 years). Labour-driven drop-outs are more likely to be low in the early grades. NSS data have confirmed that lack of attraction and the lacklustre teaching is the main reason for both drop-outs and low enrolments in primary schools. Why then can we not make schools and the teacher more attractive for the kids?

4

Governance and the Governed : Global National and the Local

Ulrich Beck of Munich University in his book *Democracy Without Enemies* says "that people acquire' a taste for democracy by practising it. Freedom begets strengthens and expands freedom. What all this means is that we have to invest in civil society. We have to delegate power and authority to it in every respect:technologically (information media) economically (basic investment) and educationally (skills and knowledge). Public work (where public is supreme) in this sense means an odd blend of politics, care for others and everyday co-operation. We need a citizen-state alliance for civil society." India' s panchayati raj system has emerged as one of the potent instruments for building a vibrant civil society in the days to come. Thank to 73rd and 74th Constitutional Amendments, village/town republics/governments have been constituted and in MP there are at least 30,922 village panchayats spread over in 45 districts (zilla panchayats) and 459, (janpad panchayats). In MP thousands of locally elected grass roots men and women are now making a difference to the lives of the people (good or bad depending on the panchayat leaders).

If we go by Beck's model of democratising the democracy, the first task in MP is to strengthen these decentralised bodies. The three main areas which emerge as important in this task are, (a) strengthening the panchayats technologically; (b) managing resources both fiscal and physical; and (c) skills and knowledge of doing things efficiently and effectively by these panchayats. The method followed so far in MP is to issue 'adesh' from time to time on the powers given and not given. By the time these adeshes reach the village panchayats things would have changed totally. The previous ones are never abolished even when they are irrelevant or useless.Managing panchayats (at all the three levels) cannot be done through these centralised instructions. Let us examine each of these areas of action against the background of the experience gained in MP in the last few years. Just a year back a decision was taken to hand over the maintenance of nearly 2.50 lakh India Mark II hand pumps installed by the PHED in MP and an amount of Rs.500 per pump was given to each village panchayat. This was the most sensible decision taken by the government in keeping with devolution of powers and functions to the village panchayats (VPs). Then the PHED started a campaign of vilification of these VPs on the ground that the villagers do not know how to maintain them, they lack technical skills, they do not know the spare parts of the pumps, they will sell the spares, maintenance grant will be misused, etc.

The female panchas were very angry. Women of the village are the ones who spend their lifetime with these hand pumps and in Betul women have written a *Maintenance Manual of India Mark II Hand Pumps* by describing each spare of the pump in their own local language. India Mark II hand pumps in India are more than 30 years old. Why could not the PHED demystify the technology of these pumps in 30 years? The village mechanic of the PHED never took the villagers into confidence. Here is a hand pump which gives life to the people and this technology has been kept a secret by our public health engineers. But the people themselves understood how the pump works, where it breaks, how to grease the fast moving parts, etc. This is the classic case of how democracy can fail if technologies which sustain life and living are not 'democratised' and the earlier the technocrats realise this, better is for democracy in our country. Sam Petroda brought STD technology. Mahatma Gandhi wanted the village technology to be democratised so that large number of people use it and enjoy it.

We are on the threshold of the new information technology and if our panchayats have to perform well in MP they have to be equipped fast. Equipment does not mean buildings, tables, and chairs but equipped with technologies which are affordable and can be used to enhance their efficiencies. All 450 and odd janpad panchayats have to be provided with PCs and connected with internets. A Hyderabad-based company Kayz has developed 'Plug and Play' internet services accessible from the TV sets available in many villages. Many of the adeshes of government never reach the VPs, JPs and ZPs. All these can be off loaded on the internets. Take the case of *Rozgar*, a magazine published by Madhyam, a public sector undertaking of MP which contians many government orders and notifications. The postal distribution is cumbersome. This can be put on the internet and every janpad level member and unemployed youth sitting in a block town can access the advertisement for jobs, application forms, etc. and need not wait for postal receipt of application forms and the chances of missing the deadlines. In fact, the whole government *Gazette* can be put on the web site of the MP government. The arguments put forward against providing PCs and internets is that the janpads are not literate/educated. But how come they picked up STD technology within no time?

The State Finance Commission in MP, has made recommendations for the devolution of grants and sharing of revenues from the state to the different tiers of the panchayat and between the tiers. There are still areas of conflict and the panchayats have to be rewarded for their tax revenue mobilisation efforts. MP has to go a long way improving the planning methodology. ZPs have to plan at the district level and the district planning has remained a theoretical exercise. Each District in MP is a complex entity by itself with so many sectors like forest, minerals, rivers and roads needing close attention for improvements as well as for generating employment and revenues. The state and district level planning experts have to sit together with panchayat members and develop ZP, JP and VP level plans with the involvement of people and panchas. This was how the decentralised people's plans were developed in Kerala for which Planning Commission supported. These plans should not become blueprints like the PWD blueprints which are dumped when funds exhaust. They should become talking points for the people in the districts for developing themselves and their areas and the government playing a facilitating role. The private sector can also play a role in this district plans by picking up some activities for financial and other support. Under the 73rd/74th Constitutional Amendment District planning body has to be strengthened. Unfortunately, the sectoral departments of the government set up their own 'line' structures by by- passing the panchayats. The DPEP- the World Bank funded primary education programme has established village education committees(VECs) in their project villages when there is already a provision under the panchayats to have such VECs which can oversee all types of primary education programmes, formal, non-formal, alternative and education guarantee schools, etc. All bilateral and multilateral agencies must be mandated to work with these panchayats in India. The ZPs are never involved in any discussions with bilateral and multilateral agencies when the loans/grants are negotiated.

The third area of democratisation process is the skill and knowledge improvement of these panchayat bodies and its members. In the past 'soochna shivirs' and 'janjagran abhiyans' were held in many blocks of MP. They all turned out to be camps for the officers to tell the people about their 'yojanas'. The tactics of getting benefits of these yojanas were never told. Panchayat members are nearest to the people and their knowledge of how the state works is very important. Unfortunately, the training of these panchayat members was not done properly by the goverment. Many training centres establised under the community development programmes in 1960s are languishing for want of funds and directions in MP. They can be energised now.

The final area of concern for developing these panchayats bodies in MP is the absence of an institutionalised 'think-tank' to advocate, articulate, argue, defend the cause of panchayats in all state level policy-making fora and confabulations. There is a need for constituting MP panchayat parishad as an institutional forum headed by a professional activist who believes in the professional development of these panchayat bodies. V.Kurien helped to develop village milk co-ops through the state level milk federations. Gujarat State Milk Federation is now competing globally to sell its milk products. The panchayats are like co-operatives for promoting civil society and good governance. The state level panchayats parishad is like a state level federation for protecting the panchayats. This MP panchayat parishad will exert constant public pressures on the state for making these panchayats vibrant organs of civil society and governance. Otherwise the state level legislators, ministers, bureaucrats would make these panchayats impoverished constitutional bodies.

Global Political and Economics Security

The present world is characterised by natural and man-made disasters, insecurity, political unrest, increasing poverty, migrations, environmental degradation and what have you. Red Cross data indicate that a significant natural disaster occurs in the world on average once a week. Every three weeks, on average, there is a disaster which exceeds the response capacities of the country afflicted.[1] The World Bank has estimated current global losses from natural disasters alone at an average of 2,50,000 deaths and at least $ 4 billion in damage per year. The UNFPA has estimated that with the present rate of population increase, everyday there are also 2,50,000 more human beings needing land, food, fuel and shelter. The number of the absolute poor have increased from some 800 million in the 1970s to about 1.2 billion and are projected to rise to 2 billion over the next decade. FAO estimates that by the year 2000 over 2 billion Asians will either be without wood fuel or will be consuming more fuel than can be replenished. Large-scale human movements and even conflicts may increasingly be triggered by the scarcity of water. Modern weapons technology has blurred the distiniction between conventional and mass-destruction arms. With the modern Weaponry accessible even to a low income country, civil war can quickly devastate its weak infrastructure and thus affect its population.

The migrant worker exodus in the Gulf crisis included 5,00,000 Egyptians, over 8,00,000 Yemenis, 1,00,000 Bangladeshis (who had been remitting $ 100 Million per annum). 2,00,000 Indians (remitting 15 per cent of the Kerala state economy) and 1,00,000 Sri Lankans ($ 100 million per annum).[2] UNHCR estimated that in 1991 there were 17 million refugees and if we add to this another estimated 24 million displaced persons, who do not currently fall under refugee category, the number is scaring. The current global aggregate of 41 million uprooted exceeds the whole population of Spain or Zaire.

Against such a background the world social summit, at Copenhagen, deliberated; perhaps without any conclusions, to come to the grips of these ghastly issues. The summit had basically three themes on which to get the consensus of the world leaders, viz, poverty eradication, employment and social exclusiveness. There was also a parallel NGO forum to deliberate on these and other issues like participation of people in the civil society and what NGOs can do to tackle the burning issues affecting the world. But the most important deliberations which missed the attention of the media and the NGOs was the nature of the forthcoming world governance for tackling the worst aspects of world degradation and poverty, how to ensure what that type of governance, what instruments are needed for its functioning and what reform or restructuring of the UN system, if at all, is needed in the coming years, to tackle these global issues.

Commission on Global Governance

The commission on global governance (CGG) constituted in 1992 released its report much earlier but was discussed in the NGO forum of the world social summit thanks to the excellent initiative of the UN association of Denmark which also translated the commission report into Danish to provoke wider debate and discussion in the summit.[3] The CGG was the last in the series of global initiatives taken up in the past by well meaning 'wise men' and has coincided with the 50th anniversary of the UN. There have been in the past five major initiatives, viz., (1) Independent Commission on International Development Issues, Willy Brandt, 1980, (2) Independent Commission on Disarmament and Security, Olof Palme, 1982, (3) World Commission on Environment and Development, Gro Harlem Brundtland, 1987, (4) Independent Commission on Interrnational Humanitarian Issues, 1988, Sadrudin Aga Khan, (5) South Commission, Julius Nyerere, 1990, To mark the 50th anniversary of the UN, several efforts are underway to think on reforming and restructuring the UN and what can be done to Brettonwoods institutions like IMF and the World Bank, which are drifting away from the UN and establishing their own 'turfs' unconcerned with the world public opinion against both their style and substance of functioning. The notable work in this direction which this author has come across is that of the Ford Foundation-Daghammarskjold series of reports on reforming the UN.[4]

At the outset Shridatt Ramphal, the co-chairman of the CGG, who chaired the plenary session in the NGO forum, said that global governance does not mean global government and traditionally global governance has been viewed primarily as intergovernmental relationships." Today it must be understood that governance involves not only governments and intergovernmental institutions but also non-governmental organisations, citizen's movements, multinational corporations, global capital market and the global mass media. States and governments remain primary actors but they do not bear the whole burden of governance. Likewise the UN must play vital and central role but it cannot do all the work of governance." "A new world order must be organised around the notion of governance of diversity, not uniformity, of governance through democracy not dominion, of governance at all levels within society and not just from above. By definition global governance implies a decentralised system built on the foundations of a common set of values." [5]

According to the CGG the foremost of these values must include the duty of care for one's neighbour. In a neighbourhood all are neighbours. In our global neighbourhood, therefore, our duty of care is owed to all who share the planet. The CGG has emphasised the following rights and responsibilities for a successful world governance. Rights: a secure life, equitable treatment opportunity to earn a fair living and provide for own welfare, definition and preservation of our differences through peaceful means, participation in governance at all levels, free and fair petition for redress of gross injustices, equal access to information and equal access to the global commons like sea, sky and the planet earth. Responsibilities: to contribute to the common good, consider the impact of our actions on the security and welfare of others, promote equity, include gender equity, protect the interest of future generations by pursuing sustainable development and safeguarding the global commons; preserve, the humanity's cultural and intellectual heritage, be active participants in governance and work to eliminate corruption. Security of state and its people has emerged as the most difficult task to handle by the present UN system which has not shown its effectiveness in identifying, anticipating and resolving conflicts before the use of force becomes necessary. At present the UN intervention is used simply as a cover for the intervention of major powers. In Somalia even before the issue was discussed in the UN, one million people were dead. The war torn regions and states have suffered much more in the post-conflict stage, than in the pre-conflict days. Landmines are the worst landmarks of post-war conflicts. It is estimated that 100 million landmines have been planted in more than 60 countries and another 100 million are stockpiled for sale and use.[6] How will the world governance change this? The CGG says, "To improve global capacity to prevent confict, there should be mechanisms to alert the world community to situations that could lead to humanitarian tragedies unless timely preventive action is taken. NGOs and grass roots organisations in the field are often in the best position to alert the international community to potential conflict situation, but have no channels through which to activate international attention. We propose that a Right of Petition should be made available to international civil society to bring to the UN's attention situations that imperil people's security. A Council for Petitions should be established within the UN system composed of five to seven independent persons, to entertain petitions by non-state actors" (CGG *Report,* p. 24).

State actors have failed to resolve and prevent civil and ethnic conflicts because states always *ipso facto* defend their actions. Hence, a third party through the petitions, like our Indian public interest petition, can always throw lhe light. One can recall here the individual petitions filed by people like Archbishop Tutu of South Africa in different world forums against White regime in South Africa and who played a significant role in the abolition of apartheid. Right to petition is not to replace the UN but to strengthen the UN's initiative. At present the UN is bankrupt both in terms of soldiers and resources to prevent and handle conflicts/ civil wars/

emergencies. Ford-Dag Hammarskjold Foundation study by Urquhart and Childers have pleaded for a rapid-response emergency fund of $ 50 million. Chartering only one large transport aircraft, for example, can cost one million dollars a month before fuel and landing cost. The CGG has suggested a UN volunteer force that could be deployed at an early stage of civil strife. But the states would not accept UN force at an early stage. Wars and conflicts arise due to fear and to protect one's own territory states build up arms/weapons. World total military expenditure was $ 815 billion in 1992 but the UN peace keeping expenditure was just $1.9 billion. The world global military spending also declined between 1987 and 1994 at an estimated average annual rate of 3.6 per cent but nobody knows where the cumulative peace dividend of nearly $ 935 billion went away.[7] Defence is a highly secretive business and even the most professional NGOs have no access to this information. CGG has, unfortunately, not thrown any light on how the peace dividend can be ensured and how the money saved can be made known to the people at large in the world community?

Another serious issue is that of bringing to book and punishing those despots, military and civil rulers who conspire and perpetrate the killings of innocent men, women and children, during civil unrest and inter-regional wars. The UN war crimes tribunal at The Hague - the first big international effort to pass judgment on man's savagery to man since the Nuremberg trial in 1945-46 - has records of some 150 mass graves in ex-Yugoslavia, each holding about 350 corpses. The tribunal has 65,000 pages of documents plus 300 hours of video tapes all computerised on CD-ROM *(The Economist,* March 11, 1995, p. 19). The UN is now in the process of setting up a second tribunal to deal with the slaughter in Rwanda and is headed by Richard Goldstone, a distinguished judge of South Africa. But The Hague tribunal lacks political support to go ahead with prosecutions. No long lasting reconciliation between enemies can come about without a proper accounting of war crimes. Peace has to be built upon truth. Such a process re-establishes confidence in the rule of law. If such tribunals are to become a part of international ethic, governments must provide something better than their current lip-service. Many would now accept that to already existing offences, such as shooting military prisoners, there should be added the concept of crimes against humanity and the mass murder of civilians. Unfortunately the CGG has not come out with any suggestions on trying war criminals, except to suggest the setting up of an international criminal court. In particular whether the right of petition includes the right of any citizen affected by the war crimes, to ask for prosecution of the guilty? There cannot be any world governance without punishing the war criminals of the world. It was surprising that in the NGO forum, despite the presence of many from Rwanda NGOs, none raised their voice against the human killings.

Economic Security Council

Once there is peace and physical security in the world, people look for economic and livelihood security and planetary security. The interest of future generations are today placed at risk by the overuse of common environmental assets - the global commons like atmosphere, outer space, oceans beyond national jurisdictions and related environmental and life support systems that underpin everyday human life. Poverty issues cannot be separated from these environmental issues. The CGG has suggested that the UN trusteeship council would be ideal to hold global commons trust, now that the council is no more in charge of trust territories. The CGG wants the council as a global environmental custodian acting as an umberella for the administration of environmental treaties.

The present UN economic and social council (ECOSOC) has become in the words of Ramphal 'talk-shop' and some more UN agencies like the UNIDO have lost their utility and have to be closed down. It was pathetic to see how in the NGO forum in Copenhagen some UNIDO officials were trying to lobby, with the members of CGG, not to recommend such a step. The CGG calls for a more powerful economic security council since the pollicies towards equitable sharing of resources of the world and directing pro-people policy changes across the world cannot be left to a few brains in the World Bank/IMF who have demeaned themselves in the eyes of the majority of the NGOs and the governments of the world. There is no culture of co-ordination between the UN and these Brettonwood institutions.

The World Bank's operational track record should also form part of review about its future place in the UN system. "In an internal assessment of 1,800 current Bank projects in 131 countries involving loans totalling $ 138 billion, it was reported that 37.5 per cent of projects completed in 1991 were deemed failures".[8] In the words of Childers and Urquhart, "It is extremely difficult to envisage the scope of reforms in the World Bank that would make it compatiable and appropriate specialised agency of the UN system. Beyond austerity air travel not only the Bank's present lavish meeting style, but staff remuneration would have to be brought into line with the UN's common system. The heavy-handedness of Bank loan approaches, with staff arriving in developing country capitals with projects already designed in Washington DC, is equally incompatible with the principles of respect, co-operation and partnership on which all UN system development activities are based."

The proposed economic security council as an apex economic body within the UN family would have the same standing as the security council of the UN. The CGG rightly says. "The group of Seven, a self-constituted club of the nominally richest countries, formed to look after their own rather than global interests, cannot claim to be a sufficiently representative forum to take on this responsibility". ECSOC has failed to influence the G-7 and the developing countries are desperately dependent on the west for money, skills, technology and information. World economics cannot survive in this lopsided fashion and hence, much discussion was centred around the resources for social and economic development of the world as a whole in the NGO forum. At present, resources of the UN are fast depleting. When the UN was founded only one method of financing was envisaged, viz, a percentage of the budget allocated to each member state calculated on the basis of 10-year average of its gross domestic product with downward adjustments for low per capita income and high foreign debt. It was based on the principle of capacity to pay. At present, the US share has been adjusted at 25 per cent and the contributions of the poorest countries cannot fall below 0.01 per cent. Based on 25 per cent of UN budget the US is paying $ 310 million. France 6 per cent, UK

5 per cent and India 0.36 per cent. All UN contributions have to be paid in US dollars. Impediments to earning hard currency in the present adverse trading and monetary system makes this more difficult.

Any reforms of the UN towards world governance has to set right the principles of contributional and make it more equitable. If it is strictly on per capita levels of national income then many oil producing countries would pay more than what India is paying at present. But the more vital issue is that of raising resources for poverty eradication, employment generation and social integration of the developing and least developed countries. Several suggestions for global resource mobilisation which were floating around in the social summit were UN surcharge on (1) all arms sales and sale of land mines produced after a certain date (There is now a UN arms register but we do not know whether any country is registering the arms in that register); (2) surcharge on the use of global commons like sea lanes, international airspace, etc; (3) UN levy on international air and sea travel: (4) One day collection charge named as UN communication day, when all postage charges and telephone calls would carry levies accruing to the UN.

The hotly debated resource issue was that of Tobin tax, named after James Tobin, Nobel laureate in economics, who suggested a tax on foreign exchange transactions 16 years back. The present estimated forex transactions around the world per day is more than $ 1 trillion. "The questionable nature and composition of the capital flowing through financial markets arise from the fact that only about 5 per cent is for the financing of trade and less than 15 per cent for investmenl. *The Wall Street Journal* (September 18, 1992) has ventured to state that less than 10 per cent of this staggering sum has anything to do with trade in goods and services. It would seem that the remaining 80+ per cent of the ebb and flow is attributable to speculative and/or money laundering motives that are in large, measure beyond the bounds of serving any beneficient social purpose and which revalidates Keynes's references to the casino society. Capital movements have only a weak tenuous' connection to societal objectives; major financial decisions are made without references as to whether the projects being financed are or are not productive in the broadest social sense of that term".[9]

David Felix's 'back of the envelope' calculations are illustrative of the astonishingly high revenue potential of a globalised Tobin tax (*Futures,* March 1995, p. 205).

	Taxable Foreign Exchange 1.0 Per Cent Tax	*Annual Tax Receipts 0.5 Per Cent Tax ($ 10.9)*
41 trillion * 240 trading days		
less 20 per cent tax exempts = $ 192 trillion		
less 20 per cent evasion= $ 144 trillion		
less 50 per cent reduction of trading volume = $ 72 trillion effective		
tax base	720	360
50 per cent kept by collecting govts.	360	180
Distributed to the UN, IMF World Bank	360	180

Now the politics of Tobin tax is whether the G-7 countries will have the political guts to initiate such tax measures given the power of multinational investment banks and several transnational companies (TNCs). The 500 biggest TNCs account for 30 per cent of global production, 70 per cent of global merchandise trade and 80 per cent of international investment. The World Bank guidelines on foreign direct investment are insufficient because they discuss only the rights of investors, not their obligations. The south needs investments which neither enrich investors at the expense of the poor nor create dependency and exploit natural resources. The first step is to have a code of conduct for TNCs.

The final important issue which received attention of the participants in the NGO forum was that of leadership of the UN and those who make up the world governance. In the words of CGG, "Whatever the dimensions of global governance, however renewed and enlarged its machinery, whatever values give it content, the quality of global governance depends ultimately on leadership. At national, regional and international levels within communities and in international organisations, in governments and non-governmental bodies the world needs credible and sustained leadership" (*CGG Reports,* p. 45), But how will we get such a leadership? The leadership issue within UN and its sister agencies is itself beset with innumerahle problems. One of the most vocal criticisms of the UN is the size and quality of its bureaucratic leadership. But the reality is different. In the words of Erskine Childers, "The entire UN staff - professional, general service, spread over in New York, Geneva, Vienna, etc, is now about 9,000, which is less than the civil service of the city of Winnipeg in Canada. It is less than the staff of the international advertising firm of Saatchi and Saatchi. The total regular and non-permanent staff of the entire UN-excluding World Bank and IMF- and the contributed peace keepers is about 51,500. That is less than the total governmental staff in the state of Wyoming; it is less than the civil service of the city of Stockholm, it is less than the district health staff of the principality of Wales in the UK."[10] Article 100.2 of the UN charter says". Each member of the UN undertakes to respect the exclusively international character of the responsibilities of the secretary-general and the staff and not to seek to influence them in the discharge of their responsibilities". But the very fact that the candidate for the head of UN, i.e. the secretary-general, must first be acceptable to five permanent members of the security council has fundamentally weakened respect for these charter provisions from the outset. Once the top leadership post in the UN is politicised, all posts down the line get politicised.

Any move towards world governance, in the words of Shridatt Ramphal, has to be within the broad framework of the present UN charter. The UN, according to him, is like a sun; we cannot avoid it, we have to live with it. But the question is, can the type of world governance that is envisaged or dreamt by the CGG make the life of the poor and the marginalised on this earth a happy place to live in? The entire discussion on world governance in the NGO forum at Copenhagen reverberated the warning issued as early as 1969 by U Thant, the former secretary-general, "I do not wish to seem overdramatic but I can only conclude from the information that is available to me as secretary-general that the members of the UN have perhaps ten years left in which to subordinate their ancient quarrels and launch a global partnership to curb the arms race, to improve the human environment, to defuse the population explosion and to supply the required momentum to development efforts. If such a global partnership is not forged within the next decade then I very much fear that the problems I have mentioned will have reached such staggering proportions that they will be beyond our capacity to control".

References

1. Nordic UN Project, *Responding to Emergencies,* report no. 14 Stockholm, 1990, p. 13.
2. Inter Alia, Overseas Development Institute, Briefing Paper, London, March 1991.
3. *Our Global Neighbourhood - The Basic Vision,* The Commission on Global Governance, PO Box 184 CH 1211 Geneva 28, 1995.
4. *Development Dialogue,* 1994: I, Uppsala, Sweden.
5. *Op.cit.* p. 7.
6. *UNICEF Annual Report,* New York, 1994, p. 37.
7. Manu N Kulkarni. 'World Summit on Social Development - Choice of Agenda Issues', *EPW,* September 24, 1994.
8. The assessment was led by Willi Wapenhams as chairman of a portfolio management task force appointed by the Bank president Lewis Preston in February 1992.
9. Morris Miller, 'Where is Globalisation Taking Us-Why We Need a New Bretton Woods', *Futures*, Vol. 27, No. 2, March 1995, Special Issue. *The UN at Fifty: Policy and Financing Alternatives*, Harlan Cleveland et al (eds), Butterworth-Heinemann released in the World Summit, Copenhagen, March 6, 1995.
10. E Childers, 'Financing the UN', *Futures*, Vol. 27, No. 2, March 1995, p. 163.

Managing Human Development Programmes : Challenges and Opportunities

Schemes and projects designed to serve basic human needs such as health, education, food, etc do not directly contribute towards an organisation's business objectives. As such corporate enterprises have tended to shy away from making investments in such projects and no serious effort has been initiated towards indcluding modern management techniques as an aid to the efficient running of these 'human development programmes'. The article brings home the importance of introducing these techniques and methods in HDPs and discusses their varied dimensions.

Human Development Programmes (HDPs) are attracting increasing attention from politicians, planners and industrial enterprises. While the politicians look for political gains in these programmes, the corporate bodies look to them for creating markets and through them augmenting profits. Basically designed towards fulfilling the basic needs of the poor, like water, health shelter, nutrition, education and a minimum level of income to meet their consumption needs, HDP are soft programmes that indirectly contribute towards the achievement of an organisation's business objectives.

The poor are a diverse group, difficult to stereotype and classify. They comprise small farmers, landless field hands, urban construction workers, migrant workers, nomadic shepherds, members of scheduled caste and tribe. They are scattered in different geographical areas and are not easily accessible to formal state service structures. Service functionaries of the state are either inaccessible to the poor or cannot understand their needs, thus creating a big gap between the poor and the development bureaucracy (Korten, 1983). This gap is found in almost all sectors of economic activity like banking, trade, commerce and public distribution system. The poorest of the poor who are illiterate and starved are in a worst situation.

HDPs, which are meant to serve thc poor in particular and thus help towards removing their disabilities arising from the above gap, are difficult to design and implement. Unlike petroleum projects where technology is precise and where work (oil exploration and drilling) is subjected to precision analysis and control and the results (oil output) are predicted with accuracy, in HDPs, while inputs are quantifiable, outputs are countable and outcomes are unpredictable. In the area of health, we have the example of primary health centres, where doctors, auxiliary nurse mid-wives, drugs, etc. are the inputs for providing health care, and the number of patients treated, quantity of drugs distributed, and the number of beds occupied are the outputs. The extent of health improvements brought about as a result of health centre visits, is an outcome indicator and cannot be easily quantified. While the number of handpumps installed, water tanks built, and the number of people who have used the taps, are input indicators, the *magnitude* of the reduction in water-borne diseases among the protected water users and its effect on the health of the people are all output indicators.

Sectoral HDPs

HDPs could broadly be classified as either sectoral (dealing with individual sectors like water, health or education) or multisectoral (where these are grouped together as a project for implementation). In both these there are trade-offs, advantages and disadvantages. Depending on the choice of alternatives, HDPs unfold themselves in different patterns (e.g., family planning programme during emergency, antodaya programme of Janata regime and the new Twenty-Point programme).

The managerial dimensions of HDPs are more ,complex than those of pure business and or enterprises.The nature of these dimensions could be gauged in terms of the following issues: (a) How to manage HDPs in a fast-changing political and social environment? What strategic choices are to be adopted by managers of HDPs? (b) What organisational structures are best suited for managing HDPs - vertical, horizontal and football type in which managers can tackle all problems simultaneously - human and material? (c) What are the investment implications of HDPs? (d) What are the rates of return and sources of finance? (e) What types of management information system are suited for HDPs (f) How can HDPs and their components be monitored and (g) What are the gains of HDPs and who benefits most from implementing them.

HDPs evoke popular appeal because they cater to the essential needs of the general public. This also makes them politically attractive - the location of these centres is determined by the political dividends they bring in rather than considerations of economic feasibility. But the managers of HDPs face the problems of rationalising these choices. Although many of the locational decisions may not be rational, *a priori,* but if well managed the facilities wrongly located would always prove useful to the people. (e.g., a health centre across a bad road, if well served, would be frequented by the ailing public). *Thus, although locational decisions are politicised, the strategy of managing HDPs has to be evolved by managers of HDPs.*

The present organisational structure of the HDPs in India are the off-shoot of history, politics and economics. No serious thought has been given to the structuring of outreach health services such as water and sanitation and a range of basic services. The consideration that has guided the planners in designing organisations for HDPs is that of proximity to the people - the nearer the location of services to the people, the better it serves. Although it is true, as revealed by World Bank studies, that distance is a critical element in the use of health outposts, in the absence of an effective organisational back up the services offered are sub-optimally used. HDPs cannot be vertically controlled like military check posts. The frontline workers in HDPs are the real leaders. Unfortunately all organisational development interventions in HDPs that have been attempted so far are based on 'bureaucratic therapy'- with emphasis on control, rewards and punishment. The team building approach practiced by OD specialists and MBO strategies have yet to be accepted and tried out in HDPs.

Modern P.R. Techniques

In view of the fact that HDPs deal mostly with people and less with machines, the organisational structure of HDPs has to be responsive to the needs of a diverse type of clientele. It is here that the modern PR techniques could be profitably used by HDPs in designing their organisational strategies. This aspect could be illustrated with reference to mass immunisation programmes in the field of health care. Today, we find that a majority of rural mothers are not convinced of the importance of immunising their children against killer diseases like diptheria, tetanus, whooping cough, tuberculosis, measles etc. Social marketing theories and tecniques are not used by health authorities in India to *generate* demand for this service. Rather, the emphasis here is on cold chain equipment and hardware building. Indeed, public health establishments in India have much to learn from the corporate world in fields like cold chain system, marketing logistics and computer software. Unfortunately, corporate bodies in this country have not tapped the area of primary health care for introducing these concepts. Health has been equated, regrettably, with drugs and pharmaceuticals in the world of business.

If health-related industries offer to invest in the business of primary health care, then the investment returns can be tremendous. In India alone the total number of new borns were estimated at 24.84 million in 1982 and cumulative births at 27 per cent. The immunisation coverage of children under 1 year of age is very low—39 per cent for three doses of DPT, 18 per cent for three doses of Polio, 10 per cent for measles, 18 per cent for BCG and 24 per cent for tetanus of pregnant women. According to WHO, the supply of vaccines used in the expanded programme of immunisation is *adequate* to meet world needs. (Henderson, 1984). But the week spots in the area of public health relate to : availability of materials and methods for transporting and storing vaccines at *correct* temperatures from the point of manufacture to the point of use at the child's arm/mouth, sterilisation techniques for needles and syringes, refrigeration facilities in areas with less than eight hours' electricity per day, accessories such as unbreakable thermometers, voltage regulators and alarm systems, vaccine carriers, cold boxes weighing 20 kg. and capable of transporting and storing up to 3000 doses of vaccine at temperatures less than 8°C for seven days, etc.(Henderson).

New Strategy

As a first step in the effort to overcome these inadequacies health directorates and business enterprises could jointly evolve a strategy for mass immunisation whereby tenders could be invited from corporate bodies to immunise all children in specific areas on 'turnkey' basis, on the pattern of PWD inviting tenders to build bridges and highways on a 'turnkey' basis. Alternatively, health department personnel could be made responsible for droppings and injecting vaccines leaving the work of keeping the cold chain in perfect order to enterprises specialised in cold storage and refrigeration. Yet another option could be to identify a marketing company to generate demand, and a refrigeration company to administer the vacceine while the health department could provide the vaccine at a *cost* to the child's family. This is an area where business enterprises have hitherto shyed away from active involvement perhaps because of profitability considerations. In this context it is noteworthy that costs in established health care programmes average only $ 5.00 per fully immunised child (Henderson), and that these activities are remunerative.

There exists a widespread belief today that human development is the sole responsibility of the State. The Indian Minimum Needs Programme, Integrated Rural Development Programme, 20 Point Programme are the biggest HDPs ever undertaken by any developing country in the world both in terms of public outlay and complexities. In the last two decades the Governments of India and the States together have incurred a capital expenditure of more than Rs. 3000 million in projects for potable water, primary schooling and rural development in terms of giving assets to the poor, mid-day meals, school feeding programmes, etc. While capital investments are attractive for getting political mileage, in terms of so many KMs of road built, so many school built, etc. The maintenance and recurrent cost burdens pose a threat to the financial stability of the States.

Need for Effective Maintenance

Today, there is a dire need for a strategy for the effective maintenance of HDPs in the country, in terms of manpower requirements, maintaining standards of service and the cost recovery. There is a false notion that health services should be free for all because of the strategy of *health for all.* Good management costs 'something' and that 'something' is a matter to be decided by Managers of HDPs. It is here that the application of techniques of cost accounting, cost recovery, etc., become relevant. It is this 'grey' area that needs proper investigation by managers and executives who have specialised in these areas.

If HDPs have to survive on their own, cost recovery bases have to be built into their design. In the past some incentives were given for industrial enterprises to invest in rural development activities, but the coverage of in respect of both people and area was inadequate. Industries took to rural development for claiming tax incentives rather than for the purpose of promoting human development as such. This emphasises the need for a fresh approach to attract corporate investment in HDPs. The demand for HDPs arises basically from basic human needs - the minimum needs of those whose purchasing power is negligible. Hence conventional, theories of market demand do not apply to the production of goods to fulfill these needs.

Another area where the skills of enterprise management could be profitably applied is that of information gathering, storage and retrieval. The present methods of information gathering in HDPs are based on the theory of controls, which requires that HDP managers collect information irrespective of their functional utility and value to improved performance of HDPs. As already noted earlier information on *outcome* indicators of HDPs are not collected and what we have is a plethora of progress reports with *progressive* totals on various components of HDPs, which do not lend themselves for meaningful analysis of management problems and trends.

To conclude, the management movement has not caught up among the managers of HDPs and it will not do so unless agencies like All India Management Association and a number of corporate bodies make a conscious and deliberate effort to generate management ethos among the policy makers and managers of HDPs in the country.

References

1. R.H. Henderson, "Vaccine Preventable Diseases of Children- The Problem" in "Protecting the World's Children—Vaccines and Immunization within Primary Health Care" Bellagio Conference Report, Rockfeller Foundation, New York, June 1984.
2. David Korten and Felipe B. Alfonso, "Bureaucracy and the Poor- Closing the gap" Kumarian Press, USA 1983.
3. Mahabub UL Haq, "The Poverty Curtain", Columbia Press, 1976.

Consulting for Social Development in India

With the growing concern of the State to improve the lot of vulnerable and deprived people of society, through programme interventions like minimum need programme, education, health and family welfare, the needs for pre-investment feasibility studies, on the situation of the target groups has assumed importance.

State and funding agencies are increasingly concerned with better pay-off on their investments, in terms of "social development" or "social advance". Consulting for social development has been need a great, in several states, and of national and international funding agencies committing substantial resources to basic services for rural and urban poor through mother care, nutrition, school education, water supply and sanitation.

Historically, investment by the State in the social sector was treated mostly as of low return with low impact. The emphasis was on social welfare, rather than on social development. The latter is now expected to proceed with agricultural and industrial development, reflecting in better quality of life. Social indicators are increasingly recognised as critical for increasing productivity in several sectors of the economy. Official, voluntary, national and international agencies are increasingly turning towards consultants and specialist who can undertake feasibility studies and project formulation for social development programmes.

There have been Consulting Associates, Syndicates and System Groups for advising corporate and industrial clients but the clients in the field of social development are finding it hard to get sound management and system consultants to advise and offer diagonistic projects in social development programmes. In the fifties and sixties, when India launched massive agricultural modernisation programmes, international agencies like the Rockefeller and Ford Foundations provided both resources and consulting expertise to design and implement agricultural development programmes. To some extent, social science departments in universities and individual social scientists provided the expertise on an *ad hoc* basis to these funding agencies. This expertise, however, was loaded with too much knowledge disciplines like sociology, agricultural economics, soil science, and extension techniques, without providing the much needed managerial skills in solving social development problems flowing from agricultural modernisation.

The Agro Economic Research Centres and the university departments in social science provided some inputs for designing social development programmes through village surveys and micro-economic studies. These studies were confined to selected rural areas characterised by high economic activities. With the establishment of the Centre for Management in Agriculture of the IIMA some organised thinking was initiated, with the support of the Ministry of Agriculture of the Government of India, to provide management and skill oriented techniques for agricultural projects/ programmes across the country. Besides health and education, research units in all management institutes were also organised for skill improvement among educational and health administrators. With the establishment of ICSSR, the science of social development was also given fresh impetus. But the impetus provided was more for social scientists to get rehabilitated in universities and centres of social studies, than for helping the programmers in social development at the Centre, state, and other levels of public policy formulation.

The corporate consultants in India have not found consulting for social development an attractive 'fee'-earning proposition. They have not made sustained marketing of their skills to get assignments on project and feasibility studies in social development for the clients'.

In some large metropolitan development authorities, which have complex technological problems like erecting sewerage disposal plants, water filteration plants and city fleet operation, the consultations have been mostly for technological know how rather than for identifying management skills for social development in these metropolitan areas.

Hence sustained professional consultations for social development in India have been either *ad hoc* or *sporadic.* (They have not been sought by the clients like state/Central/local funding agencies/voluntary bodies engaged in rural and/or social. development.) Social development programmes are increasingly being subjected to, what is termed in industrial parlance, the feasibility test. One may question the feasibility test for basic services, since the need for basic services like health care, protected water supply and sanitation, basic education and nutrition are beyond question. While the need is not in doubt, the mechanics and systems of delivery of these services time and cost of delivery, and the maintenance of these, are never analysed in a management perspective.

There is need, therefore, to analyse the various 'dimensions' of the 'process of consultations' on social development programmes. The term 'social development' broadly includes the following components:

(a) improvement in health status of vulnerable groups of people like children (0-6, 6-14 age groups), visible pregnant and lactating mothers, reduction of infant mortality rates;

(b) improvement in consumption levels of busic services like protected water supply, sanitation, nutrition etc;

(c) fulfilment of learning needs for children and adults;

(d) improvement in the overall quality of life of the vulnerable groups in particular.

The term 'consulting' in this note refers to :

(a) process of consulting for assessing the magnitude and dimension of basic service needs of vulnerable groups of population like mothers, children and the aged;

(b) assessing the gaps in the delivery systems of these services and design improvements for them;

(c) assessing the cost-benefit implications of extending these service;

(d) suggesting manpower training needs and skill development programmes for the personnel engaged in the delivery of these services;

(e) designing, installing, operating, and evaluating appropriate management information system for the programme/projects for basic services;

(f) suggesting policy options and pay-off strategies for the funding, agencies for social development.

The above 'process consultation' operates between the two systems, viz, the client system (funding agencies, state/Centre etc.) and the consultants system. The client group includes the following types of agencies :

(a) Central state and local bodies engaged in health care sanitation and water supply and nutrition oriented activities;

(b) international agencies like World Bank. UNICEF, CARE, WHO,DANIDA, UNFPA etc. engaged in funding activities under (a) above;

(c) voluntary non-governmental agencie. like CARE, Mafatlal Foundation, Tata Trust, corporate bodies engaged in funding and extending basic service programmes.

The consultants group include the following types of professional bodies/ associations :

(a) University professors, fellows in research centres, faculties in institutes of management;

(b) Associate corporate groups engaged in corporate enterprise consultations;

(c) Computer-based, agro-based and technology based consultancy agencies, marketing and operational research groups;

(d) Freelance social scientists engaged in social science research either on their own, or on behalf of social science research institutes.

The 'process' of consultancy for social development takes place between the clients and consultancy groups within national and/or international settings. There could be process consultancy too for a consortium of national and international agencies.

Process consultancy for social development qualitatively differs from consultancy for industrial and agricultural development. The broad differences are :

(1) Social development needs are pronounced in, highly diffused rural communities which are not organised, and the target groups generally lack purchasing power to pay for the basic service, unlike the urban-based organised groups.

(2) Conventional tools of cost-benefit analysis and the internal rate of return are generally not useful for measuring the impact, or quantifying benefits flowing from provision of Basic Services. The special difficulty in planning the health sector is that although it is quiet possible to measure health inputs in terms of money, buildings, etc, there is yet no convenient methodology for measuring the output in improved health in response to these inputs especially for countries with weak health statistics, as is the case in virtually all parts of the Third World. It is necessary to make additional use of output as measured in terms of the volume and type of services offered and taken up as the next best available indicators of health[2].

(3) The organisers of basic services are not professional managers, nor are they trained in management discipline to understand the complexities of social development process They are good men, but are not technocratic

(4) Voluntariness and mission objectives characterise the non-governmental organisations engaged in social development. In contrast, the corporate enterprises view social development objectives as inputs for furthering corporate image and objectives. Consultancy therefore, assumes a different dimension.

(5) Maximisation of benefits to the clientele, rather than profits to the service organisations, is the characteristic feature of social development organisation. Hence consultations have to be towards maximising benefits than profits though the latter is important for ensuring viability of the social development organisation.

(6) Social development is a joint venture product of the state, the funding agencies, the voluntary bodies, non-govornmental organisations (NGOs) and the beneficiaries. No one agency can, by Itself, ensure development, and has to depend perforce on partnership. How to ensure this partnership, what are the relative shares and responsibilities, are matters for consultation. The partnership programming is a difficult process which needs careful designing by the consultants.

To meet the demands of client groups who are concerned with proper investment opportunities in the area of basic services, the consulting groups have to make proper methodological choices to evolve sound recommendations. The consultants generally face the following types of methodological alternatives in designing social development programmes:

(a) Embark on time-consuming indepth household surveys in the client identified areas, and aspect certain basic service needs and gaps in their fulfilment.

or

(b) Assess them based on secondary data and obtain feel of the situation after talking to as cross section of families in the area.

or

(c) Talk to the programme operators and beneficiaries to understand the operational dynamics and assess the gaps in basic services. This calls for a dispassionate assessment of the programme impact on beneficiaries and problems of programme management.

Perhaps there could also be a varying combination of (a) to (c).

Household surveys to assess nutritional, health educational status of famliy members would be of limited value, since the majority of rural households do not keep 'account' of social consumption. Even on tangible, assets such as land, buildings, livestock, etc, rural surveys in the past have not covered much ground. As instruments of data-gathering despite refinements in sampling techniques, household surveys leave much to be desired. The programme designers do not get much inkling out of these surveys. However, these household surveys are good as a benchmark to assess the levels of social development at a point of time. If these are repented after five to ten years, one can gauge the extent of change or stagnation in the levels of social consumption among the target population.

For purposes of programme planning, budgeting, and monitoring, these family-oriented surveys cannot possibly provide any clues to the social services bureaucracy which manage the social development programmes. In specified areas/districts, basic needs of vulnerable groups like self-employed artisans, agricultural labourers, women and children are well known. What is not known is how to effectively manage the, delivery of services like primary health care, water supply, school education and feeding. Programme planning need not depend unduly on family-based surveys, and these surveys could become part of the programming activities than the programme itself.

Another important issue that a consultant group has to face is the choice of organisational designs and structures for programme planning and implementation. As, stated earlier, social development programmes are joint-sector activities with the share of the State (Central or provincial) being more than, 50-60 per cent, in the total cost of the programme. Specialised funding agencies generally share the capital cost of buildings, equipment, training and knowhow. The recurring costs are in principle borne by the State. States are generally reluctant to shoulder the burden of recurring costs and the funding agencies are reluctant to lend to programmes whose recurring budgets are not borne by the State. Here begins the rub. How will the consultants design budget systems which would take care of both the creation and maintenance of assets for social development? How do we make the state agencies restructure their investment on social programmes to incorporate more recurring budgets and also to make necessary managerial position changes to meet the requirements of funding agencies?

Unfortunately; at the state/district/cient personnel. Over a period of time, a reservoir of rejected personnel have been pooled to manage social welfare programmes at the field level. The so-called Harijan Welfare Department has paved the way for what is called the department of Social Defence, but the personnel are the same. Some of the funding agencies are choosey about the project personnel, particularly in those projects which receive massive assistance. Social Development Programmes need much more skilled manpower in view of their complex relationships with the target groups, sponsors and funding agencies.

The process consultations would need to identify the type of skilled manpower required to manage the programme and to suggest placement of such manpower in the programmes. This would help the funding agencies to monitor the programmes more effectively with the programme personnel.

Monitoring and evaluation of social development programmes are more complex than industrial and agricultural projects, since a number of variable get mixed up while monitoring and measuring the impact of the programme. Management tools, like PERT and CPM, perhaps are, required to the reotooled because each of the programme partners have different set of operational procedures, different set of people, to implement different components of the programmne. Each of them are accountable to different set of departmenta heads. In such a complex web of inter-relationships among programme personnel, one is not sure about the choice of conventional monitoring techniques. This is where consultants can advise the social development agencies about the proper monitoring techniques to be applied and management information system to be installed.

Similarly, techniques of evaluation in social development programmes are difficult to apply. The Agro-Economic Research Centres in India conducted a number of benchmark surveys of villages across the country and re-surveyed them after a gap of five to ten years to find out the impact of economic development, on families in the selected villages. The focus was more, on economic impact in terms of assets accumulated/depleted, immigration/outmigration, production gains/losses at the household level. The basic needs or social consumption data on these families were not adequately gathered however, to measure the impact in the levels of social living.

There is need to evolve evaluation techniques to find out the impact of investment activities, on infant mortality, health, and nutritional status' of vulnerable groups such as mothers, children" and the aged. The funding agencies need to know how their investment, in specific areas/districts, has resulted in the well being of their target groups.

Besides, the states and a number of voluntary agencies are also investing in the areas/districts for social welfare. The question arises as to how to delineate and correlate the impact to the agencies in the area. This is where the consultants could suggest evaluation techniques/methodologies for measuring impact in the creation of which several agencies have been involved. This would help to suggest improved methods of spending on social services in the agency area.

The consulting process for social development is, therefore, beset with several complex methodological and managerial problems. Further the process could lead to better investment opportunities for the funding agencies and help build up local-level managerial capacities for implementation of social development programmes.

Globalised Business and Local Bodies

In the last few months, two big events took place, one in Bangalore (Jan 5 to 11, 2002) and another in New York (Jan, 31 to Feb, 4, 2002) where leaders of industry, prime ministers and ministers and a few civil society groups deliberated on the shape of the world economy. The event in Bangalore was that of the Confederation of Indian Industries (CII) Summit to deliberate on how Indian Industry leaders can increase their bottom lines in the wake of world-wide economic slowdown and the September 11 attacks on the US. The theme of the CII Summit was how to do business in "local boundaries" with global capital, technology and human skills and the star speaker was none other than British Prime Minister Tony Blair. The New York event was the famous Davos gathering of big players in world capitalism organised by the World Economic Forum (WEF). Its theme was "Leadership in fragile times", and top speakers from Hillary Clinton to Bill Gates to pop singers and philosophers like Sri Sri Ravi Shankar attended and spoke.

I attended both these mega events and a majority of Indian Industry captains led by Yashwant Sinha and Chandrababu Naidu attended the New York WEF gathering. Both these events clearly point out that, globalisation is unstoppable and it will impinge on local people, local institutions and local resources. In the US and Europe, local institutions are powerful. New York Mayor Rugio Guliani was more powerful than US President Bush when the World Trade Center was attacked. Guliani was declared Man of the Year by *Time* Magazine because of his work for helping the victims of the WTC. It was the recognition for a local institution, the New York Metropolitan Council.

Hearing local voice

In Bangalore, the Mayor was nowhere to be seen when the CII Summit was held. It was all S.M. Krishna and his ministers rubbing shoulders with Tony Blair. The CII Summit discussed at length how in local areas factories, are being closed due to labour and other problems and the dynamic economist of the CII, Onkar Goswamy, brought to light how in many "local areas" of Karnataka, factory inspectors create more problems for local industries. The industry minister of Karnataka explained to the CII members how the government is extending a red carpet for foreign direct investment. In all these "political power point" presentations, the local boundaries are treated as very important but the "representatives" of these local boundaries are forgotten.

In India, through the 73rd and 74th constitutional amendments, we have defined local boundaries through a three-tier panchayat system and nagara-palikas. These local bodies are now constitutional entities in their own right and they have to be heard, respected and involved in all economic/social development programmes affecting them. Europe and the US have 'their own strong decentralised systems of governance. Switzerland is a classic example. The WEF for the first time was held outside Davos in Switzerland to show to the world that New York is still important in global capitalism. The head of the Swiss Confederation - a representative of local bodies in Switzerland - flew all the way to New York to join hands with the WEF to tell the New York audience that the Davos spirit is still alive even if the WEF is held in New York. That is how the status and prestige of the Swiss local bodies have been recognised.

Many multinationals are concerned with local health and development issues. They want to do business with a human face and with due regard to "local" culture and spirit. But they don't know how to go about it. One multinational CEO attending the WEF meeting asked me: "What is this panchayat in India? Is it a temple?" I laughed. India has such vibrant "local boundaries". Our zilla panchayats and nagarpalikas have to be aware of the consequences of globalisation. Unless they are sensitised on. this count, they will be faced with innumerable problems like dumping of toxic goods, sale of unwanted products and several development problems.

Redrawing Boundaries

Take the case of BT cotton in Gujarat. Ten thousand acres of genetically modified BT cotton have been sown and farmers have enjoyed the fruits of biotech cotton crop with less pest attacks and high yields. The ministry of agriculture in New Delhi wants the crops to be destroyed because the genetic engineering approval committee has not approved the cultivation of such crops. If the ZPs are involved right in the beginning all these remote control methods of regulation can be avoided. If Zurich airport can be managed by Swiss canton, why not our ZPs and nagarapalikas manage many development projects in their "local boundaries"?

The CII summit in Bangalore proclaimed that the summit would redraw "the boundaries of doing business in the millennium and add fresh perspective to the corporate planning process from' financial budgeting to strategic and interactive planning". How can there be interactive planning if those who manage the local boundaries, are kept away? The World Development Report-2002 quotes research results showing that corruption is lower in the presence of more decentralised governance; free and fair elections and press freedom. The CII could have invited mayors from some cities to understand how these nagarapalikas can help industry players to do better business in their local areas.

Yashwant Sinha at the WEF meet at New York said India had panchayats which are being used to distribute resources of the Centre and the states. Honourable Finance Minister, this is not a good view of the panchayats! Panchayats are units of self-government. They do not depend on the mercy, of the government which unfortunately is the situation now. We have to change it. To do so we need the panchayats and nagarapalikas to think beyond elections, grants, yojanas, and schemes. They should become more global in their outlook. The civil society groups should also help these local bodies instead of running parallel projects and programmes. Then only we will have a good and enduring global order.

Makings Gram Sabhas Tool of Governance

The Constitution has created village panchayats as units of self-government along with the three-tier structure of panchayati raj with the district as a unit of planning and development. The gram sabhas are supposed to be vibrant and actively supported by efficient gram panchayats/taluk panchayats and zilla panchayats. Today these PR bodies do not have any integrated information system at any level. Hence their planning capabilities are also limited. At the village level we have to have an integrated information system which serves the needs of villagers of all occupational and interest groups. Take the gram sabhas. If e-governance is to make any sense the first step should be to build an efficient information system at the gram sabhas and not collection of piecemeal information by a VA or an anganwadi worker or a school teacher to be fed to his/her superior officers at the district and state level.

At the village level a typical family wants to know the job opportunities, the prices it may get for its produce from season to season, the nearest good maternity hospital, the seasonal rain forecast for crop sowing, the new crop technologies available like genetically modified ones, the various risks involved in them, ways of getting old age pension, entitlements like food-grains from fair price shops and so on and so forth. Today, if the village child in Karnataka wants a caste certificate or a young man wants an income certificate to get admitted to a professional college, he has to bribe the village accountant E-governance is supposed to be not only efficient and effective but also honest and transparent.

Integrated System

The best location to bring all the relevant, village-level, information in one PC window is the level of a gram sabha. After all in every taluk there are some 100 villages and at best 50-60 gram sabhas. If each gram panchayat secretary is given not just a simputer but a mandate to keep all the relevant information, including land records at the gram sabha level it will serve the purpose of all villagers and the purpose of village level planning. All the Village level functionaries have to be instructed by the government to feed the Gram Sabha Information System (GSIS) which can be accessed by any villager or any outside visitor, researcher or an activist.

Each gram sabha can load all its information in their own website which is not difficult to do. We do not have any good websites even for zilla panchayats in Karnataka. Today the STD is available to any villager within a walking distance. But the integrated information system connecting all the sectors in a village from agriculture to trees to ponds to tanks to cattle to kids to mothers to weather to temples-all in the nature of connecting one another is missing. The government always talks of "single window" delivery of services. Why not make the village gram sabha a single window information system where every information of that village or group of villages is loaded and anybody can access that information any time, at a price if necessary.

There is a need for the GSIS like the Geographic Information System (GIS) which can provide at one go all, the information that is needed for every villager and the planner at any time of the year. Today IT is developing fast and it is unfortunate that with all the IT talent in Karnataka our villagers and constitutionally created bodies like the gram sabhas are not developing a user-friendly GSIS. The Bhoomi project leaders should rethink of providing a simputer to the VAs just to digitise land-related transactions and transmit them to the taluks.

Building Linkages

The present Land Revenue Act and other similar laws in Karnataka need amendments to provide "space' to the gram sabhas, gram panchayats, taluk panchayats and ZPs to link up and "connect" with other development sectors. Most of the time, VAs, in approving mutations of land transfers, have to do village level enquiry. Why not the VAs do this type of enquiry in the gram sabhas where the buyer and the seller of the land are known.

The GSIS can perhaps pro-vide the needed connectivity for bottom up plannilig and development from the village to the district. Today our villagers are not getting the benefits of modern technology, whether it is in agriculture or medicine or nutrition or education. Our Constitution wants the gram sabhas to become the effective. Instruments of governance. By establishing the GSIS, we would be able to load the latest information on how the village lands water bodies and forest wealth are shrinking, enabling us to decide how the biodiversity in the village boundaries should be protected.

Our scientists use these digital and satelite pictures to present papers in International conferences but the average villager does not know what is happening around her/his own surrounding, environment. Karnataka has hundreds of villages in the Western Ghats and in ecologically fragile areas like coastal areas, if the GSIS is well prepared the villagers in these areas would know through it what is happening to their immediate environment.

The gram sabhas are also pivotal for human resource development. Families, in villages are now clamouring to fall below the poverty line and if gram sabhas can by good information system weed out the better off families from the BPL list it will go a long way to focus on the really destitute families for help and support.

There is no linkage at present between self-help groups and panchayats because the SHGs have been formed by different departments of the State. Both have to be connected for getting the best synergy and benefits. Women in the SHGs have saved crores of rupees but they do not know how to leverage with other productive sectors to process and produce and thus increase their incomes. If the GSIS is well developed, such SHGs can be linked locally and globally.

Whither e-governance in Karnataka?

Our new President Dr. A. P. J. Abdul Kalam, in his latest book *Ignited Minds-Unleashing the Power Within India,* makes a pointed reference to the mission mode style of development in the country by establishing what he calls "connectivity" between people, processes and sectors so that the present "tunnel vision" devlopment within one's own sector is stopped and we the people of India develop as a whole and not in parts. He has quoted several holistic development experiences and systems approach that he implemented during his career.

One is the agricultural development in Bihar as part of the work of the Technology Information Forecasting and Assessment Council (TIFAC)- a body of 500 members who have given thought to what should be next vision for India. TIFAC examined five areas- agriculture, power, education and health care, information technology and the strategic sector of nuclear, space and defence technology. Action in these five areas, if properly integrated, would lead to food, economic and national security. But the key to success lies in what he repeatedly terms "connectivity". It is however unfortunate that TIFAC did not examine e-governance as a tool to bring about sustainable development although they did examine the role of IT in the development of the country.

Karnataka is now in the fore front of establishing what is called electronic governance or e-governance that is expected to provide efficient and effective governance at the village, taluk, district and State levels. Yuvacom and Bhoomi are cited as the flagship experiments in the State. Bhoomi is supposed to provide just at Rs. 15 record of rights copies to land owners and cultivators. The village land owners and cultivators need not be at the mercy of village accountants (VAs) in getting their pahni and record of rights extracts. They just walk into the taluk office kiosks, just pay and carry their titles to their lands without hassles.

Data Collection

Bhoomi is now expected to enter phase II by the end of this year by introducing simputer-a low cost hand-held computer developed by the IISC in Bangalore. VAs who play a pivotal role at the grassroots level, are expected to use it to collect data digitally and transmit them to the taluks instantly instead of the current practice of dispatching written reports to taluk headquarters which takes months to reach the tahsildar's offices in taluks. According to a press release, "the current network created by Bhoomi is to be exploited to disseminate other information digitally like lists of destitute and handicapped pensioners, families living below the poverty line, concessional foodgrain card holders, mandi rates and weather information".

This is good as far as it goes. But today we are talking of good governance through the use of IT and other technologies to help the villagers and urban dwellers to make their lives qualitatively better. VAs are one of the government functionaries in the villages of Karnataka and are not the only ones. In all villages we have now a plethora of fuctionaries like anganwadi workers, auxilary nurse midwives (ANMs) of primary health sub-centres, school teachers, police constables, irrigation and tank-related fuctionaries, forest guards and gramsevaks of the agriculture departments.

Finally we have created the village panchayat secretaries to help the effective functioning of panchayats and gram sabhas. We also have hundreds of self-help groups (SHGs) and civil society pressure groups spaning several villages. Besides, we have several inspectors and government orderlies who make the life of the villagers not happy but miserable by forcing the villagers to comply with umpteen government orders which now touch every aspect of village life.

Debatable Question

Hundreds of vertical schemes and programmes of the Centre and the States reach the villagers and none of them are "connected" at the village level nor they are converged at the same time on the same families or the same groups. These schemes have been reduced to "stand-alone" type of programmes. Vertically they are good but horizontally they are useless.

What is the rationale of providing simputers only to VAs and tell them to digitise all the relevant data at the village level and make them to transfer the data to the taluks and then to the districts? VAs by the very nature of their work are only concerned with land-rights work and land-related policing work and not related to land development, land resources management and so on. They protect the land rights, note the encumbrances on land, note the disputes related to land through mutations that are settled or certified by the revenue officers above them. The Land Revenue Act of the State regulates all these functions.

In the past, and to some extent even now, VAs and school teachers are burdened with so many functions which are unrelated to their job-descriptions. VAs also carry out cattle census, human census, do the work of revising electoral rolls and so on. School teachers are saddled with much non-teaching work like motivating couples for adopting family planning methods!

VAs by training and motivation are not disposed towards good governance or people focussed work. They are trained for revenue recovery work where coercion and force have to be applied. Now we are trying to make them collect data related to village planning and development and make them people-relationship managers in the village. It is debatable whether these VAs are well-suited for the development tasks. It is not a question of possessing a simputer and doing this bhoomi work. But the very purpose of providing them with simputers may not be cost-effective and serve the purpose of good governance at the village level.

The two-part article by Minister for Panchayat Raj and Rural Development M Y Ghorpade on panchayat raj in Karnataka (DH October 5 and 6, 2006) leaves one with an impression that the Government has done its best to give the panchayats all powers' short of making them units of self-government as enshrined in the Constitution under article 243 (G). Mr Ghorpade's innovative step to organise vasati sabhas before the villagers meet in bigger gram sabhas is laudable. The gesture of the Government in giving Rs. 5 lakh to each panchayat for preparing annual plans based on the needs of the villagers should also be appreciated. The revamping of the Sampoorna Grameen Rojgar Yojana and leveraging it with the Jalarakshana Programme are laudable. But all these are just cosmetic gestures to make the panchayats to work as agents of the Government at the State level and not as units of self-government. The basic thinking has not changed although Mr. Ghorpade keeps emphasising that "what is appropriate at a given level of the three-tier system should be done at that level and not at a higher level".

Dichotomy

Let us examine how the Government is doing precisely the reverse of what has been stated so elegantly by him. As per Schedule I of Section 58 of the Karnataka Panchayat Raj Act 1993, the gram panchayats have been entrusted with almost 30 tasks and activities and if all of them are to be done by the village panchayats there would be no need for any State-level development functionaries to be doing their jobs in the panchayat areas. All of them have to be done or supervised by the gram panchayats and the State-level functionaries in the panchayat jurisdiction have to work under the orders of the panchayat president, the subject committees and so on. A sample of the tasks entrusted to the village panchayats as per Schedule I is, providing relief in natural calamities, promotion and development of agriculture and horticulture, development of fisheries, construction, repairs and maintenance of drinking water wells, tanks and ponds, ensuring full enrollment and attendance in primary schools, participation in the implementation of women and child welfare programmes, promotion of school health and nutrition programmes and monitoring the public distribution system. The village anganwadis have been under the control of the State women and child welfare department. the anganwadi worker is a local village woman and is answerable to the child development project officer and not to the panchayat. The anganwadi feeding and what food is given when, how much with what ingredients and with what nutritional values and so on is still decided at the state level and the sarpanch cannot even go and see what the village children are eating. Pre-school and school feeding in the villages are best done by women in self-help groups (SHGs) which are in hundreds now in the villages of Karnataka. How come these SHGs are still monitored by the women and child welfare department in the grab of a state-level programme called Stree Shakti, and not leveraged by the village panchayats for the good health of mothers, and children?

Raithara Santhe is a pioneering programme to help the farmers to get better prices for their produce through digital information. The farmers get ID cards so that they can enter the market. The ID cards are given by a team headed by the sub-divisional assistant commissioner and the horticulture officer of the Government and not a single panchayat member is involved. Agriculture is the sheet-anchor of the panchayat system and the panchayat members are kept away from the Raitar Santhe!

On paper and in theory all the 29 department works have been delegated to the panchayats but in practice there is no 'connectivity' and 'convergence' of streams, of State-level departmental works at the level of the panchayat. Karnataka is proud of its IT and e-governance and the bureaucrats boast of many digital dividends they have obtained through computerisation. If we make a 'spread sheet' of the actual powers and authorities given to the panchayats to hire and fire the different functionaries of the development administration and the powers vested in the panchayats for drawing and disbursing powers of all the schemes that fall under Schedule 1 of Section 58 of the Panchayat Act 1993, we will know which are the schemes and programmes which are under the panchayats and which are still independently working under the State departments. The Minister for Panchayats could direct his department to prepare such a 'Spread Sheet' for all the 5600 gram panchayats in Karnataka which would provide at a glance the actual status of the devolution and delegation and how it is working.

Each department of the State has a invested interest in protecting its 'turf' and its 'silos'. In 1931 when Mahatma Gandhi visited England in connection with the Second Round Table Conference he was asked at Oxford, "What is the greatest obstacle in the way of swaraj". He replied: "It is the British officers' un willingness to part with power and our incapacity to wrest power. from unwilling hands. "In 2002 AD, 71 years later, the same answer would remain valid if one substituted the word 'British' with 'Indian' in respect of non-empowerment and sometimes disempowerment of constitutionally mandated panchayats" (D Bandopadhya, former secretary Rural Development Department, GOI).

Need for New Reforms

Development departments in Karnataka have over the years built their own systems, enacted their own Acts and are wary of integrating them with the panchayats in all the three thiers (village, block and the district) because they fear they will lose their autonomy and their power.

There is need to bring in the second set of reforms for panchayat governance and Mr. M.Y. Ghorpade, with his commitment for decentralised governance, should immediately set up a task force to look into the relevant Acts. Unless this is done early panchayats will just remain spectators and we will keep hearing pious pleas to strengthen them.

Relevance of Human Development

MP was in the forefront of initiating several people centered programmes during 1999-2000 under the leadership of the Chief Minister Mr. Digvijay Singh. In fact, MP was the first State in India which brought out its first Human Development Report in 1995 (HDR). It was followed by another in 1998, third one followed by all this was done when, even at the Government of India level nobody thought of bringing India Human Development Report. The first India HDR came in 1999. Karnataka, Rajasthan then followed suit. HDR concept was the brainchild of late Dr. Mahboobul Haq - a pioneering Economist of the 20th Century. At the global level the credit for bringing out a global situation of children every year should go to the visionary Executive Director of UNICEF late James P. Grant. He brought out the first Report on the State of the World Children way back in 1979. After this every UN agency started a sort of their mouthpieces every year. After the State of the World's Children Report, the UNDP under the inspiring leadership of Dr. Mahboobul Haq started bringing out every year the HDRs and now they have become like any other agency reports. World Bank is bringing their World Development Report, UNDP their HDRs, FAO the State of the Food and Nutrition, the WHO The State of Health of the people of the world and so on.

For common people these reports make no sense because they do not solve their survival and livelihood problems. UNDP and World Bank spend Millions of Dollars for bringing out these reports because round the year the Staff are employed, specialists are hired to write specific themes and highlight specific problems of regions and countries, narrating successful and unsuccessful stories. So an intellectual industry is thriving in the production of these reports worldwide. The latest controversy in the World Bank's World Development Report was around the resignation of their Economist Dr. Ravi Kanbur just at the time of the release of the report in 2000 because he did not agree with the contents of the report!

Several questions are raised on these reports at all levels. Why at all we need them? Who reads them? Who will monitor the several suggestions made in them? What are the costs involved in bringing them every year — both human and financial? How does these HDRs differ from several Government Reports brought out by respective State and Federal Governments? Do they have any policy implications? How attractive they are for Politicians, Media, Academics and the Corporate World? Is it necessary to bring HDR Reports at the National level or the State level or the District level? These are some of the frequently asked questions (FAQs) when we talk of bringing out HDRs from time to time.

HDRs particularly at the State level as in M.P. is not like bringing an Audit Report of the State Accountant General. First it has no legal Status nor it is mandated by the Constitution. It is not even a part of the budget of the State or the Centre, nor is like a State of the Nation or any particular "State" of the State report in India. Second, is it necessary to bring such Reports every year at the State or the National level as is done by the UNDP or the World Bank at the Global level ? Third and important is how to make it accountable to the government for implementing several suggestions and ideas marshalled in the report. How do we use them to assess the performance of our MLAs and MPs in respect of their constituencies? It may not be like an election Manifesto which will contain promises made but unkept all the time.

Let us examine the two HDR reports of M.P. which were well brought out by an outside Research Agency under the guidance of the State level body which consisted of people from academics and government departmental heads. The 1995 report that was brought out for the first time by any State in India, was released with all the fanfare and media blitz at New Delhi. The report stressed in the context of M.P. education for all, perspectives on health and nutrition, gender issues and empowerment of women, information base and human development issues and the State level strategies on poverty reduction decentralized governance and the Rajiv Gandhi Missions on watershed, Fisheries and Education, followed by technical notes on building Human Development Index in M.P. The report was definitely a feather in the cap of the State. The 1998 report was released by Dr. Manmohan Singh and included themes on Panchayati Raj achievements, water management and livelihood security, Joint Forest Management processes involving people how the State is getting out of BIMARU trap, followed by technical notes on Gender Index and ratios, Infant Mortality Rates, and district profiles, etc. The 1995 M.P- HDR was more focussed on human development issues like education and health and being the first one it was like a benchmark for the future HDRs in the State 1998 HDR should have compared the human development situation that was prevailing in 1995 so that we could have got the performance of the State government in respect of human development indicators. It is true that in a span of many years, not much improvement could be seen. The most crucial indicators like Infant Mortality Rates and Maternal Mortality Rates cannot change dramatically in three years. But at least one could get to know the efforts made by the State in reducing these crucial indicators. We cannot during the critical importance of policy changes and mobilization of the State machinery for creating impact on these important of forests on the lives of the people of the State but that is a subject which is can be addressed in any other document but not in a HDR report of the State, which is specifically focussing on human development issues and human development indicators.

M.P. has made headlines in the country for its innovative programmes like Education Guarantee Scheme, Padna-Badna Abhiyan, Rajiv Gandhi Missions on Watershed, Fisheries and so on. Mr. Digvijay Singh has been acclaimed as an environment friendly, Panchayat friendly and pro-poor Chief Minister. There was criticisms that the corruption in the State was at its height. One can go on adding a list of issues to be addressed. However HDRs are not for bashing the government or for praising the government achievements. They are meant to present in an honest manner the successes and failures in an unbiased and objective manner keeping the "human" side of the situation of the State as the main objective. Hence the following suggestion are made for future HDRs in the State. Four areas of relevance to the State are suggested. First, the area of environment which includes all the work done by the State on watershed, protection.

Competitive politics for good governance

Principle of corporate governance can be productively used for the governance of the country too. Indian politics is undergoing rapid changes and the days of single party rule are over. Coalition politics involving alliances of disparate groups will be the scenario of the future both in Parliament and the state assemblies. Coalitions are a type of competitive politics. Just as competition in a market economy leads to better production and services competitive politics should in theory at least lead to better governance.

Many countries in Asia and Africa will face these types of coalition politics and governance. This is to be viewed in the context of the world trend in competitive business and corporate governance with complex set of roles for global companies who wield enormous power of generating wealth and influencing political power. The largest 100 multinational' $ 2000 billion in foreign assets outstrip the combined GDP of China, India, South Korea, Malaysia, Singapore and Phillipines. The multinationals' power has increased greatly and they have to face many complexities to survive. Similarly political parties have to face various complexities where money and peoples' choice play a crucial role.

People decide

In competitive politics it is the people who decide the fate of governments and in corporate governance the shareholders decide the fate of CEOs and presidents. Both in competitive politics and. corporate governance old men nearing retirement are threatened by young leaders. Michael Waldrop in his book 'Complexity; the Emerging Science at the Edge of Order and Chaos' has explained how this theory of complexity works and makes a strong case for decentralisation and empowerment for competitive advantage of flrms. Kelvin Kelly, 'Wired' magazine editor, has listed nine.principles to take advantage of the phenomenon: (1) Decentralised operations and networked models only work in the long run. (2) Control from the bottom up. (3) Invest in education. (4) Grow by chullking and build the system in pieces, not all at once (5) Focus on randomness and unpredictability that leads to progress (6) Honour errors. Look for accidents that are competitive advantages (7) Pursue no optima; have multiple goals. Have alternative plans. (8) Seek persistent disequilibria.Industry revolutionaries create turbulence to open spaces for their product. (9) Change changes itself. Static or incremental strategies often fail.

Political parties may benefit a great deal and may also be able to deliver "development" if they follow some of these principles. Delivering development to benefit people is not going to be easy and the state need not exactly be run like a corporate structure. But there are certain techniques from the corporate world which have relevance to governance. Let us examine the principle of decentralised operations and networked models. Rajiv Gandhi's biggest gift to this country was his passion to decentralise power to the panchayats by making them units of self-government. Mahatma Gandhi dreamt of gram swaraj. India is too vast a country to be governed by a few ministers and bureaucrats sitting in New Delhi and state capitals.

Networked models

Networked models only survive in the end.If all these gram sabhas and panchayats are properly networked we get a shining India. NDA,s networking is for power sharing and not for networking the 500,000 villages. Unfortunately the same Congress has not bothered to reiterate the decentralisation mantra in 2004 election manifesto. Instead it has picked up six pedestrian slogans to win the voters hearts. The Congress calls these unfortunately the six basics of governance Samajik Sadhbhavana, Yuva Rozgar, Grameen Vikas, Arthik Navotthan, Mahila Sashaktikaran and Saman Avsar. Most of these are outcomes and not techniques and instruments of governance. What are those strategic choices which will promote Saman Avsar, or equal opportunity? How will you give Yuva Rozgar when half the Yuva are illiterate? This is linked to education and empowerment. In corporate governance investing in education is a big" step to accelerate your competitive edge in knowledge economy. Education alone can usher a knowledge driven society and polity. None of the parties has emphasised education to lift masses from poverty.

Our politicians are not in the habit of honouring their errors. For instance, not once has Narendra Modi said, "sorry" to the Gujarat violence victims. Another principle of the complexity theory is you cannot forecast accurately and you have to have alternative plans. Look at the recurrent drought situation.The only alternative plan the Prime Minister has, is to link India's rivers, which has technical complexities. There are better ways, to use the phrase of management guru Gary Hamal, to bring change through a "tornado of innovation". There are no such innovations adopted in government systems.

Let us hope we get a government which means business for helping the people and just not getting votes. Let competitive politics lead to better governance.

Liberalisation with a Human Face

In the wake of liberalisation, many industries are booming in the country. We hear a lot on 'JAMES', that is joint venture, Acquisitions, Mergers, Euroissues and new shares. Trade visits and CII sponsored dialogues on the style of Devos meetings are now fashionable. Junk food advertisements, Pepsi and Coke and cornflakes popularisation are now the 'in thing' in all discussions. The mass media like TV, FM radio and the press are all busy praising the virtues of Liberalisation. The poor do not comprehend JAMES. What they understand is whether the prices of onions, tomatoes, chillies, condiments are coming down or not as a result of liberalisation and fiscal adjustment in the country. The poor do not understand how many power project MOUs are signed by this State or that State. The poor farmer understands whether his pumpset gets *bijli* or not and whether in the height of summer his crops get water through his electric pump or not.

We still hear about plague, measles epidemic, polio eradication initiatives, energy for the poor, fuelwood crisis, increasing infant mortality in some States, literacy and primary education, water crisis and insanitary surroundings in slums and shanty towns. A large number *of* the poor and the marginalised people in thousands of villages/slums are not affected by these economic reforms. They are passive onlookers to the reforms. Several questions come to the fore: (1) We want reforms because reforms bring growth and growth brings employment and employment brings income. But is this automatic? Are we hearing about the sarne old trickle down theory? (2) How can the process of getting growth to reach the poor be hastened? (3) Whether markets can be pro-poor? (4) Whether the essential human services and the price of getting them can be made poor-friendly? (5) Whether as a result of mechanisation and modernisation of industries/labour will be displaced? (6) What will happen to the large mass of illiterates who can't get into the job market? (7) What will happen to the social services provided by the state if the state stops providing them? (8) Is the private sector interested in running schools and health centres, water supply and sanitation services?

We do not get the right answers to many of these questions. Lessons from different countries in Latin America and Africa are not very happy. In the words of Kevin Watkins, Senior Policy Advisor of OXFAM, observing the reforms and adjustment process in Africa:

> People enter markets as unequal participants and leave them with unequal rewards. More specifically because poor people are denied access to productive inputs, marketing infrastructure, information and

capital they are severely disadvantaged in the market. That is why whatever the efficiency of the price mechanism as an instrument of resource allocation, market reforms can be associated with increasing, poverly and inequality,

He further add:

If the objective is to reduce poverty, we should not take it as axiomatic that the withdrawal of the state is in all case the best option. Nor should we assume as Adjustment in Africa tends to, that market interventions by the stat are inherently inefficient.

Meanwhile, the Indian observation was as follows:

The bulk of the increase in employment that took place between March 1990 and 1992 had occcureed in contract and other forms of non-regular employment, the share of which in total employment had gradually risen to one-third by March 1993 and regular employment fell by 3 per cent in 1992-93 even as the value of fixed assets of the sample companies rose by some 27 per cent.

We are not against the reforms per se. In fact, the virtues of the market as an institution should percolate down the public administration and help the public. The virtues of the market like cost consciousness, efficiency and effectiveness, paying for the services/products, etc, have to be encouraged by those who run our vast public bureaucracy. Today the urgent need is for revamping and improving our public bureaucracy which comes in contact with the poor and the marginalised people. Public-oriented bureaucratic systems are basically the following:

Public health, public health engineering and sanitation; public primary education; raliways, public distribution and public banks which deal with the poor, public road transport and public highways; public utilities like electricity and public distribution supplies.

Whatever reforms that keep going at the macro level should percolate down the layers of the public admistration and should reach the poor, which unfortunately is not happening. All the good things of reforms are siphoned off by the top creamy layers society and the bad fallout is reaching the poor.

Our public health system should improve its culture and get into the habit of doing business with poor people more efficiently. Our health subcentres are devoid of manpower as well as drugs. Poor people who need small treatment facilities like treatment of diarrhoea by getting a small ORS packet do not get it and are forced to go to a private medical practitioner. Our hand pumps in the rural areas are rendered non-operational for want of minor repairs. Our public roads are in shambles despite the toll tax that is collected round the year. Our schools have leaking roofs and children do not get attracted to them. We can endlessly list the failure of our public administrative systems down the line. The buck stops at the level of the poor and Mr Poor or Mrs Poor will express his or her anger at the ballot box when the elections are held.

For the common man and woman of this country what is needed are the fruits of reforms. They are not convinced that these reforms and liberalisation are for them. The state has to undertake the task of educating and informating the public about liberalisation if it is to succeed. At present this is not happening. There is a sense of fear among the poor. They even feel that they may not get drinking water but would only get Coke or Pepsi to drink! Satellite TV has done more damage to the liberalisation process than helping it.

Where do we go from here? Will the corporate sector take the lead and bring the fruits of reforms to the poor? They should not do it in a cosmetic style like digging a well here in some village and building a school in another village. Corporate management values must help and benefit the poor. They must extend 'hand holding' to small and tiny sectors and informal sectors. The state and district administration must learn to be efficient.

In the words of M.B. Athreya, the management guru of India,

> State governments must believe in enabling, facilitating and not controlling restricting and directly doing, must believe in delaying removing unnecessary levels in the hierarchy from the LDC to the Chief Secretary, must improve delivery of existing services, must encourage the reporting of the truth and not just palatable whitewashing.

Liberalisation must help Sustainable Human Development which not only helps economic growth but also distributes its benefits equitably. Liberalisation with a human face is one that is pro-poor, pro-nature, pro-jobs, pro-women and pro-children.

World Summit on Social Development

World summits are getting popular. From World Summit for Children in 1990 to Earth Summit in 1992 to the Population Summit in 1994 and then Social Summit In 1995-UN Agencies have generated enormous information and worldwide thought processes and actions and also gained expertise in holding such summits. Agenda 21 of the Earth Summit was a massive document and even now nations which ratified several agreements and conventions have still to understand the implications of the agreements, which they signed leave apart, the implementation of these convention? Preparations for the Social Summit have been launched with, the release of UNDP's *Human Development Report (HDR)1994.* In fact, the report itself reads like an agenda for the Social Summit and the choice of issues for discussion in the Summit is thrown open to the world audience. Unfortunately, the kind of uphoria which Earth Summit generated even at the time or prepcoms, is not to be seen in the case of Social Summit. The NGOs stole the limelight, not only in the prepcoms but also in the Earth Summit at Rio. In fact, the suggestion to constitute an Independent Commission for Sustainable Development was, from the NGOs.

If the World Social Summit has to be 'owned' by the people of both the developed and developing countries, then NGOs have to be in the forefront in the forthcoming Social Summit. But from a careful reading of the *HDR 1994* one gets a feeling that the Social Summit will be packed with UN bureaucracies and donors/creditors and the third world debtor/countries would be onlookers in the Summit.

The UNDP suggested a seven point agenda for the Social Summit in March 1995. These were (1) Approve a world social charter as a new social contract among all nations and all people. (2) Endorse a new development paradigm of sustainable human development with economic growth centred on people and sustainable from one generation to another. (3) Give the UN the mandate to draw up a comprehensive blueprint for ensuring global human security and protecting people from threats in their daily lives like poverty, unemployment, etc, (4) Agree on a targeted reduction of 3 per cent a year in global military spending for the decade 1995-2005 and credit the savings thus accrued to global security fund, (5) Approve a human development compact of 20:20 for the next 10 years by countries, aid agencies, (6) Recommend to ECOSOC that it examines the feasibility of various forms of global taxation-especially taxes on global pollution and speculative movements of capital to raise adequate financing for setting up a new global fund for human security. (7) Urge international community to strengthen UN in socio-economic field by establishing what is called UN Economic Security Council to manage the new dimensions of human security.

This itself is a complex and exhaustive agenda, and if in this Summit, the world leaders either agree or come to some sort of consensus, then it would be an achievement. Otherwise, the Summit is a failure. Nobody disagrees with the concept of human security-job security, income security, health security, environmental security and security from crimes. The *HDR 1994* captured the people's feeling of security. A woman in Nigeria says, "My security is only in the name of Lord, who has made heaven and earth. I feel secure because I am at liberty to worship whom I like; how I like and also because I can pray for all the people and for peace for all over the country."

A secondary school child in Mongolia says, "Before, education in this country was totally free, but from this year every student has to pay. Now I do not feel secure about, finishing my studies. "A man in Ecuador says". What makes you feel insecure above all, is violence and delinquency as well as insecurity with respect to the police. Basic services are also an important part of security. Insecurity arises basically from threats from the state (physical torture) threats from other states (war) threats from other groups of people (ethnic tensions) threats from individuals (crime and street violence) threats against women (rape and domestic violence) threats to children (child abuse). Ensuring safety and security to the citizens in any given country is not just the look out of the state but also of the citizens as well. Many developing countries have poor record of human rights protection. Developed countries are abetting the crimes by setting up one ethnic group against the other. How can the leaders in the Social Summit agree to ensure security to its citizens? Human and civil rights activists are always in loggerheads with the states. What is going to be the consensus in the summit? Will there be an international civil/human rights commission to oversee the security problems of civilians in the developing countries? Yes we want security but how do we ensure it? Such questions need deliberations by a wide section of human rights activists across the world before the Social Summit to bring practical orientation to the issue of security in the summit. The *HDR 1994* does not throw light on such questions on how to go about in the business of providing life protection and security? This issue will be hotly debated in the summit if civil rights activists have their way!

Global military spending declined between 1987 and 1994 at an estimated average annual rate of 3.6 per cent yielding a cumulative peace dividend of $ 935 billion-$ 810 billion in industrial countries and $ 125 billion in developing countries. "But it is difficult to track where these funds went. And there has heen no clear link between reduced military spending and enhanced expenditure on human development". Of the current arms supplies 86 per cent originate from the five permanent members of the Security Council. India and Pakistan accounted for more than 18 per cent of world's arms imports-nearly twice as much as Saudi Arabia's share. "The Report has made radical suggestions to reduce the military spending make aid allocations dependent on the recipient country's ratio of military to social spending-progressively reducing aid as the ratio becomes greater than. But what is the prospect of enforcing this? Who will sign this treaty? When the *HDR* 1994 says we do not know where the peace dividend went, how will we know from time to time what is the arms reduction taking place? Defence is a highly secretive business and even the most professional NGOs, have no access to this information. We will have to depend on the governments and the heads of the state and when there is no transparency there is no accountability and no peace dividend. Armament industry provides the biggest kickback to the politicians and the bureaucrats alike. One wonders, how in the forthcoming summit any decision will be taken at all on this sensitive issue.

Oscar Arias, winner of 1987 Nobel Peace Prize says in the *HDR 1994* that a global demilitarisation fund should be established to add dynamism to the current demilitarisation trend by rewarding primarily, but not exclusively the efforts of developing countries, to disarm and demobilise their armed forces, promote arms control, reintegrate military personnel into society, etc. These are very laudable ideas but are not implementable or enforceable. We have to learn from Earth Summit experience. What is happening to Global Environmental Facility (GEF). We have yet to see what it is doing and who is benefiting from GEF in developing countries. These initiatives would attract bureaucratisation and the original intentions are never realised. Defence issues are generally beyond the understanding of common people and unless these are discussed in a transparent manner, the ideas never get translated into action.

Human development programmes are person-intensive and not capital-intensive. It is true that 20:20 compact is a good tool for investing in human development programmes by aid agencies and national governments but the problem is not with initial 20 per cent but the subsequent 30 or 40 per cent needed for maintenance of human development structures like school buildings, health centres, water facilities, etc. It is a common sight to see broken school buildings, health centres without drugs and water pipes without water in all third world countries. Maintenance burden in human development programmes is heavy. How can we address this? No answer is forthcoming in the *HDR 1994*. Global prescriptions are not relevant for local problems and unfortunately human development is more local than global. Can the Social Summit provide answers to these local problems?

The use of existing foreign aid in the recipient countries is a more serious issue than the quantum of aid. The development fund of UN (UNDP, UNICEF, UNFPA, IFAD, WFP) provides nearly \$ 5 billion a year to developing countries. If all this had been used effectively, by now, mortality and quality of life would have improved significantly in many developing countries. But the capacity of aid-receiving countries to improve their systems and procedures of handling and using aid has been poor. In fact the World Summit should discuss more seriously developing countries, capacity in using aid effectively.

The agenda on global taxation, economic security council and ideas like establishing global safety net, world income tax and, Tobin tax on foreign exchange movements, Islamic Science Foundation, are all grandiose but are they implementable? In the words of Abdus Salam, Nobel Laureate in Physics, who has proposed this Foundation, "The Foundation would be sponsored by Muslim countries and operate within them. It would be non-political, purely scientific and run by eminent people of science and technology from the Muslim world". Salam also suggests that it would build links with UNESCO and other UN bodies. In the days of secular movements worldwide, one wonders whether moves to create 'Islamic-science' and 'Jewish science' and 'Hindu science' and 'Christian science' are really the right steps .

If the World Summit discusses science and technology for human development, it should also include in the agenda the role of religion in human development because religious institutions have played critical roles in promoting human excellence in many developing, countries. In the Earth Summit at Rio, Buddhists monks from Thailand, Bahai International and Ramakrishna Missions. Christian missionaries played a significant role in providing inputs to various sessions. All these issues need to be widely discussed among a cross-section of the people around the world to make the World Summit people-oriented.

Where the Sky is the Roof

The flight to Bhuj from Mumbai was delayed because the airport in Bhuj was still under repair. I was anxious about the few tents and lanterns that I was carrying from Bangalore for two non-government organisations (NGOs), the Sevadham India Foundation and Yogi Divine Society, working in Anjar, and wanted to ensure their safe transfer to Bhuj. Indian Airlines (IAC) refused to carry my gift to the NGOs free of excess baggage charges. They said they would lift for free only the material sent through the relief commissioner, government of Gujarat at Ahmedabad. What a tragedy! The material sent by well-intentioned people to the relief commissioner, on the other hand, is rotting in Ahmedabad airport, because nobody knows what these packets contain and who they are meant for. Here, I was paying heavy cargo and excess baggage charges on relief material meant for NGOs.That the management of earthquake relief by the IAC, the government of India and the government of Gujarat nearly 20 days after the disaster!

When I landed in Bhuj, my friends who work with NGOs took me straight to the tented shelters in Bhuj town. The first photograph I took, was that of a 10-year-old girl with multiple fractures on her hands, shoulders and legs. A beautiful hospital had been set up by a team from Red Cross in a fully air-conditioned tent. While I was taking pictures, one of the Red Cross doctors asked me if I had a license to do the same. I did not, I replied, and as an NGO relief worker I was not committing any crime, I told this person.

Soon after, an interagency meeting was convened by WHO functionaries. However, the meeting did not provide any answers on what was to be done next. Some of the NGOs present were sure what was to be done when the Red Cross team left. The representatives of the state health department met in this WHO concerened meeting to plan for the next cycle of relief and rehabilitation (R & R) since rescue operations were almost over.

The feeling I got at this meeting was that the left hand of the government did not know what the right hand was doing. In the words of a Kutchi businessman, who was also working with a NGO relief team, "The government does not know whether it has any hands at all" I went to the collector, Anil Mukhim, to tell him that he must allow the Indian Airlines to accept consignments sent to NGOs in Bhuj by other NGOs free of cargo charges or excess baggage charges, if accompanied by passengers. He seemed like a good man but harassed man. He was positive to my suggestion but said he could not do anything because the IAC would not listen to him.

Next, I went into the UN on-site camp for relief operations. The tent looked like an international conference hall, where all you could see was people sending e-mails and trying to feed the foreign media and UN headquarters on all that was going on around them.

Late in the night, I reached Anjar Vivekananda High School ground where my friend Sudhirbhai, of Sewadham Foundation, had pitched his tent. I fell asleep wondering how people could sleep in tents. The next morning, I went around the big shelter in Anjar in which hundreds of families were staying since the quake struck the town of Anjar. The town is now a flatland of rubble and debris. The Reliance group banner "Cleared by Reliance" speaks volumes for the publicity sought by relief workers.

In another shelter, small children, old men and women were lying down not knowing what to do next, where to go, where to eat. They had lost all tears and emotions. They just smiled and laughed away questions. When I clicked photographs one young man asked me where the photos will be sent and what will he get from these photos! Another young girl, Shilpa, who had lost her mother said her father is a clerk in a private firm and he had incurred debts to build the house which was now rubble and brick powder. The sky was now the roof for her and her father, she said. Shilpa is now scared to stay in a house of any kind. Ramesh, a young boy of 13, was one of the few children who survived the flag-hoisting ceremony in his school in Anjar where 400 children died. The plaster on his left leg functions as a slate, a drawing board to draw pictures and scribble anything he likes.

There are three big shelters in Anjar - one run by a team of RSS workers, another by a Swaminarayanan team along with Sewadham, and the third by a Jamait Islamic group. There appears to be a feeling of rivalry between them. In Ratlam, a small, roadside village with a roaring lorry business carrying lignite has perished completely. We find tents set up by the Congress and many other groups, but nobody takes shelter in them. However, there is no shortage of people wanting to take credit for putting up the tents and being in the limelight.

Finally, the homeless will go to what is now known in Anjar as *'Sparsh Sewa'*, which literally means 'doing service by touching'. The activity here consists mainly of helping people to walk again and physiotherapy. The Yogi Divine Society and Sewadham has opened the Physiotherapy Centre for quake victims and extends all general medicine and small surgery services like dressing wounds, tending to bed-sores on those rendered immobile by fractures, etc.

Sanitation and provision of potable drinking water are going to be the worst problems, faced by those who stay in tents, at least till next February. That means they have to fend for themselves in the tents through the summer and the rainy season. They need dry pit toilets which require little water. The Safai Vidyalaya in Ahmedabad is a pioneer institution in building such easy-to-build leach pit latrines, but one has to coordinate and plan for them right now before infectious diseases start spreading. There is a great demand for all-weather tents and tarpaulins. Even those families whose houses have not collapsed, are demanding tarpaulins and plastic nets, because they are all sleeping outside their homes due to fear and tremours in Kutch district.

In Anjar, the relief team from Poland left last week and handed over the tents and medicines to my NGO associates of Sevadham Foundation of India and the Yogi Divine Society. Valuable medicines have been stored away by an NGO which doesn't know what to do with them because the instructions are in Polish. So, there are medicines but one does not know what they are for!

Swami Tyagvallabh Das of Yogi Divine Medical Office of Anjar has done a quick survey of the affected and there are nearly 1000 orthopedic cases which need physiotherapy treatment for which phsyiotherapy equipment for treatment like Interferrential Therapy, Short Way Therapy, Cervical Traction, Continuous Passive Mouts, Suspension Therapy and others are immediately needed. These were urgent needs but no one seemed to have any idea where they are coming from.

Reliance Industries is supposed to be in charge of the relief and rehabilitation of Anjar town and were involved in debris clearing and mechanical clearing of sites. One wonders about issues such as human resettlement. Who will provide the human touch to these trautamised people, who will care for the young ones who have lost their families? These were long-term problems that require long-term solutions. Will Reliance remain active for the next five years in these areas, trying to tackle these issues? We should be worrying about these things.

Everybody is in a hurry—land, take pictures, smile and console the affected and depart. Of course, we cannot expect doctors, nurses, and physiotherapists from states like Karnataka, Madhya Pradesh, etc. to remain working in Anjar for months together. This is where the need for a Central Control Room in each taluka is essential in order to keep disseminating information to the Indian and foreign aid agencies - individuals, and institutions - about areas in which they can help, areas in which they cannot, the various requirements from different agencies.

There was a lot of *atta* (flour) and food stuff, but who will make the *rotis?* The point one is trying to make is that giving money is the easiest thing to do but giving time and providing "touch" and empathy is the most difficult. If the Latur experience is any guide, physical resettlement by providing homes, will be done by the government, but providing emotional support and settling families will be the most difficult. Only local NGOs who can speak the language can help the affected to rebuild their lives.

Social Audit

Elected representatives in our country represent the people of our republic in different legislative, executive and decision-making bodies. We have people's representatives in the Indian parliament, state legislatures, zilla parishads and district-level, local bodies, block and village panchayats.

We have about 540 members of the Lok Sabha and at least at an average of 200 members in 22 state legislatures, we have 4,400 MLAs. In about 600 district zilla parishads, assuming 20 members in each, we have 6000 ZP members. In at least 5000 development blocks (assuming all of them have panchayat unions, at 20 members for each union), we have100,000 elected panchayat union members.

Thus we have in our republic, on a rough approximation, in different popular bodies, a staggering number of 1,50,000 elected representatives representing 1000 million Indians in different fora. Besides there are a number of cooperative societies/bodies where farmers all over the country elect in thousands their representatives to safeguard their farming interests, (e.g. sugar cooperatives, milk coopetatives, marketing federations etc.).

Roughly, once in every five years, people exercise their franchise to elect their representatives to these bodies in different cycles provided these elections are held regularly! These elected representatives, therefore, constitute the "core decision group" who determine the content, pace and direction of the country's governing process. What is the method by which their promises and performance are judged? Who assesses their performance? What performance indicators are available to evaluate their work? Who, monitors their performance and what are the instruments presently employed for monitoring the accomplishment of their tasks?

The Tasks

These are some of the issues which citizens in a representative democratic form of government should be concerned with. We are more and more concerned with, getting better "value" to the citizens franchise. At the end of the tenure of every 'elected representative', every citizen, who has exercised his/her franchise, is expected to know the tasks accomplished/not accomplished by the elected representative.

Let us examine the tasks of one set of representatives, *viz.* MPs. These are varied and complex and do not lend themselves for classification into neat boxes. These could be broadly classified into bubbles,which are loose, flexible, and evolving. A typical MP has to divide his time between:

(a) Attending to the grievances of the inhabitants of his/her constituency, answering letters which generally seek MP's favours for getting jobs in public sector undertakings, issuing testimonials and character certificates, seeking transfers, hoping to let licences and permits, getting gas and telephone connections, rail reservations, allotment of scooters and cars on priority basis and playing host to people from his/her constituency, who once a while visit New Delhi. All these tasks are in the nature of "Personalized Services" by MPs and those who are benefited alone can evaluate the MP on these counts.

(b) There are constituency development tasks, like getting public works (bridges, roads, electrification etc.) sanctioned and executed, monitoring the flow of centrally-sponsored schemes and their benefits to the poverty-stricken families in their constituencies (IRD, CHV, 20-point programme, employment guarantee, rural housing, rural industrial estates etc.) An inventory of centrally sponsored schemes at the district level would reveal that majority of them are either not availed of by the district administration or are not implemented vigorously.

An MP would be the best person to monitor the implementation of these projects in his/her costituency and this would fetch high "value" benefits to the people of the constituency. By constant interaction with the district administration, an MP would ensure fuller utilisation and better implementation of centrally-sponsored schemes. Most of the MPs are nominated on the district councils and MPs could keep track of the development trends in their constituencies, which partly or fully coincide with the district.

(c) There are policy-oriented tasks in Parliament and they spend much of their time in Parliament debates, (if they wish to participate) and in attending consultative committee meetings of the ministries to which they are attached.

Evaluation

These mix of tasks generally do not lend themselves for quantification and easy evaluation and we have yet to see any indicators of performance assessment spelt out by MPs or by their party headquarters. In the absence of a formal mechanism to assess the performance of an MP, voters are to fall back on value judgements, image and visibility of an MP in the constituency and personal help rendered (specific relief).Some MPs nurse the constituency by frequently visiting the area, by attending official meetings which review the development programmes in the constituency, attending to social functions like marriages and funeral ceremonies.

A time has come, when voters and MPs together have to evolve a mechanism or a process by which, an informed and objective account of the performance of an MP has to be presented at the end of every five years or in the terminal years of their term. This cannot be done purely by the party's monitoring device or by sending observers before the party nominates its candidates for the election. Party observers group cannot also monitor/evaluate the performance of an MP because it saps objectivity and takes, a 'party' view of the performance.

What is needed is a process of social audit of the performance of MP in a particular constituency beyond the party mandate. Such social audits have been tried, for example, to assess the performance of TISCO by a group of eminent "public men" who were not connected with the enterprise, with very good results.

Limitations

When an MP gets elected he/she should announce a social audit group from his/her constituency, representing the cross-section of the voters, like leaders of agricultural labourers, artisans, teachers, voluntary agencies, intellectuals, small traders, and all, those who constitute the 'vote bank' in the constituency. The group should be free from party loyalties and predelictions, so that a fair degree of objectivity is ensured in its assessment. The group should issue at least three reports in a span of five years, which could serve as a concurrent evaluation of the MPs performance, covering abroad spectrum of MP's activities in the constituency.

However, there are some inherent limitations in the functioning of this group. First is the extent to which an MP shares information on his/her accomplishments, doings and non-doings etc. Greater the information sharing, better the social audit. Secondly, there are certain, tasks and accomplishments of an MP like his/her contribution to the Parliament debates on budget, economic policies, defence, foreign policy which are not directly connected with the constituency-related work performance.

How does the social audit group evaluate or give weightages to these? But given the broad-based composition of the group, we, could expect a fair assessment of the performance of an MP in his/her constituency. MPs who have been returned to the Lok Sabha, could go back once or twice in their, tenure and present a social audit of their performance, so that both partners in the development-voters and the voted-together improve the quality of service to everyone in the constituency.

Once this approach of social audit is accepted by our elected representatives, the voters can apply the social audit principles to all representatives in different elected bodies in the country. The big question, however, is who will bell the cat, voters or the representatives?

Some Pre-requisites of Reform

With independence and planning, the character and structure of Indian administration have changed significantly. The district which was the administrative unit for policy formulation and implementation has now lost its former autonomy and viability. Instead, a highly formalised pattern of ambivalent objectives has been superimposed on the traditional district set-up. An undesirable dichotomy has been created between development administration and general administration which includes maintenance of law and order) when, in fact, general administration should have been geared to development administration in many ways.

The existence of two Collectors - for instance, in Maharashtra - one to look afler land revenue recovery and the other to work as Secretary of the District Development Councilor the Zilla Parishad, is a retrograde step because it frustrates the task of integrated administration of the district. The dichotomy between development administration and general administration has led to considerable multiplicity both of staff and line agencies, with serious consequences for administrative overheads and public relations. Co-ordination, which is the acid test of administration, has to be sought either through acrimonious debates or through pious resolutions doomed to be ignored or forgotten. Decentralisation of decision-making can be laudable, but the execution of development programmes through Panchayati Raj bodies by a civil servant who is answerable both to the State and to the Panchayati Raj body, makes the civil servant's problems more than just administrative. He has to strike a balance between the competing claims of the panchayati Raj body and the State.

The tehsils or taluks -the constituent units of a district - have a similar dual set-up in most States. The Block Development Officers and Tehsildars or Mamlatdars are both supposed to work for the welfare of the general public. But here again we witness a dichotomy between development administration and general administration. Maintenance of law and order is qualitatively linked with economic development. Food riots are basically the result of food shortages, and an effective control of such riots demands an effective boosting of food production and its satisfactory distribution. Implementation through separate departments is likely to frustrate the benefits of an integrated administration.

Divided Loyalty

Under the British, the district was the basic unit of administration with the tehsils or taluks as subordinate units, which made for speedy execution. The district set-up played a crucial role not only in the maintenance of law and order but also in the implementation of the broader policies of the State. The District Collector occupied a pivotal position in the administrative hierarchy. Any legislation or rule was formulated after taking into account the opinion of the Collector. The grievances of the public were never redressed without consultation with the Collector. And Collectors had the fullest discretion in deciding matters falling under their jurisdiction. Autonomy in defined spheres was also delegated to the lower echelons of the administration. The bonafide of decisions made in the discharge of duties was never questioned. While there was perfect accountability for various commissions and omissions, the discretion allowed made for official loyalty, subordination and discipline at various levels of the administration. Even now this formal pattern has not changed significantly, but little room has been left for discretion. Today's dissipation and proliferation of accountability leads to divided loyalty and responsibility, and frustrates smooth implementation.

Today, the absence of adequate discretion has resulted in a labyrinth of office procedures, inter and intra departmental consultation and consequent delay, lack of vision among officers for making summary decisions and taking responsibility wherever possible. There is, instead, a proneness to enquire and report vague complaints or petitions to higher-ups, even when the petition can be disposed of summarily at a junior officer's level.

Public petitions and grievances may be broadly classified in two main categories: specific allegations or demands supported by facts, and general and habitual complaints against the conduct of officials or policies of the Government. The failure to receive a certain grant, a piece of land, certain permits or minor benefits are inslances for specific petitions; while allegations about the general conduct of an official, that such and such an official moves about with x, y or z or that he is harassing the public", etc, are a few instances of the vague and general petition. The point to emphasise is that, vigilance bodies against corruption should be more selective and imaginative in investigating complaints. They should summarily dispose of petitions of a general character and investigate only the particular ones.

An important consequence of the earlier system was that grievances of the public were redressed on the spot by personal visits and delegation of powers of enquiry to subordinates. Allegations about officials were enquired into with regard to particular circumstances. Allegations of a purely general character were summarily filed and dismissed. It is this selectiveness that is lacking in the post-Independence set-up.

The need to reform the structure of administration for better performance towards Plan targets and to evolve a machinery in the administrative hierarchy for redressing the grievances of the public and for enquiring into serious allegations about officials, has assumed considerable proportions. Institutional measures like the Ombudsman, Vigilance Commissioners, Lok Pal, etc, are in the nature of indicative reforms. They are intended to provide the necessary organisational framework to investigate allegations of corruption. Prompt attendance to the grievances of millions of farmers, consumers, petty traders, labourers, office-goers, etc, forms the core of administrative justice. The evolution of machinery to attend to such grievances should, therefore, brook no delay. But the machinery has to be more discriminating and choose only the specific and substantive allegations for redress.

Moreover, administrative reform implies reform of the entire fabric and structure of the governmental machinery which comes into direct contact with the public. Success in changing the complex structure of a society in accordance with a Plan, and in increasing productivity at the village and taluka or tehsil, depends largely on the efficiency with which the lower echelons of the administration function. The image or the nation in the minds of millions of farmers, petty traders and consumers is influenced and moulded by the smaller officials engaged in field administration. Unless the structure of administration at the level of the district and its constituent units, *viz.* taluka or tehsil, is overhauled to suit the requirements of a fast growing complex community, we need have no illusions about the coming social order. Reforms confined to a few ministries and secretariats do not have any practical significance. Men of the Indian Administrative Service and its allied services have received much attention in the past decade as regards training opportunities and facilities; but men at the levels of the talukas or tehsils have remained in a state of dry rot. A purposeful administrative reform must proceed from the lowest rung of the administrative hierarchy. A top-heavy and bottom-loose structure of administration is unlikely to provide a solid base for a welfare state.

Towards this end, apart from administrative training, delegation of powers and selective admission of only the specific charges of maladministration should help significantly in toning up the administration.

Mending the Links

The inappropriate use of social communication apparatus to reach the people, is an outcome of the poor access that Panchayati Raj bodies have to official documentation. This calls for greater interaction between the government and local groups.

With the 73rd and 74th amendments to the Constitution, Panchayati Raj has been given a wider berth. Some states, which can claim an enlightened political leadership, like Madhya Pradesh, have held elections to local bodies and succeeded in lakhs of people in power in their villages, zilla panchayats as well as in urban local bodies. Many panchayat leaders are now attempting to decentralise decision-making. Several cases of friction have been reported between the panchayat leaders and the bureaucracy. One of the reasons for this is the lack of information and knowledge among the panchayat leaders on "how to do things". The bureaucracy, at whatever level, is tightlipped about information. The only way to be provided with details is to ask for them in the right manner, at the right time, and at the right place, by the right person and from the right source.

One of the ways of empowering panchayat leaders is through provision of information. The right to information is fundamental for every Indian citizen, although this has unfortunately not been enshrined in the Indian Constitution. People (particularly the gramsabha) have a right to know whether the resources meant for development projects and schemes are actually being used towards such ends. The case for demanding accountability from government functionaries who are responsible for the disbursement of such funds can hardly be contested. One keeps hearing that the collector and block development officer (BDOs) withhold telling panchayat members about the schemes that are available, and the money that has been earmarked. Information on central and state government schemes are never shared with these panchayat leaders in a manner they understand.

The Madhya Pradesh government recently launched the Chaupal Programme for sharing information. But this was treated by the bureaucracy as providing lectures to panchayat leaders. Lecturing is not the right method of sharing information. Information has to be disseminated within a 'context' to be absorbed correctly. Such dissemination requires good communication, verbal, non-verbal and visual. "All behaviour, verbal and non-verbal, in the presence of someone else of whom we are aware is communication".

Print communication materials miss their mark when their target group is largely illiterate. Among other means, verbal communication, does not mean oratory alone, but it is perhaps the only way out till panchayat members can learn to read print material. Unfortunately posters and pamphlets are printed for the use of panchayat leaders, without assessing their impact. The question of usefulness apart, there is no proper planning about the distribution of this print material to individual panchayat members in far-flung areas of the state. An enormous amount is spent on printing materials without planning for their distribution. Anything not read is as good as not printed. Much of the printed material does not go beyond the BDO's office. Despite the availability of good postal facilities, individual mailing is never done by the authorities who use their line departments to distribute the material, a system which fails.

Communication and information is critical to the success of Panchayati Raj. The needs vary from one tier to another. What is relevant for the gramsabha and gram panchayat is not relevant for the janpad and zilla panchayat. The bottom tier requires hard, factual information on who gets what and from whom. The local bureaucracy is always reluctant to divulge this information. The information on programmes and allocations can be communicated without requiring any special skill. There is no marketing involved in it.

But when we want to convey low cost health messages like child immunisation, the use of oral rehydration salts and the use of iodised salt, we need to use appropriate communication channels so that the essential technical content is not lost. For instance, this author was involved in training folk artists of Punjab to make messages on the value of breastmilk and infant-feeding practices, It is difficult to convert technical knowledge into a simple message for the common folk. But one artist was successful in conveying the richness of breastmilk through a simple song "Mothers" milk is always available at any time and place is always at the right temperature, does not need refrigeration and most importantly no cat can come and drink it! Only the child gets it and nobody else!" The message on the value of breastmilk was immediately understood by the illiterate mothers in a slum in Patiala, thanks to the song.

Communication and Information therefore, has to be relevant to the culture of the audience. While it is easy to offer simple information to the gramsahha on school attendance attendance of an anganwadi worker and the number of beneficiaries under Indira Awas Yojana, it is difficult to convey simple but critical information on health, the use of pesticides, construction of leach-pit toilets, home hygiene and animal care. It is here that comminication techniques assume importance.

Hence, rethinking on the use of print materials s required if one is concerned with effective communication. Interactive training is one method which has proved effective for information sharing and building management skills. To be a good trainer one has to be a good communicator. "About 70 per cent of all communication is non-verbal. The proportion rises when feelings are expressed. Words convey about seven per cent of the message the rest is about feelings, 38 per cent is conveyed by intonation, and 55 per cent by facial expression. For a full understanding of non-verbal language one should always take the situation into account. In all communication the content aspect is usually expressed with words, the emotional and relational aspect with non-verbal signals". (Frank

R Oomkes and Richard H Thomas, *Developing Cross-Cultural Communication).* At the gramsabha level, there are both men and women. Women are shy of coming out and asking questions. How does one communicate with them? Some communicators suggest using participatory rapid appraisal (PRA) to learn more about the village and the problems through social mapping, etc. So, what follows after the maps? Gramsabha members want solutions and decisions from the village panchayat president and members.

At the gramsabha level questions which are generally asked are why is the village road or a culvert not built, why is the school teacher not coming, why is electricity erratic, which affects irrigation, etc. In the course of answering these questions the communicator/ trainer has to share the relevant information. For example, while talking about the doctor's carelessness in not immunising the village kids, information on the do's and don'ts of immunisation has also to be shared. In the last nationwide Pulse Polio Immunisation drive, where millions of kids were administered the polio vaccine, it was not the print media which helped, but television and the village mohalla level "neighbours", who geneated both the information and the actual polio administration by bringinng the kids to the polio immunisation centres.This is one example of how information and communication can and should go together.

Unfortunately although the gramsabha is the most critical level, its Communication and Information needs are not properly assessed. At gramsabha meetings in Madhya Pradesh which this author has attended most questions pertained to seeking essential information on the village, births, deaths, watershed, water resources, land rights, debts, and benefits received by whom and how. Unfortunately it is at this level that the village *patwari* and other village functionaries remain absent and avoid information sharing. One has to link the life-survival information like land records, land rights which people seeks, with life survival information like health, nutrition, etc. Simple life-*survival* information is not attractive enough for villagers. A transparent government has to inform the gramsabha members about everything that has happened in the village, to create credibility. It is here that information becomes the right of every villager.

At the village panchayat level, the Communication and Information needs are different. If we want its capacity to be strengthened, members have to have the right to information. Here again, the village *patwari* and all functionaries of the village have to share information from time to time, which is not happening at present. There is a panchayat gazette of the Madhya Pradesh government of but it should reach every panch/sarpanch, so that every member knows or at least takes an interest in state-level happenings. Unfortunately the postal system has not been used by the state to distribute their material. Once this essential information is shared, communication of developmental issues follows suit-, how to develop a village watershed plan, its costing and so on. At present, there is no planning at the village level. What we have is a distribution plan for the village for distributing central/state level funds under the JRY, the IRDP, the DPAP and such schemes. The management capacity of the panchayat members cannot be improved unless interactive training is given to them where appropriate C&I needs can be met. Training is the best form of communication.

At the janpad and zilla panchayat level, what the members need are skills for planning and management of all types of programmes. Unfortunately, here again, there are no plans made by these bodies. Money is distributed on the basis of norms which may or may not be relevant. Communication and Information needs flow from the planning processes of these: two tiers. Besides, all the three tiers are not organically linked. One hears a lot about the gramsabha and its ability to question the decision-making of the village panchayats, but nobody talks about the position of the village panchayats to question the janpad and zilla panchayats. Democracy is a process where people question the elected representatives and not just the bureaucrats.

The Communication and Information needs of the Panchayati Raj therefore are complex and have to be anlysed at each level by a mix of experts in print, audio, video and folk media. We also hear about satellite-based training. Each member of the panchayat is an institution by him-self or herself. We cannot adopt a mass-based learning approach when it comes to individual excellence and building capacities. Interactive training is the best option and needs to be pursued in order to strengthen Panchayati Raj.

Voluntary Sector

Voluntary agencies (non-government organisations or NGOs) in India have been recognised as active partners in development along with the private sector and the all pervading public sector (government organisations or GO). Their numbers, composition, coverage and management styles vary from state, districts and region. They could be generally grouped under four broad categories. (a) advocacy NGOs which are engaged in advocating causes like environmental degradation, ecology, pollution control etc; (b) relief and rehabilitation NGOs, which are generally active in providing relief to earthquake, flood and famine victims, and they fold up the operations when the relief is over; (c) grassroots NGOs, which are engaged in actually doing development work in a defined geographical area (district, state or villages, e.g., doing afforestation, wasteland development, watershed management, dairying, training villagers, handicraft production etc.) (d) multipurpose NGOs as against single purpose ones. Those who are engaged in a mix of social, rural or urban development activities and not confined to single objectives.

These NGOs all over India have played constructive and innovative roles in the past. Just as there are good and bad GOs, there are good and bad NGOs. The general tendency of government policy-makers is to romanticise the role of NGOs and make paternalistic references to them like "involvement of NGOs", "consultation with NGOs", which are no doubt good intentions. But good intentions are no substitute for efficient use of NGOs in country's development process and providing them a 'defined' role.

Not all NGOs are good or efficient in all spheres. Some are good (honest) but may not be efficient. Some are one man/woman shows. Some do not have even typewriters to correspond. Some are bureaucratic large organisations, resembling GOs, and imitating management styles of government. Some NGOs have leftist or rightist tendencies, without aligning themselves to any political parties. Some only keep 'friends' in political parties and some are totally neutral in politics. Some NGOs are dragged in political witch-hunting, without their involvement in politics. Some NGOs, which are either Delhi-based or state capital-based, get all the plums of nomination on national and state advisory bodies. But those who are in the hinterlands, always remain in the hinterlands of power centre. Some are religious and some are secular. Some are registered societies or trusts or legal entities and some are loosely organised associations.

Thus if one were to make a SWOT analysis of NGOs in India, one would get an interesting scenario of little islands of excellence and flickering polar stars here and there across the country, trying in their own ways to improve the lot of the poor in urban and rural areas. They may not have contributed to the reduction of poverty levels, but have contributed to the equitable sharing of benefits and to the quality of life of those whom they have serviced or helped. What is it that the state and GOs want these NGOs to do for the national development? What are the thrust areas in which government wants these NGOs to enter or consolidate their activities? What are the patterns of financial and R& D assistance to them? What mechanisms are needed to monitor their performances? Who and how will their management capacities, skills and training are to be built?

The five-year plans have not clearly identified the critical thrust areas in which NGOs were to function. The role of public and private sector enterprises were clearly defined, but the role of the voluntary sector was left to be defined by several ministries/ departments in the centre and states. These ministries brought out their own guidelines and patterns of assistance to NGOs which did not take into account 'holistic' nature of NGOs. The ministry of forests/environment through NWDB has evolved guidelines for assisting NGOs engaged in wastelands development. The ministry of rural development has also evolved guidelines for assisting NGOs engaged in or trying to take up social forestry through CAPART. Thus some NGOs go to both NWDB and CAPART for the same set of activities, although care is taken by both to avoid assisting for the same set of activities of the NGOs. But the efforts are a waste of time. Similarly, we find the Central Social Welfare Board, Central Child Welfare Council, State Child Welfare Councils all duplicating assistance to NGOs running *balwadis,* creches, etc, whose impact on the status of children are doubtful. The thin spread of resources does not take us anywhere. The ministry of health and family welfare, family planning association of India, family planning foundation, Indian Red Cross are all assisting NGOs in family planning activities in their 'own ways'. One is not sure whether this is an efficient method of allocation of resources to NGOs.

A sound policy towards NGOs has to be based on a few basic action areas. Scaling up NGO activities: NGOs doing pilot projects can never go to scale. By the very nature their activities, they are localised and their experiences are location and region specific: The GOs, have to learn, from NGOs on how to universalise NGOs experience. The Comprehensive Health Care Project of Jhamkhed in Maharashtra piloted by Dr. Arole became a forerunner for the Community Health Volunteer and Village Health Guide Scheme of the Government of India. Similarly, many NGOs are presently engaged in wasteland and common property resource development in villages. Their experiences are worth universalising. Therefore, the policy implications are that GOs should universalise the experience of NGOs and for that purpose certain NGOs and GOs have to work in partnership towards defined objectives in defined areas. Taralabalu Rural Development Foundation in Karnataka has involved itself in school nursery programme for the past few years. Their experience is worth universalising for a countrywide programme of sapling raising and plantings through school children.

Just as GOI has defined thrust areas for small-scale industries, for joint and private sector industries, there is need for reserving select development areas for NGO participation. In industries it is the "investment criteria" but for NGOs the best criteria is the length and depth of "service" rendered in an area. Past, experience has shown that person intensive service activities like child care and health services, demonstration of better farming practices, running of schools, and literacy programmes are better done by NGOs. NGOs are a via media sector between profit oriented private sector and not so-efficient public sector.

Appraisal/scrutiny of NGO projects/proposals by *GOs:* This is an area which has not been looked into carefully by ministries/

departments at the centre and states. What we see at present is standard application forms to avail of financial assistance from different ministries instead of sound appraisal methods and processes for screening projects, proposals. The best appraisal methods/processes which this author has come across are the one adopted by Society for Promotion of Wastelands Development, New Delhi, and the Ford Foundation. Both these have not prescribed any standard application forms but the NGOs' can put informal request, which are appraised through discussions, personal visits to the NGO area, discussion with beneficiary groups which the NGOs intend to serve or help. It is true that GOs are accountable to Parliament and legislature for the money advanced to NGOs and are to ensure financial propriety. But it is possible to do that by adopting imaginative appraisal methods so as to get the best project outcomes from NGOs in lieu *of* standardised application forms. A majority of NGOs are not trained to write project outlines with graphs, bar diagrams, outcome and input objectives and with all the blueprint niceties. Mostly by talking to NGO workers, and getting insights from the area real appraisal can be made. Such appraisals could also be used for better monitoring and evaluation of project activities more meaningfully.

Finances of NGOs: Another area *of* concern for the NGOs is the financial patterns of assistance adopted by different GOs to the NGOs. There are a number *of* boards affiliated to central ministries like Central Welfare Board, Wasteland Board, and all of them have evolved their own patterns of assistance. Most critical issue is the recurrent cost burden that NGOs have to face, once the non-recurring one time costs are withdrawn by funding GOs. Just as in the states non-plan maintenance cost burden is high, similar is the case with NGOs implementing large-sized projects in water supply or sanitation or health. Some NGOs have solved the recurrent cost burden by involving peoples contribution and pricing the products/services. Large NGOs with their 'connections' in GOs manage to get recurring costs but smaller NGOs suffer a lot.

If GOs can think of devolving resources to panchayats (recurring and non-recurring) from state sector plan outlays, why not NGOs also get resources devolved on well established principles from the state sector from time to time. Years ago Panchayati Raj finances were thoroughly examined by late K. Santhanam and principles of devolution of resources were evolved. Unfortunately, voluntary agency finances have not been examined systematically. It is high time the Eighth Plan strategy evolves some principles for devolving resources to NGOs by GOs for development activities. In the absence of these principles 'arbitrariness' and 'ad hocism' would guide the GOs towards NGOs.

Manpower development and capacity buildings : NGOs need two types of skill (a) technical - "how to do" type of training (b) management to empower them to do better what they are already doing. The solution is not to set up an all-India training institute for NGOs attached to a ministry in Delhi which would be a disaster! If we analyse the management development programmes of prestigious management institutes (IIM, A, B, C & L) we hardly come across any NGO functionaries being trained by them. Those NGOs who are nearer to the seat of power in New Delhi, get nominated either to undergo training abroad or in prestigious management institutes. But a large majority of grassroots NGO functionaries who can understand only regional language cannot set the benefit of management training in these institutes. There are a number of state level administrative training institutes, which can impart management and functional training to NGO personnel, not separately, but along with GO personnel, so that interaction between the two can take place. The Department of Personnel, Training Division, GOI, at present is charged with the designing of training programmes for all-India service officers. Why not the same division think of long-term training programmes for NGO personnel. It should be noted that NGOs at the field level have no resources to spend on travel and *per diem* during the course of training nor they have a 'parent department' to foot the bill. If the GOs are concerned with the quality of manpower among the NGOs, then training becomes crucial and a clear training policy has to be enunciated.

Code of conduct for NGOs: In the past a code of conduct was sought to be evolved for NGOs to get the development funds and assistance available with the GOs by confirming them to the code of conduct. This was no doubt a good intention for weeding out power brokers among the NGOs. If the working of codes of conduct of professional bodies like Indian Medical Council, Chartered Accountants of India etc. is any guide, these codes are observed more in the breach than in observance, Code or no code, human nature will behave in its own way. Integrity and honesty are the two qualities of NGOs and the voluntary sector. A policy towards NGOs and the voluntary sector has to promote voluntariness and not regulate its intentions by state fiat.

Management by Legislation

In sixties, the rapid growth of industries, trade and commerce led to a phenomenal rise in management education and training programmes.

The change agents identified by the management institutes are those who manage corporate finances, organizational behaviour, industrial personnel and those dealing with industrial relations and a host of problems affecting the present and future industrial scenario. In fact, more training programmes are evolved than the managers available for being trained!

The most important change agents in this country are the Legislators, Parliamentarians and Ministers, who constitute the 'core' of the top brass in decision making in the country. They represent the clients (public) in a representative democracy.

They constitute a cross section of public opinion in the country and they get the first hand information on what the people need, their aspirations, sufferings and rising expectations. They get feed back from the electorate to whom they are finally accountable.

Through this process of articulation, changes in the lives of the people are sought to be brought about in living standards and productivity in farms and factories.

This articulation finds its fullest expression in the legislative and law making processes. It is the laws of the country, which have assumed the role of instruments of change; and the Legislators have assumed the role of change agents The spate of legislation in this country in the last decade is baffling.

Between 1971 and 1976 alone the Government of India made 19 amendments to the Constitution, passed 463 statutes, promulgated 96 ordinances and 30 regulations and enacted 114 President's Acts under Presidential Rule. The Law Ministry drafted 36,515 Rules, Orders and Notifications (N.A.Palkhivala - The Tasks Before a Free People-Lecture at Bombay May 1977). If we add the various laws passed by the States, laws of the country would truly form a jungle.

What is the competence of these change agents to effect changes in the society through the laws of the country? What is the expertise that goes into the making of these laws? What is the management context for these laws? How these laws are conceived and the amount of planning and thinking that goes into these laws? These are some of the issues which have eluded the attention of management educationists.

Management by legislation and by ordinance is the new style of the Ministers. There is need to understand the nuances of management by legislation, because legislation has assumed the role of a vital factor in production relations.

Bad laws are a hindrance not only to the participative democracy but also to the economic advance of the country. Imperfect laws are still worse. There are perfect laws and incomplete laws and certain fads and fancies of the ruling politicians are also pushed through in the form of ordinances.

The typical law of a State Government in our country is the product of will of elected representatives. They try to keep up their promises to their 'clients' (voters) by legislative gestures. Very little of planning, organising, staffing, directing, cordinating, reporting and budgeting (POSDCORB) enters into the process of legislation.

Let us take the case of land reform and tenancy laws of a typical State in the country. The objective of such a law is to improve man-land relations to confer ownership on the tiller of soil and to abolish absentee landlordism. All these are purported to achieve increased productivity of land.

There need not be any dichotomy between equity and productivity. In other words, the land reform laws are to be conceived as laws which would promote sound production management in agriculture and not piecemeal social reform of the peasantry.

If we consider land reform laws as those concerning production relations in agriculture, then the management perspective for this piece of legislation becomes clear. It is this management perspective which is lacking in all legislative processes in the country.

Before the intentions or objectives of the legislators (whether at the Centre or the State) are crystallised into law, the process passes through several stages.

A Bill narrating the objectives, scope and applicability is first brought before the Assembly or Parliament. If there are certain clauses which are found controversial then the Bill is referred to a select committee. The select committee would discuss in more detail, visit places and institutions to study operation of similar laws and then bring the Bill back to the Assembly. Parliament, where it will be passed after discussion because the party in power wants that law to be passed. Once the Bill becomes an Act, then the rules are framed to implement and execute the law.

In this process of legislation, management problems of the particular law are never thought for instance, in passing the land reform laws no thought is given to managerial problems like how will the tenants manage the lands which would come under their ownership? What would be the range of inputs needed to bring the tenant owned lands into high production range? What is the concentration of tenant turned owners in drought prone areas, areas with assured irrigation and areas with scanty rainfall ? What is the arrangement for financing the acquisition of ownership rights by the tenants?

These issues are not properly analysed nor attempted to be answered by the law makers. Instead, these are treated as incidental to law-making. The only level at which some analysis is done is at the drafting stage of the law and in the rule making stage subsequent to the enactment. But the analysis is confined, in the former case to the legal niceties is like definition repugnancy, applicability, exceptions, jurisdiction, limitation, repeal and savings.

In the latter case, the analysis is confined to the implementation procedure like who is the appropriate authority for admitting the petition, time limit for filing the petition, what constitutes the forum, procedure for admitting the petition, powers of the presiding officers, etc.

At both these stages, no managerial questions are raised. They are left to be raised and answered by the executives who interpret the law and execute the objectives of the act and judges who check the dangers of executive excesses.

This makes the task of managing the law much more difficult because of incongruence in the preception of goals and objectives by the various personnel involved in the process of legislation and its execution.

What are the key managerial issues in the legislative process? The pundits on management execution would raise, impromptu, concerns like management by objectives, management information system, audit and financial control, monitoring system and so on.

Management by legislation is not the same as Management by objectives. The latter may perhaps prove to be mythical and useless if we have to practise it in the field of legislation.

Though the stated objective of any public law in this country is public good and welfare, there would be as many objectives of the law as there are groups of personnel involved in the execution of the particular law.

The Ministers, the prime movers of the law have their own objectives in passing the law. With all the public welfare pretensions, their objective might be to get more funds for their political party or for themselves.

The threat of nationalisation issued by a Minister is more dangerous than nationalisation itself. For the bureaucrats, who execute the laws, the objective might be that of using discretion and benefits of doubt to their advantage instead of to the advantage of the citizen or the public.

The field personnel may find certain lacuna in the law to thwart the entire due process of law. That might prove to be their objective. The judges who interpret the law in case of dispute might consider the objectives of equity and jurisprudence than of production.

The lawyers who help the clients (public) consider seeking maximum adjourments to get more fees from the clients as their objective. It is this incongruence of objectives in managing the law that makes the task of bringing about changes in the chosen field of public system difficult.

Management of the laws need altogether different skills. Ministers, parliamentarians and legislators are the new class of managers emerging in this country. Unfortunately, our elite management institutes have not shown any concern for management training and education for this class of managers. We have had several years of experience in managing this country through the Ministers. We have yet to see a single 'case study" of a typical Minister viewed as a manager.

There have been courses and programmes for hotel managers and housewives, but not a single programme for the elite of this country who guide the destinies of the nation.

The legislative process has become more complex like all other economic and technological processes. A lot of planning and thinking has to precede the enactment of law. If management by legislation is to prove effective the managers who conceive and manage the laws are to be exposed to the various techniques of management.

The foregoing is a plea to the management educationists to explore and research the field of management by legislation. We have outstanding Ministers in this country. They have pioneered many laws and have contributed to the growth of food and agriculture, defence preparedness, fiscal management, administrative reforms, tourism and industrial development. Except their biographies, which are political in nature, their styles of management, their perception and information system which they built in their organization are not known.

During the tenure of their office they do not have time to share their experience with others and when they are out of office they have no interest in documenting their knowledge and experience. When they die the circle is complete and we have lost valuable information and knowledge on management by legislation.

It is time management educationists do some serious thinking on complex processes of management by legislation, so that the laws and those who frame them really become the instruments of change and change agents respectively.

Panchayati Raj in Mysore

Under the Mysore Village Panchayats and Local Boards Act Panchayati Raj institutions were turned into bureaucratic cells. there is no organic link between different tiers of Panchayati Raj nor do the sources of revenue allocated to each bear any relation to the functions it has been charged with.

In fact, the Act was so full of shortcomings that what is necessary is not to amend it, but to draft an altogether new Bill. The recommendations of the Government appointed Study Team on Panchayati Raj should form the basis of the new legistation.

The working of Mysore Village Panchayats and Local Boards Act 1959 has revealed glaring imperfections which affect the basic tenets of the Panchayati Raj like decentralisation of decision-making power, organic relationship between different tiers and democratisation of administration. The objective of increasing people's involvement in the development efforts of the State has not been attained because of the unrepresentative character of the District Development Council. The DDC is composed of the Deputy Commissioner of the District as the chairman, all the presidents of the Taluka Development Boards, Members of Parliament and State Assemblies, government officers not exceeding 15 in number, a member of the scheduled castes and a woman member nominated by the Government. The inclusion of directly elected members in addition to the *ex office* and nominated members would have established a link between the DDC and the masses. The DDC is not an executive body with financial and executive powers but an advisory body at the district level meeting once in a quarter to review the work of the TDBs, scrutinise its budget and to attend to "any other work entrusted by the Government relating to the work of the TDB". The non-deliberative and non-executive nature of the DDC has made the third tier superfluous. Genuine decision-making that is expected from such a body is not possible without executive powers.

Under the Act TDBs are composed of members directly elected by voters in each taluka. This precludes the representation of the village panchayats on theTDBs which is necessary to link the lower and the middle tiers. As for village panchayats, villages with populations not below 1,500 have panehayats, the rest form group panchayats. Group panchayats have led to groupism in the villages and as a consequence the development of villages without panchayats has suffered considerably. Besides, the Act has no provision for the constitution of Nyaya Panchayats and Gram Sabhas. Gram Sabhas can wield considerable influence on the activities of the panchayats. The objective of "arousing popular consciousness" of Plan programmes will be better accomplished if the Gram Sabhas are vested with functions, like approving the annual budget of the panchayat, supervising panchayat production plans, etc.

Functions and Resources

Functions assigned in the Act to the three tiers do not bear any relationship with the finances and resources at the command of each. The DDC does not have any independent sources of revenue nor any independent functions. The TDBs have certain obligatory functions like construction, repair and maintenance of public roads, primary school buildings, minor irrigation works, establishment and management of dispensaries, rest houses, etc, and certain discretionary functions like running of primary and secondary educational institutions, encouragement of cooperatives, granting of loans to industrial enterprises, etc. The statutory separation of functions into obligatory and discretionary has resulted in the complete neglect of discretionary functions which are no less important for the economic prosperity of the taluka. The main sources of revenue of the TDBs are the local cess of 12 Paise in a rupee on land revenue and on water rates, a stamp duty on transfers of immovable property and a tax not exceeding 25 paise per animal brought for sale in the markets within the jurisdiction of TDBs. The TDBs have a so a 25 per cent share in the land revenue collection of the taluka, and 5 per cent share in that of the State. In view of the inelastic sources of revenue and the wide functions assigned to the TDBs, there has not been any significant improvement in the development of the taluka since the launching of the Panchayati Raj.

Village panchayats likewise have obligatory functions like construction, repair and maintenance of village roads, public wells, allotment of places for storing manure, laying out village extensions, etc, and discretionary functions of a broad nature affecting village' life and prosperity generally. The panchayats have been assigned other 'agency functions' by the TDBs and the Government like execution of construction works, distribution of irrigation water, management of minor forests, pasture and common lands. The main sources of revenue of the panchayats are taxes and grants. The Act empowers panchayats to impose a building tax not exceeding 8 per cent of rental value, land tax at the rate of one rupee for every 100 sq yards un-assessed to agriculture, and tax on professions, trades, callings and employment at specified rates. The panchayats also have a 30 per cent share in the land revenue collection of the village and 5 per cent share in that of the State. Although the tax coverage appears fairly wide, tax receipts invariably fall short of dues because of the inefficient recovery machinery of the panchayats.

Study Team's Report

The study team on Panchayati Raj, which recently submitted its report[2] on the working of the Panchayats and Local Boards Act, has suggested far-reaching changes. The teams recommendations include, among others, reorganisation and renaming of the DDC on the model of the Zilla Parishads of Maharashtra, reconstitution of TDBs by making it a partly directly-elected and partly indirectly-elected body so as to link it to the village panchayats, and constitution of Gram Sabha and Nyaya Panchayats. The team has also suggested measures to strengthen the financial position of all the tiers and recommended certain criteria for allocation of grants-in-aid and other revenue.

Role of Zilla Parishad

The team suggests that the third tier, the Zilla Parishad, should be a more effective body than the DDC is today and must consist of directly-elected members, with a non-official as chairman. The District is to be divided into electoral divisions with a population ranging from 35,000 to 50,000 and one member will be elected from each division. Members of Parliament and State Legislature, and the Chairman of the District Cooperative Bank will be associate members without the right to vote. The Zilla Parishad will have a chief executive officer of the rank of the Deputy Commissioner as its Secretary and the president of the Parishad will exercise administrative supervision over him. He is liable to be withdrawn by the State Government if not less than two-thirds of the total number of members other than associate members vote in favour of such a resolution. The Parishad will have development and administrative functions. Under the former are in-cluded administration and management of primary and secondary education, opening and maintenance of seed farms, maintenance of veterinary hospitals and dispensaries other than district hospitals, construction and maintenance of minor irrigation works, registration of cooperative societies whose working capital does not exceed Rs 5 lakhs. Under administrative functions are included power to incur expenditure on education or medical relief outside its jurisdiction, Contribute to associations at national, State Or interstate levels and to render financial or other assistance to any person carrying on work in the district related to any of the functions of the three tiers.

The study team has recommended that the TDB should consist of partly directly elected and partly indirectly-elected members, the latter from among members of the panchayats in the taluka. By far the most important recommendation of the team is the' constitution of Nyaya Panchayat and Gram Sabha for each village panchayat. The membership of the Nyaya Panchayat should be restricted to the residents of the village and each panchayat should elect from among its members 5 persons, one being a member of the Scheduled Castes. Offences like obstruction of and encroachment on public streets, grazing lands, etc, offences under the Mysore Compulsory Primary Education Act like failure to send a child to school or employing the child in a manner which prevents it from attending school, may be tried by the Nyaya Panchayats.

III
New Sources of Finance

The team's recommendations on the finances and resources of Panchayat Raj bodies do not touch upon the problem of exploring the possibility of imposing-new taxes in addition to or in lieu of existing ones whose administration is found difficult or whose receipts fall short of realisation. This is particularly important in the case of panchayats. Now that it is the obligatory function of the panchayats to prepare panchayat production plans, and production of cereals, etc, is likely to go up, there is scope for the imposition of a grain tax. The grain tax. if levied by the panchayats on the basis of per acre yield. is sure to increase the panchayats' resources in kind. If the tax receipts are marketed through the village cooperatives, that tax will achieve the dual purpose of increasing the resources of the marketing societies and stepping up the marketable surplus.

The team has enunciated certain principles to govern grants in-aid to Panchayat Raj bodies by the State. It suggests that the entire land revenue collection, including the surcharge, without deduction of the cost of collection should be assigned to the three tiers in the following proportion: village panchayats 30 per cent, Taluka Develapment Baards 35 per cent, Zilla Parishads 20 per cent. The balance of 15 per cent will be paid inta a State Equalisatian Fund which is meant to make good short falls in land revenue as a result of suspensian or remissian and to assist bodies which have very small resources so as to reduce inequalities. This 15 per cent is to be allocated thus: panchayats 5 per cent, TDBs 5 per cent and Zilla Parishads 5 per cent.

Grain Tax

If the principle of percentage distribution of land revenue is accepted, poor regions with lower land revenue will get a smaller share, and regions with higher land revenue will get more. Even an equalisatian grant of 5 per cent may not substantially after the position. A more rational principle would be to distribute grants on per capita basis. The per capita formula has to be linked with the taxable capacity of the people residing within the jurisdiction of each tier. If this principle is accepted, the larger the population and the lawer the taxable capacity of the people, the higher will be the grant. The acceptance of this principle will achieve two purposes. First, grants will be made contingent upon tax contribution and, second, regions with lower income from land revenue but higher income from forestry or mining will not suffer because of their low land revenue share.

There is also the problem of financing the agency functions assigned to the different tiers. If the Zilla Parishad assigns more agency functions to the TDBs and Panchayats, the resources have also to be assigned to them to carry out the 'agency functions'. The main sources of revenue for the Zilla Parishad are the cansolidated cess of 40 nP in a rupee an all items of land revenue, excise and other items of State and local revenue and the tax an animals braught to its markets. The team has not however examined the financial implications of assignments of agency different tiers.

These shortcomings notwithstanding, the team's recommendations will make Panchayati Raj far more genuine in Mysore. As it is, the Village Panchayats and Local Boards Act has made a mockery of Panchayati Raj and has turned Panchayati Raj bodies into bureaucratic cells. The introduction of an altogether new bill in the light of the team's recommendations is more desirable than the amendment of the existing Act which will create more ambiguities and make the task of those in charge of implementation more difficult.

Panchayati Raj : The Potential For NGO-government Partnership M.P. Leads the Way

Madhya Pradesh was the only state in 1995 which has passed the 73rd and 74th amendments and installed democratically elected bodies. As many as 5 lakh leaders chosen from the people in both rural and urban areas are now sitting in position to "do what voters have asked them to do". Unlike the assembly elections which are fought on party lines, the gram panchayats and municipal elections are fought on local issues and the voters are influenced by the contestant's family background, connections and what the candidate can do for his/her area.

Thanks to the constitutional requirements of the 73rd and 74th amendments a large number of women have been elected as panch and sarpanches in the rural areas and as councillors of municipalities in urban areas. We do not have details on the social background of these elected members. But many of them are doctors, lawyers and graduates and one can expect that the quality of decisions which they would be taking are not going to be no worse than what it is already prevailing!

The Government of M.P has taken several steps in delegating powers and functions to the Panchayati Raj bodies in the last several months. The first generation problems are mostly in terms of who is who in the zilla panchayat set up i.e. whether the collector, who is the chief executive of zilla panchayat, is subordinate to the president of zilla panchayat or whether he is independent.

Personality Clashes

The government has declared that presidents enjoy the status of the state ministers and hence the Z.P. presidents feel that they should supervise everything in the district. Many personality clashes have been reported from many districts of M. P. Similarly, at the janpad (block) level there are administrative problems of not getting the chief executives in position. Many who have been posted have not reported. At the panchayat level there are old secretaries who have felt threatened with the coming of the new panch and sarpanch.

Panchayati raj in M.P. has come to stay. Even when the government is changed, no political party would dare postpone the panchayat elections or scuttle the powers that have already been given to them. Given the size of M.P. the panchayats are the only hope for administering the state efficiently. The governance by panchayats has therefore to be strengthened and in this process not only the state but a large number of professional bodies and NGOs have a role to play. Unfortunately serious debate on how to involve the NGOs in development activeties in missing.

Madhya Pradesh has as many as 1200 NGOs spread across its 45 districts. Many of them are small and medium-sized ones engaged in running schools (Shiksha Samitis), creches, Balwadis, managing village resources and asset creation programmes, etc. Some are engaged in socially sensitive issues like preventing child prostitution and child marriages and promoting child rights. UNICEF has been engaged in improving their capacities for project formulation, training, constituency building and experience exchange.

Areas for NGO Involvement

What are the areas with reference to panchayati raj that NGOs could be involved in M.P.? There is rich potential for NGO-government collaboration in this field as the various activities listed below will indicate.

Training This is very crucial for the success of Panchayati Raj in the State. Very often when we talk of training NGOs and government bodies we think of infrastructure and hardware but not training manuals, training skills, training materials, etc. UNICEF is developing training manuals for all the three levels of the panchayati raj system i.e village panchayats, janpad and district panchayats. These manuals give details on whom to train, how to train, place and content of training, use of training materials at all the three levels, etc.

We have found that at the panchayat level the group training of panchayat secretary, upsarpanch, panch and female panch is very important because they have to take joint decisions. Panchayat secretaries being government employees have to be exposed to the dynamics of the panchayati raj system and they have to be transformed as facilitators of the system at the village level. At present the janpad and zilla panchayat presidents and members are trained at the Academy of Administration, the state's apex training institute, located in Bhopal.

But the most difficult and important part is the training of village panchayat members. Nearly two-thirds of the members of the village panchayats are women and some of them being illiterate and not exposed to the art of decision making would be slow learners. Therefore, the trainers have to be both patient and gender sensitive.

Sound Technical Knowledge. NGOs who are keen on taking up training of panchayati raj members must have sound technical knowledge which the villagers/members of these bodies would demand of them in training sessions. For several decades members of local bodies have been denied the knowledge of technologies and right information on the maze of government schemes and particularly information on who gets what is these schemes. Government functionaries believe that information is power and withholding information is superpower. Hence NGOs who want to build partnership with panchayati raj bodies have to be up-to-date with government programmes/schemes so that the information monopoly is broken. This helps the NGOs to gain credibility in the eyes of the panchayat members.

Planning Skills. A large number of village panchayats, janpads and zilla panchayats would be involved in planning for rural development and in sharing of powers and resources. Simple planning skills are very much needed for members of these bodies.

Legal Literacy. The decisions of all panchayati raj bodies at all levels would be subject to scrutiny of the legal process because many would be affected by the decision of the panchayats. Ours is a democratic system and everybody has a right to question every-body else's decision. Hence the basic principles of natural justice, legal process, etc, have to be understood. Hence NGOs have to impart such basic knowledge of law and how to observe natural justice principles.

Monitoring Networking and Experience Exchange. This is another important area where NGOs can play a critical role. The biggest problem of village panchayats is their lack of information on what the "other panchayat" is doing. They need to know about both success and failure stories in order to improve their own performance.

Between government and NGOs, the latter are better placed to inform the panchayati raj bodies about both the truth and the untruth. Monitoring of programmes and the outcomes have to be continuously shared across and within panchayats. The janpad and district panchayats have to know how others are doing. A newsletter brought out at the top by the government may not be able to capture all the nuances at the local village panchayat level. Some NGOs in M.P are successfully bringing out local newsletters covering many issues affecting the poor. "Disha Sawand Seva" is a newsletter produced by Mr. Suresh Diwan of Hoshangabad with many fascinating stories and issues.

At present panchayati raj bodies and government functionaries feel threatened by each other. The NGOs are a third and independent force and they can play the bridging role between the two.

If NGOs believe in strengthening the panchayati raj system in the country they must first understand the system and then help to strengthen it. The NGOs have now before them limitless opportunities to get themselves involved with the third force in the governance of this country. If they miss out they are the losers and have only themselves to blame.

Learning to Rule

Training village level leadership in the finer points of panchayati Raj has to be a priority with the state if power to the people has to become a reality. It was a sultry afternoon when Mohan Singh Rathore, member, zilla panchayat, Gwalior, and Uma Rathore, janpad president of Ghatigaon Block, took me to see the training programme they were conducting for the panchas and sarpanches.

Kulaith is a fairly big village, half an hour's drive from Gwalior. Nearly fifty men and women panchas and sarpanches of Ghatigaon block, Gwalior district, were waiting in the temple premises to attend the final day of the three-day training.

After the usual "Ram Ramji", Mohan Singh started off by telling them about gram vikas (rural development) and what it meant, in Bhojpuri mixed with Hindi. *Vikas,* he explained, was not just drainage, or the construction of roads and culverts, but mostly about how people survived - what they ate, whether the children went to school and whether they were protected from diseases. A heated discussion was sparked off while he was talking, among the women whose heads were covered with the traditional *ghunghat* or veil.

The ghungats were gradually lifted when the functioning of anganwadis was discussed. One woman bitterly complained about an anganwadi worker who gave tuition in the aganwadis to village children, pocketing Rs. 30 per month from each child. She said children were not fed or weighed and there was no playing or singing. Another woman wanted to know how under TRYSEM, instead of giving stipends to youth trainees, the trainer himself charged the youth Rs.100 each. How come in Kulaith, she continued, the anganwadi was held in a temple when the new building for housing it was locked and not handed over to the panchayat for the last eight months by the Rural Engineering Service Department attached to the BDO.

The atmosphere was charged and the training team handled the questions very skillfully by putting counter questions to the trainers on the lines of what they had done to supervise the anganwadi worker, school teacher and the health worker. When the topic on immunization came up, the trainers used examples which the people could identify with. "Just as you offer fruits/ coconuts to Hanumanji every week you have to offer polio drops to the child when there are fixed days or immunization sessions every Tuesday."

The anganwadi worker, who is herself paid a pittance, and the nurse are held in contempt by villagers who resolved to closely monitor their activities in the future.

Kulailh village is somewhat overpopulated. I asked one sarpanch how many kids he had. Seven, he replied. When I asked whether they were not too many, he said he regretted it now. Another trainee got up and said he had only two children because he practiced family planning. Then the discussion centered around child spacing and family planning. One sarpanch said, *"Jyada santan* is like *shaitan.* The *shaitan* will ruin us. Women are illiterate and their "gunghats" have created *more jhanjhats* (problems) for them. Men were equally illiterate," he added.

Problems of literacy and school education were raised and the discussion led to the state of primary schools. A common problem was the teacher not turning up. Now that the panchayats were empowered to supervise schools, they could enforce some discipline on the teachers. Singh said empowerment through *shiksha* had to replace empowerment through the gun. He said the days *of* the gun were over. In Gwalior district, every fourth or fifth person carried a gun on his shoulder as a sign of his strength. In the training session itself there were many sarpanches with guns. By the time we discussed many such issues, the sarpanch of Kulaith, Papan Singh Yadav, announced that lunch was ready. It was already 4 pm and after consuming hot *puries* and *alu sabji*, the entire training team took a round of the village.

Papan Singh said that there were three anganwadis in the village and all of them had no pucca buildings. When we went to see that new anganwadi building, Papan Singh took a stone and broke open the lock of the door and asked Mr. Rathore to declare it open. Instead of the more common cutting of the ribbon, Papan Singh resorted to this somewhat unorthodox method. He proudly said all government buildings in his village belonged to the panchayat and since the anganwadi building was ready, why shouldn't children use it instead of the dharamshala. He instructed the anganwadi worker to function in this new building and declared it open.

A hapless government functionary argued that this was trespass as it was forceful taking over of state property. What happened if the BDO charge-sheeted the sarpanch for trespass or willful violation of law? However, under Panchayati Raj, such incidents are bound to take place all over the state. The bureaucracy will not hand over its powers on a platter to the panch/ sarpanch. But if the local leadership did not assert itself, or waited in the forlorn hope that power would be decentralised, then it may be in for a disappointment, despite pious resolutions and government orders. This is the paradox of Panchayati Raj governance.

This Panchayati Raj Training Module was designed by Anita Das, IAS, former secretary of panchayats and social welfare, and short-term consultant to the UNICEF. It is adopted by 60 NGOs for imparting training to nearly 20,000 village panchayat members in Madhya Pradesh. Its strong point is that it focuses on leadership training that is imparted to women panch/sarpanches and the importance of context, content and the interactive process of training.

Out of nearly 18,00,000 women panchayat members elected in the state, nearly half of them are not only illiterate but also in "purdah". When they attend panchayat meetings, their husbands also accompany them just to see how their wives speak and behave. Many of these womcn, given the freedom to speak, are prepared to throw away their veils and join the mainstream discussion. But they are not allowed to by their husbands and elders.

The veil also inhibits the free flow of ideas and a veiled woman cannot see the posters or the blackboard or videos in the training session. If there is no eye contact there is no discussion, no dialogue and chances of interaction are hampered.

This training therefore, lays a lot of stress on these interactive processes. The initial reports from 60 NGOs who are involved in training, have revealed exciting interactive experiences throwing up many issues of empowerment.

Many questions have been raised on the training of Panchayat Raj members in MP. How will the state train such a large number? Who are the trainers? What should be the content of training for the members of all the three tiers of the system viz. village, block and the district? The training materials required? The follow-up and quality control of training? While the State Academy of Administration in Bhopal has taken the initiative for training zilla panchayat and janpad panchayat members the content and the quality of training of gram panchayat members has not received the required attention.

The gram panchayat is the cutting edge for achieving results on all fronts at the village-level. UNICEF involvement is just an experiment to learns the processes involved in empowering women men in the new dispensation. But training will have to be scaled up by the state using available talent to make the Panchayati Raj in MP a strong force of governance.

Women and the Panchayats

Madhya Pradesh presents an unusual paradigm of development in terms of many indicators of development-low women's literacy, adverse sex ratio, high poverty ratio and high maternal and infant mortality. The state political leadership has been trying its best to reverse these trends by involving people and women in particular. It is in this context that the efforts of the state leadership in MP to involve women in panchayats both as a method of grass roots governance and also to empower them has to be seen.

Lakhs of women, in different tiers of the panchayats *(zilla, janpad* and *gram)* are participating and learning to rule and make a difference to their lives and the lives of their-communities. Cynics of the *panchayati raj,* are quick to snub the whole idea of women in panchayats as something of a joke and the men folk in these panchayats are always ready to treat them as *behans* (sisters), who can be silenced easily by intimidation.

Before we analyse the experience of M.P we need to understand the whole issue of local and grass roots governance. How is local governace different from state and national governance? How and why is governance through the *panchayati raj* system better than remote controlled state and central level governance? Are people more involved in grassroots governance or in state-centered governance? Are wisdom-based, simple and rustic people better suited for grassroots governance than the more street smart politicians of the state Vidhan Sabhas and national Lok and Rajya Sabhas? Is direct democracy through voting once in five years and sending representatives really helping the redressal of peoples' problems or are people-centered panchayats better suited to run local level establishments Like Swiss Cantons)?

Women's role in panchayats is not just the problem of M.P. but the whole country. The best way to highlight the difference between panchayat governance and state/national governance is to identify their main characteristics, especially that of the leadership in both cases:

S.N	*State Vidhan Sabha, National Lok Sabha Leaders*	*Zilla/Janpad/ Gram Panchayat Leaders*
1.	Concerned more with one time vote catching. Once in 5 year appearance before their voters.	Have to be visible always to the voters round the year
2.	Busy more with drafting, debating laws and policy making.	Concerned with actual implementation of laws
3.	Tendency towards favouring a few and selected party men. Party-affiliation strong.	Less party affiliation and more concerned with local groups.
4.	Less transparent to the local voters and people. More secret dealings.	Forced to be transparent all the time Cannot bide from the public gaze.

(Contd.)

(Contd.)

S.N.	*State Vidhan Sabha, National Lok Sabha Leaders*	*Zilla/Janpad/ Gram Panchayat Leaders*
5.	Can conveniently hide the assets / wealth. Voters are not able to see the wealth accumulation. Tendency towards capital accumulation.	Cannot hide the wealth made during the tenure. Fixed assets always visible to the local people
6.	Tendency to bluff local people since they cannot verify the facts and assertions.	Cannot bluff local people Assurances verifiable locally.
7.	More concerned with National State level resources, funds than with local resources. Not accountable to local resources/environmental resources.	More concerned with local resources/local environment problems
8.	Survives more on assurances than on finding solutions.	Cannot afford to live on assurances. Has to find local solutions for local problems.
9.	Can do anything in the name of Public/voters interest without telling the voters,	Cannot do anything in the name of public interest-only local interest reigns.

Direct democracy all over the world is now being termed as part-time democracy, says the Economist. In most of the democracies the voice of the people is only heard once every few years, in elections, in which the voters choose the President or send their representatives to an elected parliament and that between those elections,(five or seven years), it is the President the parliamentarians who do all the deciding, while the rest of the democracy is expected to and more or less quietly on one side, either nodding its head in irrelevant approval or growling in frustrated disagreement. Swiss Cantons are almost like our panchayats. Kilchberg is a Canton of 7,000 people. It raises its own income and property taxes, runs a school upto the age of sixteen, appoints teachers, disburses old age pension, runs its own fire brigade, maintains its police force and does everything that a modern state government in India does. People are so honest in Kilchberg that if the fruit seller is out for lunch, you just leave your money on the counter! The government in Kilchberg consists of a seven person council, elected by 7000 people which supervises a modest staff of professionals. The real power is wielded by the voters who assemble upto four times a year to listen to the Council's recommendation and decide whether it is handling things properly. It is at these meetings that tax levels are fixed, new laws are passed, and anything else anybody wants to bring up discussed. Voting is by show of hands but there can be a cross on paper vote if a third of those present demand it. If somebody feels the Council's ideas are useless, he or she can, by collecting fifteen signatures, insist on putting a proposed new law to the voters. This is *real* direct, grassroots democracy.

Cynics now will say, "Oh this happens in Switzerland and not in an Indian panchayati. It cannot happen here." Yes it cannot happen in an Indian panchayat because we do not want it to happen! State MLAs, ministers and bureaucrats do not want to part with the powers of hiring and firing school teachers, auxiliary nurse midwives and village *patwaris*. *Gram sabhas* in Indian panchayats are in no way different from Swiss Cantonal meetings.

I have attended several *gram sabha* meetings in M.P. and found that a rustic and illiterate man or woman has more earthly wisdom than any of our MLAs and MPs and can ask intelligent questions on governance. They can grill the village panchayat *Pradhan*. But at present, they are not allowed to take simple decisions on village water supply systems or punish an absentee school teacher. Take the case of the Local Area Development Scheme in India where an M.P. gets Rs. 2 crore to spend as he/she likes in their political constituency. The activities allowed are construction of school buildings, health centers, *anganwadi* centers etc. Aren't these matters better left to the decision of village panchayats? Why should an M.P. be given powers on these? An M.P. is supposed to think of policies and law-making and not be worried about village roads, hand pumps and school buildings. This is usurping the power of the panchayats. Similarly, state MLAs are given discretionary powers to spend money in their constituency. All this shows that we believe more in indirect rather than direct democracy. Naturally *panchayati raj* can never succeed in Indian soil.

Where do women fit into this scenario? The present controversy on reservation of seats for women in parliament and, state assemblies makes little sense in the context of direct democracy. If we want to build grassroots and direct democracy, panchayats are the best instruments. Women in panchayats can make an enormous difference to the solution of local problems like water supply, sanitation, health, education, ecology and the environment. Women at the local level can be powerful leaders and once they graduate from the local level, they can outshine any male leader at the state and national level. It is in this context that we have to view the present debate on the magical figure of 33 % reservation for women at the state and national levels. Some states, like Madhya Pradesh, have now encouraged women in large numbers, to represent their village communities in local panchayats. However, two years is just too short a time to pass any judgment on how well they can do, given the opportunity, at the state and national levels. In this period of the *panchayati raj* goverance in M.P, despite the hurdles in the form of state politicians and bureaucrats, women have played a dominant role in improving the lives of their communities.

The Women's Empowering process in Madhya Pradesh (Ghunghat Ka Janjhat and Sarpanch Pati syndrome)

When in 1994, for the first time, thousands of women in M.P. got into panchayats, their first obstacle was their *ghunghats* (veils that covered their faces) and made eye contact with the panchayat *karmis* (workers) impossible. Many women panchayat members, fresh from their homes, were a little afraid of lifting their veils and talking straight at panchayat meetings. There were several atrocities on women panchayat members in several parts,of the state. The SC/ST women panchayat *Pradhans* and some UP *Pradhans* were even physically abused by upper caste male *panchas.*

Massive training for women was spearheaded by UNICEF and the M.P. government in forty five districts of M.P. through the network of local NGOs, setting in motion the process of empowerment. So far, 20,000 village women panchayat members have been trained. These three-day training sessions were interactive and were organised by local NGOs known to the women *panchs* and their husbands. The first day was all anxiety and suspense. Husbands *(sarpanch patis* - SPs) were hesitant to leave their wives alone and would accompany them to training sessions. This was only natural because it was the first time that their wives ever left home.Gradually, the *ghunghats* were lifted and they felt free. After two years, when we interviewed these 'veiled' women they said, "We keep *ghunghats* only in *our* houses, when we come out in panchayat meetings, *we* remove them. We are no *more* worried about our veils - we know when to put them on and when to remove them". "Men have *ghunghats* too", says a panchayat lady from Betul district. "Men have closed minds *(purdah*-mind) and they can never lift their mental-veils, while women can lift or remove their veils easily, and speak with feelings."

The second empowerment process was the liberation of panchayat 'seals'. The *sarpanch patis* carried the seals on behalf of their panchayat wives, and they misused the seals for issuing false certificates. Now the women panchayat presidents and vice-presidents have captured their seals back and are keeping them in their custody. This is slow but sure empowerment.

Women Learning to Rule

The whole *panchayati raj* experiment in M.P. is teaching women how to rule. Rather, how to *govern* has been the main theme right across the forty five districts of the state.Two trends are emerging among women panchayat members (1) issues of health, education water and sanitation, fuel wood and energy are all getting priority, because as women they have suffered, and as *sarpanchs* or *upasarpanchs* they want to solve these problems in their villages (2) Men *panchs* are more concerned with Jawahar Rozgar Yojana and other Yojanas coming from New Delhi and the state capitals. They are more concerned with buildings, roads, culverts and running a full establishment with all the attendant problems of sanctions and audits and what have you. If our concern is with human development, we should encourage more women at these local levels where peoples' problems are more acute.

Panchyat Governance and Women's Policy

Madhya Pradesh is a state where an explicit Women's Policy has been prepared and its implementation is monitored. Women in panchayats do not know as yet, in great detail, the main features of this Policy and how it could further the cause of women. In a recently concluded panchayat women's convention, many panchayat women expressed their lack of understanding of this' Policy, what it contains and what they can do. Many women have been instrumental in bringing together all the disparate. programmes and schemes that have not, been implemented either because of lack of political will or human inefficiency. For instance, many women panchayat members took up the task of popularising iodised salt and monitoring its sale and consumption in many villages and towns of M.P. as part of the Rajiv Gandhi Technology Mission on elimination of iodine deficiency disorders (like goiter, cretinism and other disorders). In hundreds of villages, women took up testiny iodine tesing the salt in village grocery shops and ensured the sale of only iodised salt. In Sehore District, a woman panchayat president carries the test kit in her bag all the time and keeps testing salt wherever she goes - in shops, kitchens, *anganwadis* and midday meals in schools. These invisible, but life-saving interventions are of far greater significance in the lives of people than power stations, bridges and dams. If we want to give life to peoples' governance, then women can make a difference to that process.

Women, Panchayats, People and Pumps. Nearly three lakh hand pumps installed by the Public Health Department of M.P were transfered one fine day to the panchayats in the state, without any readiness on the part of these panchayats. Rs. 500 was given for each hand pump towards its maintenance. India Mark II hand pumps are generally sturdy but with bad handling they can break. The entire maintenance was handled by block level mechanics and for a hundred villages there are just one or two block level mechanics. It is humanly impossible to attend to all the 2000 hand pumps in a block. Hence, training of village level mechanics, particularly women, has been a felt need. Women in Betul were trained as hand pump mechanics and the breakdown rates came down. They named each part of the India Mark II hand pump in Hindi as the following:

Plunger Rod- *Chotu Chad*
Plunger Yoke Body-Pinjara
Upper Value - *Mendki*
Washer - *Bucket*
Spacer - *Katori.*
Follower - *Glassi* (Like a glass)
Check Valve Body -*Badi Pinjara*
Check Valve - *Badi Mendki*
Push Rod. *Choti Kila Kanta*
Cylinder Bodyo: *Pyle* (measuring grain)
Head - *Peti*

Women panchayat members are always concerned with drinking water issues. Here again we find a clear difference in the pattern of thinking among men and women panchayat members. Men *sarpanchs* prefer capital intensive piped water schemes because they can have their 'margins' from contractors of the piped water supply *Yojanas',* but women demand a twenty-four hour water supply available through the hand pump. They prefer to repair these hand pumps rather than depend on one *chowkidar* who can switch off and switch on the piped-water supply electric switch. The former is more sustainable than the latter.

Next to drinking water is the sanitation problem. Women are more affected by bad sanitation than men. Hundreds of women panchayats are demanding in M.P. protected sanitary facilities like leach pit toilets which do not need too much water, washing and bathing facilities and cattle troughs. Many women panchayats are demanding the use of Jawahar Rozgar Yojana funds for building toilets for women and girls' schools in particular since the national sanitation program is a centralised scheme.

Women and Education

It is not necessary, to stress yet once more the need for women's literacy and education. In M.P. the Literacy Mission has played some role but it is still too inadequate to make any into the enormity of the problem. Many women Panchayat members feel at their lack of education (not just literacy) is coming in their way of understanding the maze of literature on laws and regulation which keep pouring into the panchayat offices round the year. The panchayat *karmi:* is neither enlightened nor educated enough to make these women understand all the implications. The need for legal literacy is thus assuming critical importance. A common complaint from many harassment us. What should we do? If we knew how to file an FIR and write it properly we can fight our cases. As panchayat members they should have a minimum of legal literacy in terms of understanding which law affects them and how; course of action, whom to approach (jurisdictin) and when (limitation). Our lawyers have no time to assist these women and government legal aid is non-existent. Where do they go? This is the biggest challenge in the years to come. In South Africa, legal literacy is imparted through street corner talks, thanks to Nelson Mandela's initiative for fighting state repression through the instruments of law.

The five areas of concern affect not just women, but also the overall quality of *panchayati raj* governance in M.P. in the days to come. It is not just the problem of M.P. but that of the entire Indian sub-continent. *Panchayati Raj* is the best form of direct democracy. The 'agenda of politics' is much better handled by common people themselves on a day-to-day basis, not just during elections. Organised political parties want elections every five years and their existence depends on them. At the grassroots level, if a panchayat member can do a good job, hel she need not depend on political parties or expensive elections. Grassroots governance is the best method of cleansing Indian politics. By *giving* ordinary men and women more responsibility, it encourages them to *behave* more responsibly, by *giving* them more power it teaches them how to *exercise* power. If women are given more power, Indian politics and governance can have a humanising, if not a feminising effect.

References

1. *The Economist, Survey of Democracy,* London, Dec. 21st, 1996.
2. Manu N. Kulkarni: *Learning to Rule, Humanscape,* Bombay, February 1996.
3. Manu N. Kulkarni: *Panchayati Raj in M.P.* Action Aid, Exchanges, March 1996.
4. Manu N. Kulkarni: *Evolving a Women's Policy in M.P, Economic and Political Weekly,* Bombay, March 23, 1996.
5. My ideas of differentiating panchayat leaders and state leaders were inspired by Dr. M.V.D. Bogaert, SJ, Director of Xaiver Institute of Development Studies, Jabalpur, who in his *Watershed Management - An Emerging Leadership Paradigm,* distinguishes between watershed leaders and business -leaders'.

Evolve ZPs as 'global' bodies

India has not allowed grassroots bodies to, undertake major development projects

In the context of rapid globalisation there is need to th ink. globally and act locally so that the fruits of rapidly growing technologies, ideas and processes developed anywhere are shared by all agencies, bodies and people everywhere around the globe.

More and more local institutions are shaping up as global-local (glocal) bodies at the same time, thanks to the death of distance. Under the 73rd and 74th Constitutional amendments both the urban and rural local bodies were supposed to have been governed as units of self-government and despite the constitutional provisions and after three decades of Rajiv Gandhi's dream of making panchayat raj institutions vibrant bodies, they continue to be the agents of the state and central ministries. Now that the elections to these bodies are fought on party lines, the cycle of total subjugation of these bodies to the party bosses is complete.

Fail to draw lessons

Day in and day out we are not tired of comparing China with our own efforts in taking progressive steps in global trade and commerce. But we forget to draw lessons from China's experiment in total devolution and decentralisation despite its autocratic and centralised regime of repression and control

Chinese town and village enterprises (TVEs), actively sponsored and assisted by local bodies, became initially the major entities for foreign investment. With the central local revenue sharing system under economic decentralization, the local government bodies had a strong incentive to promote TVEs as these contributed substantialy to make revenues which the local bodies could fo retain for themselves under the revenue sharing arrangements.

Through these arrangements China has embraced the property regime and capitalist mode of production. Through such decentralised approaches China has encouraged Foreign Direct Investment (FDI) to go to the local level and help to promote and establish at the local level employment oriented industries in the rural sector.

In contrast, our central and state ministers keep harping on the dangers of allowing FDI in the rural sector or at the local level. Renowned financial analyst D N Ghosh says, "If China could manage a high rate of FDI inflow without compromising its sovereignty it does not make sense for our political class to nurse all the time a kind of vague and unspecified apprehension that FDI could erode our security and sovereignty and that we would be playing in their hands. We have to shun any kind of paranoia about FDI."

Compares with Europe

Our zilla panchayats are far stronger than the local bodies of China. The size of a typical zilla panchayat with a big agricultural area and population compares with many a European country. With the expertise of all the development departments in the district, a zilla panchayat can kickstart agro-processing enterprises to provide value addition to, agriculture and create jobs for the rural youth.

Recently the Union Ministry of Agriculture announced a capital investment subsidy in Tamil Nadu inviting entrepreneurs and agro-processing enterprises in the country to bid and quote tenders to provide direct service delivery to producers/farming community in post harvest management/marketing of their produce.

How can the babus and technocrats sitting in New Delhi invite bids, process them and award contracts when the units of self government are precisely meant for doing such work? For what have the zilla panchayats been formed?

Why can't the ministry hand over these activities to the ZPs, allow them to raise money locally or globally and get an MoU with the central ministries signed by each of the ZPs and get the business done on a revenue-sharing basis? Let the state and central ministries do the regulatory work of quality control, and make them follow central/state laws.

The presidents of ZPs, assisted by technocratic CEOs, can definitely think and access global capital and technology as has been done by China through their TVEs. The Karnataka Panchayat Act 1993 provides all the legal and political support to make them "global bodies". Will the political leaders of Karnataka show the way to the rest of the country by making the ZPs vibrant "global" bodies?

5

Food, Feeding, Water and Hygiene-Missing Synergy

Mother's Milk, HIV and the Feeding Fiasco

Every year, the Breast-feeding Promotion Network of India (BPNI) organises mothers' empowerment week in various parts of the country where the virtues of mothers' milk and the importance of breastfeeding are highlighted so that the health of the baby and the mother is protected and promoted. There is social, medical and clinical evidence world-wide to show that wherever babies are put to mothers' breast both the health of the mother and the child is forever protected and growth ensured.

There is another agency called Federation of Obstetricians and Gynaecologists of India (FOGSI) and in one of its brochures it is emphasised that HIV is transmitted to the baby before, during and soon after birth. WHO too has concluded in many of its scientific publications "breastfeeding is associated with a significant additional risk of HIV transmission from mother to child as compared to non-breastfeeding. The risk of MTCT appears to be the greatest during the first few months of infant life but persists as long as breastfeeding continues. When replacement feeding is acceptable, feasible, affordable, sustainable and safe, avoidance of all breastfeeding by HIV-infected mothers is recommended."

National Aids Control Organisation (NACO) has conveniently said "the option of breastfeeding is left to the mother to decide after counselling on the risks and benefits of various options of infant feeding practices." The Government of India, with good intentions to promote breastfeeding and stop the sale of commercial infant milk substitutes like baby foods and infant milk powder, passed a law, Infant Milk Substitutes, Feeding Bottles and Infant Foods (Regulation of production supply and distribution) Act, in 1992. This has been implemented to stop the sale of baby foods, and in the 90s, UNICEF spearheaded the Baby Friendly Hospital Initiative (BFHI) under which Government hospitals were converted into BFHI. During 1992-98, as UNICEF representative, I converted as many as 20 Government hospitals in Madhya Pradesh into BFHI ones. Under the 1992 Act, manufacturers who sell Lactogen 1&2, Amul Spray, Glacto I, Milk care, Nusobee etc. could be prosecuted under the provisions of this Act.

Confusion

One of the BPNI Publications says, "the intention of manufacturer is to persuade doctors to advise pregnant women and mothers of infants to bottlefeed their new born by providing them with free samples of their products. Once the infants start bottle feeding it affects natural breastfeeding and the infant would be caught in this trap." So we have to promote breastfeeding come what may! This was the situation before the MTCT was confirmed. The anti-retroviral drug companies, which are in the business of selling them to protect the mothers from MTCT, have not been as yet allowed in a big way to sell them because the health departments do not know whether to administer them or not.

Nevripine is the, drug that can stop MTCT if given at the right time according to 'Boehringer Ingelheim,- the manufacturer of Nevripine. This has been added to the WHO Model List of essential drugs for the indication of prevention of MTCT. This company declares that "HIV may be transmitted from the mother to child at various stages of pregnancy, including 'in-utero. A single dose of Nevripine can be given to mothers during labour and to their infants within 48-72 hours of birth. Nevripine levels in breast milk would maintain above 100 ng/ml in most of the mothers throughout the first week. The amount of Nevripine provided, to the infants via breastfeeding; although small, would have the potential to offer some protection against MTCT."

Scary situation

Against this background of emerging and scary situation we can imagine the fate of ordinary ill-informed mothers who are affected by HIV. MTCT has already killed and is going to kill hundreds of mothers and their babies and the Health Department in the State and our medical fraternity are not able to come out with a clear stand on how to arrest MTCT and at the same time help the mothers provide care and protection to themselves and to their newborns. There is no clear policy on providing anti-retroviral in large number of antenatal care centre in the State and the moribund Karnataka State Aids Society does not even know about MTCT and how to face it in hundreds of our health sub-centres across the State.

A typical mother is faced with many dilemmas. She doesn't know whether to breastfeed or not, if so how, much and when, if not what else to feed. The law prohibits, substitute feeding in hospitals. In some hospitals human milk banks are established to help the babies who cannot get mother's milk for some reasons. Can this milk be used by mothers affected by HIV. There is no answer forthcoming from anywhere. Even NACO appears helpless.

In Bangalore and Mumbai hundreds of HIV positive mothers have committed suicide after abandoning their babies. There is no proper counselling to these affected mothers and the hospital staff themselves scare them away from hospitals. Thus we can see several paradoxes and conflicting statements by different agencies involved in protecting the health of the child and the mother. There is a saying in medical fraternity that if two doctors disagree the patient dies! Southern States are floating on HIV/AIDS and Karnataka is no exception. There is no sense of urgency among our policy makers and legislators although there is a Legislators' Forum in Karnataka to fight HIV/AIDS. The State Health Department must bring out a white paper on the HIV/AIDS situation particularly highlighting MTCT, so that our mothers would know what to do to fight this dreaded disease.

Marketing of Mother's Milk

Mother's milk, is now recognised as 'amrit' for new born and infants up to the age of one atleast. In Rio World Summit 'Breast feeding is an ecological act' was the slogan put up by the Brazilian NGO health group and said Indian environmentalists are more worried about trees and city pollution than the long health of most productive human resource viz. infants. Why breast feeding is considered as an ecological act? Why human milk is precious for the new born and what is so special about it? Why bottle feeding is injurious to infants? If breast feeding is cost free and harmless, then why mothers are not taking to breast feeding? What is 'ecological' all about? What is so special about marketing of mother's milk? Mother's milk:is a 'nature product' and why this is to be sold when it is freely available? If conventional marketing theories are not applicable for selling this precious nature product, then what type of marketing strategies are relevant? These are some of the questions on which serious thinking has to be done if breast feeding is to be promoted for the good health of the mothers and the infants.

Mother's milk is much more than a simple collection of nutrients; it is a living substance of great biological complexity that is both actively protective and immuno-modulatory. It not only provides unique protection against infections and all allergies but it also stimulates the appropriate development of the infants' own immune system. Soon after the birth of the child, mother produces what is called 'colostrum' (fore milk) and subsequently 'hind milk'. Colostrum is a high density, low volume feed and is secreted from 10 to 100 rnl per day with a mean of about 30 ml per day. It contains less lactose, fat and water soluble vitamins than mature milk, but more protein, fat soluble vitamins such as Vitamin AEK and more of some minerals such as sodium and zinc. Colostrum evolves into mature milk between 3 to 14 days postpartum Comparisons of the composition of breast milk and cow's milk and tinned breast milk substitutes are generally not made properly and as a result the average ignorant mother does not comprehend the difference and the value of breast milk. For example, bovine milk proteins are different from human milk proteins, which are low but effective for optimal growth in young infants and result in an appropriately low solute for the infants' immature kidneys: Commercial infant foods, have high proteins and thus damage infant kidneys. Similarly, mother's milk is rich in long chained poly-unsaturated fatty acids, which are important in brain development. Most commercial infants' foods contain little or none of these. Mothers milk is rich in cholesterol. Mineral concentrations are lower in mother's milk than in any commercial breast milk substitutes; calcium is more efficiently absorbed and because of high calcium content in mother's milk phosphorous ratio (2.1) copper, cobalt and selenium levels in human milk are generally higher than in cows milk.

Quantity of mother's milk varies according to infant's demand. With so many advantages and no disadvantages, why the mothers are still depending on the commercial substitutes? However, the interesting question is: What are the reasons for low demand then? Marketing experts have never given thought to this aspect of selling mother's milk to infants. The breast feeding virtues are well known to the doctors, nurses and hospitals who have failed to promote the product. In the West massive advertisements are now promoting mother's milk, having understood the harm already being done to their infants by the commercial infant foods. Secondly, hospitals are also to be blamed, as the mother and the child are separated soon, just after the child's birth. Nowadays, much has been heard about 'baby friendly hospitals'. Public health policies, specially in the developing countries must be properly framed. Working mothers in the formal and informal sectors have no time to feed their infants. So advertisements alone cannot help. We need strong public opinion and legislation to sell the concept.

It is high time that the medical fraternity promote mother's milk as the best milk and breast feeding as the best practice for office going mothers as well as home bound mothers. Mother's milk has to become a 'medicine' to be prescribed by doctors. Perhaps it can be sold that way.

Mother's milk should be pristine. After all that's the one food that provides newborns with all the nutrients and benefits their growing bodies require. Nutrition experts recommend that babies be breast fed for at least the first six months after birth. Organisations such as the United Nation's Children's Emergency Fund and the World Health Organization are strong votaries of breast feeding, and many countries even have laws that forbid breast milk substitutes, such as lactogen, in maternity wards of public hospitals. But now there are aspersions that pesticide residues have compromised breast milk.

A Mother's Complaint

Writing in the US daily, *New York Times,* Florence Williams - environmental journalist and a nursing mother herself - notes, "When we nurse our babies we feed them not only the fats, sugars and proteins that help the immune system we also feed them minuscule amounts of paint thinners, dry cleaning fluids, wood preservatives, cosmetic additives, gasoline by-products, termite poisons and fungicide. Ocean and marine foods contain high mercury levels and mothers who eat them pass on to their children in one form or the other". Williams' worries are not unfounded. She got her own milk tested for polybrominated diphenylthers (PBD), a flame retardant. The PBD levels were found to be 36 parts per billion (PPB). That's seven times below the safe-level, but lets not forget that Williams' breast-feeding daughter is likely to be exposed to PBD-laced milk throughout her infancy.

Scientists believe that each suckle would add to the PBD levels in the infant's body. Says Michael Dourson, a toxicology expert consulted by Williams, "The infant is receiving one-seventh the exposure of the maximum PBD level believed to be safe. Above that level, we're not sure, but we become less confident. And at some point, it becomes unsafe." Arnold Schecter, of the University of Texas School of Public Health has a similar opinion. "No one at this time knows at what levels nursing is not the best approach, and in fact becomes harmful to babies. But such levels must exist," he contends.

Contaminants on the Rise

Experts estimate that PBD levels in Williams' milk are on the rise and at current rates of increase, they could reach 300 PPB in the next 15 years. That's the level that Tom McDonald, of the California Office of Environmental Health Hazard Assessment, says corresponds to endocrine and thyroid dys-function in lab animals. What this means, though, in human terms, remains unclear.

The worried mother's article caused much consternation. Mothers in many parts of the world had their milk tested. And to their horror, Williams was not the only one whose breast milk was contaminated. Tests on breast milk and food in many parts of Australia showed alarming levels of PBDS - up to five times higher than in Europe, where some of these chemicals have already been banned.

But not in India

Environmental activists here are more concerned with toxic crops and toxic cow milk, but not with toxic mother's milk. It's now well known that arsenic and many other deadly chemicals and minerals contaminate food and water in many parts of the country. So, worries about residues of such chemicals in mother's milk should not be dismissed as unfounded.

Before things take a turn for the worse, leading maternity and children's hospitals in India such as the All India Institute of Medical Sciences, New Delhi, Post-Graduate Medical Institute, Chandigarh and the Christian Medical College, Vellore, Tamil Nadu, should begin collecting milk sample of mothers undergoing ante natal care sessions. The samples should be tested for PBD, arsenic and other toxic contaminants, and adequate preventive steps should be taken.

More importantly, the analysis of these samples should form the basis for revamping maternity care programmes in the country. It is quite unfortunate that premier national clinical bodies such as the Federation of Gynecologists and Obstetricians of India have chosen to be silent. This is a wake up call to them to save our mothers from such deadly toxins in their milk.

Management of Services for Mothers and Children

The need for providing effective services to mothers and children has been the concern of planners since the fifties. However this concern expressed in terms of increased allocation of resource, for social services in general (from Rs. 40 million in the First Plan to Rs 2,010 million in the Sixth Plan), *is not matched* by willingness to improve the performance standards of various infrastructures built for providing such services.

Women and children constitute more than 50 per cent of the Indian population and their productivity expressed in terms of survival, protection, longevity, better literacy, etc, assumes vital importance. The adoption of National Policy in 1974 gave a new impetus at the national and sub-national levels for sustained, broad-based, long-term, integrated efforts to make children and mothers (since they live with them) the focus of development.

A number of structures for providing services to women and children have been built in the last decade both in rural and urban areas. The Integrated Child Development Services (ICDS) of the Fifth Plan has now spread over to as many as 800 Community Development Blocks, and the target in the Sixth Plan was to cover 1,000 blocks. A typical rural ICDS Block is intended to service nearly 17,000 children of less than six years, spread over in 100 villages. The coverage of pregnant and nursing mothers which goes with the coverage of these children is about 4,000 out of an estimated number of 20,000. An urban project (one or more wards/slums) is assumed to have the same demographic characteristics as a rural project. A tribal project intends to cover about 5,950 children of less than 6, and 1,400 nursing/pregnant mothers.

The objectives of the ICDS are:

(i) to improve the nutritional and health status of children in the age group of 0-6 years;

(ii) To lay the foundations for proper psychological, physical and social development;

(iii) to reduce the incidence of mortality, morbidity, malnutrition and school drop-outs;

(iv) to achieve effective co-ordination of policy and implementation amongst the various departments to promote child development; and

(v) to enhance the capability of the mothers to look after the normal health and nutritional needs of the child through proper nutrition and health education.

The whole approach of ICDS rests on the basic premise that the package of services, viz, supplementary nutrition, immunisation, health check-up, referral services, nutrition should be delivered to children/women, at a place where children would come on their own. That place and structure is the Anganwadi and the person who provides or arranges to provide the package of services is called the Anganwadi worker (AW). The Anganwadi is the single most important structure that is created by the state at the village exclusively for children and their mothers. Besides there are a number of other structures already operating in the villages which are meant for all types of farming and non-farming families. We have gramsevikas or village level workers helping the farmer-families to do better farming, animal husbandry department stockmen to take care of private livestock in the village, secretaries of village panchayats and cooperatives for ensuring participation of villagers in civic and credit decisions. Traditional birth attendants (TBAs), Auxillary nurse midwives (ANMs), community health volunteer/guides (CH Vs/VHGs), school teachers and adult literacy instructors; all are engaged in health and literacy enhancement activities. All these structures created by different vertical departments of the state are providing services to adults, children/ mothers. These structures at the village level are supported by vertical supervisory structures at the Block and District levels. The ANMs, CHVs, VHGs, are supported by sub-centres, primary health centres and district hospitals for all referral cases. The Anganwadi worker is vertically supported by Mukhya Sevikas and Child Development Project Officers (CDPOs) and also gets lateral support from PHC Doctor who is supposed to visit the Anganwadi and carry out health check up of children. In all these village level development structures the services rendered are for different age-groups of people - men, women and children. Since the needs of women and children are treated as different from adult men, the Anganwadi structure caters exclusively to the needs of women and children. The basic assumption behind the Anganwadi structure, as already pointed out, is that children/women come there on their own. The only attraction for them to attend the Anganwadis is the supplementary nutrition offered in these centres. The attendance of children (0 - 5 +) varies with the availability of food offered in these. If we stop these food offerings neither pregnant women nor children would turn up.

Tall claims have been made by nutritional scientists and experts of the All-India Institute of Medical Sicence, New Delhi, that children attending these Anganwadis have registered weight gains and thus arguments have been advanced (thanks to 20-point programme of the Prime Minister) to increase the number of ICDS to cover as many development blocks as possible. Everyone's weight will increase if free food is available through free kitchens. Children would sing not only songs but would praise the providers of such free food.

What nutritional planners really do not understand is that whether such weight gains are possible to obtain in a home environment, within the purchasing power of the household? All nutritional studies have shown that weight gains among children remain stable as long as the feeding programme keep running, The moment feeding stops their weight gains also decline. The fallacy of the so-called supplementary feeding programmes is that children are treated as guinea pigs, as disposable products or statistics for manipulating development. The structure of Anganwadis fails to recognise the fact that children upto the age of 5 are intimately linked to their mothers in the household and for them the household is the Anganwadi. The intra-household (family) dynamics of sharing food among adults and children affects the growth of children and their survival depends on the survival of their families.

In extreme poverty conditions, children, particularly girls, are the first victims of starvation. The Anganwadi structure assumes that such children, because of starvation, are attracted towards Anganwadis for supplementary or rather substitute feeding. But this approach is not a self-sustaining one and any development strategy for children should not promote dependence on off-home free feeding programmes. In terms of cost of feeding and emotional development of children, Anganwadis are inappropriate.

One of the objectives of the ICDS is to achieve effective co-ordination of policy and implementation amongst the various departments to promote child development. Already in all development blocks, Integrated Rural Development Programmes are in operation to lift 600 families above the poverty line. Health workers like CHVs, ANMs, VHGs should identify the children in these families and impart health and nutritional education so that the economic benefits which the families obtain through IRD beneficiary oriented programme, are matched by such nutritional education. In fact, Indian mothers, even in most backward areas, do not need to be told what to eat when their purchasing power goes up. In the most backward areas in India village grocery shops sell glucose biscuits and mothers buy these to feed their kids with modest increase in their wages. In the sixties during the Green Revolution, Indian farmers were criticised for their resistance to adopting high yielding varieties of wheat and paddy. But it was the small farmers who adopted them fast, when they realised the quick economic gains in adoption. They adopted all the improved/ scientific package of practices for HYVP. It was the scientist who proved wrong and not the Indian farmer. The present ICDS programme, which seeks to provide package of services to women and children, should draw lessons from the agricultural modernisation programme of sixties. On-farm successes are more durable than demonstration farm successes. Similarly, *on-family* health practices are more useful than *off-family* health demonstration in the Anganwadis or health centres.

The concept of family viability, family pot and family survival should form the 'core' strategy for child development. Anganwadis at best can be temporary structures to deal with catastrophic situations where institutional care becomes necessary. But luring children away from homes with 'free foods' is not child development. Any strategy of child development should take place *along with economic development of families* for which a number of poverty removal programmes are in operation in the villages. Unfortunately even in milkshed areas of 'operation flood' children cannot get milk and, why not tighten child care in such programmes? Even in the Amul area, according to some experts, children do not get adequate milk and the extent of malnourished children is significantly high in the area.

Whenever cold chain for immunisation is discussed the Ministry of Health talks of building new infrastructure for vaccine distribution right up to the arm of the child, without knowing that in Dairy Development Programme artificial semen is stored and distributed right up to the farmer's cattleshed and the same infrastructure could be used for distributing vaccines for children, with slight modifications in temperature control. In many tribal areas, the Forest Development Corporations have built their infrastructure for collection of minor forest produce and a large number of women and children are involved in this collection. The forest guards and depot managers could be involved in "enhancing the capability of the mothers to look after the normal health and nutritional needs of the child through proper nutrition and health education" being one of the objectives of the ICDS. All these economic programmes have built-in scope for providing basic service activities for women and children. Instead of creating specialised services and structures for the women and children in the tribal and rural areas, appropriate horizontal linkages have to be established between several sectoral programmes of the sectoral departments of the state. Women and children are a part of the development process, and are not disposable spare parts to be treated separately. Child focused programmes unfortunately treat women/children as a target group without considering them as a part of families whose survival and growth cuts at the root of survival and growth of women and children. A vertical health and nutritional care system as is done through Anganwadis cannot be truly effective or even stand by itself unless it is integrated with other development activities in a joint attack upon the problems of development and social reconstruction.

Another objective of ICDS is to reduce the incidence of mortality, malnutrition and school drop-outs. Anganwadis deal with 0-6 age group of children and the primary schools deal with 6-14 age group of children. The drop-outs take place in the latter group, basically because children are obliged to work to supplement either family income or family work. The assumption of ICDS, that those children who are provided with institutional early childhood pre-school education in 0-6 age group would automatically proceed to the primary schools is untenable. There is no data to prove this even in the PEOs evaluation of the ICDS. (See PEO, Planning Commission, GOI Evaluation Report on the ICDS, 1976-78, New Delhi 1982.) This is not to decry early childhood education, but there is no correlation between pre-school and school education. Both process take place independent of each other because of various economic compulsions. Only a sophisticated cohort analysis would alone tell us how a child born would end up at his/her 14 years of age.

The structural problems of providing services to children in the urban areas are of different magnitude. Children in urban areas are lured by exciting things of urban life outside the family. In rural areas children do not see much of excitement outside the family, except in farms and in the forest. But they are more home-bound than urban children. Destitution is more an urban phenomenon than a rural one. The structure of services for urban destitute children are based on law than on love.

Different states have passed different statutes to deal with children in urban areas who have left their parents due to a number of poverty-induced factors. Juvenile delinquents is the word used for children. In Maharashtra alone there are eight enactments, *viz,* (i) Bombay Children's Act 1948; (ii) The Children's Act 1970; (iii) Probation of Offenders Act 1958; (iv) Bombay Borstal Schools Act 1929; (v) Bombay Prevention of Begging Act 1959;(iv) Suppression of Immoral Traffic in Women and Girls Act 1958; (vii) Reformatory Schools Act; and (viii) Guardians and Wards Act 1890. In all these Acts children are treated as offenders and the type of offences committed by them are (a) running away from their homes, (b) found in railway stations and bus stands at odd hours, (c) roaming about in undesirable places, and (d) found engaging in petty thefts. The police in the respective areas are authorised under the law to identify such children and they are handed over to the Remand Homes till they are tried by the Juvenile Courts. In Maharashtra in one Juvenile Court of a metropolitan city thousands of children are facing trial. The law provides that if the addresses of the parents of such children are traceable - and a majority of such children are able to provide their home addresses -the Remand Homes should send the children back home. However, these children are just kept for nothing in such Remand Homes and they become vagrant. The police have to show cases booked by them under different Acts and Children's Act is one Act which gives them great powers to round up children. The result is that the so-called destitute children are herded in Remand Homes and the managers of the Remand Homes have a vested interest in keeping these children under trial, even when they could send these children back to their parents with a little effort. More such children mean more money for cooking contractors in Remand Homes and for managers. The

Remand Homes are the most repressive structures for servicing the needs of children in distress or destitution in urban areas. The alternatives are the homes managed by voluntary agencies which help the children to go back to their parents and live with them. Here again the strategy has to be based on keeping the children as much as possible in their homes with their mothers, not with their surrogate parents like Remand Home managers or the Juvenile Courts.

The various working groups appointed by the Planning Commission to study the planning of social services in the Seventh Plan should make some useful suggestions for improving the performance of such structure and also suggest measures for folding up such repressive structures wherever they are.

Child related services are person intensive. Unfortunately these services cannot be mechanised. The psychological and emotional development of children is by and large determined by tbe parent's attitude and their own behaviour in the family. A large number of functionaries deployed by the state in the rural and urban areas to' provide services to children are in the nature of surrogate or substitute mothers and in those specified period when the children are in their fold, they have to act as mothers/ fathers. This requires a total identity of a very high order on the part of the functionaries. Their tasks should match the needs of children and their mothers, who bring them for relief, rehabilitation, rest and recuperation.

Most important functionaries in the villages for child care services are the dais or the TBAs, ANMS, CHVs, VHGs, and now the Anganwadi Workers (AWs). Let us analyse their tasks and see how their knowledge and skills match the needs of women and children.

Of late considerable stress is laid on building the competence of TBAs in rural areas. Unfortunately, there is no single perfect job description of a TBA available. However, the Ministry of Health, GOI, has provided guidelines for her training, from which one can assess her tasks. The TBA or dai serves as a link between the families in her village and the health worker/female ANM. She is supposed to contact pregnant women in her area and see that they are registered at the sub-centre or PHC; when she receives a call for delivery she should take her kit with her, should watch the progress of labour carefully, observe aseptic techniques while conducting the delivery, make the mother and baby comfortable and attend to the nutrition of the baby, try to ensure that all infants in her area are immunised with BCG, small pox, DPT and poliomyelitis vaccine. (See Primary Health Centre Training Guide, Part III, Training of Dais, Ministry of Health and Family Welfare, GOI, New Delhi, 1980.)

All these tasks are not done in a neat fashion. The medical fraternity generally does not accept dais or TBAs as part of their profession. The dai profession is handed over from one generation to the next and while the skill is practised fairly well, the knowledge for improved health care of mothers and children is lacking among dais. The medical infrastructure is not adequate for transmission of this knowledge. The ANMs and medical personnel accuse dais of being crude in handling deliveries which lead to septics and propagating anti-family planning philosophy. In Kerala, the dais are unionised, thanks to high female literacy rate. They demand equal treatment on par with the modern ANMs. Dais are an ancient institution in village India and they are the first contact point for a pregnant woman and her off-spring. They not only attend to deliveries but also wash clothes, cook food and be a source of solace to mothers in pain. What she tells the mother gets fixed in mother's mind. Her links with other para-medics like ANMs, CHVs and Anganwadi workers are far from satisfactory. Most of the TBAs do not have modern education, and the medical bureaucracies in various states have not made a dent in enhancing their knowledge and skills in MCH care. Although there .are a number of centrally sponsored dai training schemes, one cannot draw any evaluative judgment on such training because a large number of septic cases are still reported in the rural areas.

Improved training of TBAs should reflect in their improved handling of deliveries (aspetic deliveries). There are no data to know this. The links established by other child workers like Anganwadi workers are also weak. Why not Anganwadi workers invite TBAs to their Anganwadis and persuade them to inform mothers about the importance and utility of pre-school education, so that mothers could be prompted to send more children to Anganwadis. TBAs have more contacts with mothers than AWs.

Anganwadi workers' work could be categorised under (1) health-related, (2) kitchen-related, (3) education-related, (4) book-keeping and administration and co-ordination tasks. The health-related tasks are more time-specific and need a lot of MCH knowledge. Knowledge of immunisation schedule, infectious diseases, diarrhoeal management, infant feeding practices, growth monitoring - all these need specialised skill and knowledge to be imparted, on the job. The diarrhoea episode takes places in a house and not in the Anganwadi, and the AW has to be in a position to visit the house and demonstrate how to mix salt and sugar in protected water. Then only the AW can establish credibility in the eyes of the mother. In the present job structure of AW, she cannot leave her Anganwadi premises to call on mothers in their households in emergencies. While it is one thing to learn the techniques of oral rehydration therapy in a laboratory situation, it is another thing to practice it in a home environment. What we need is the latter.

Her kitchen-related tasks are such that she has to feed 40-50 children every day around 250 days of the year. Although food articles are distributed by the state as part of the Supplementary Nutrition Programme, the mobilisation of local level food materials and vegetables, and getting local mothers involved in cooking the meal for children is not attempted. The Anganwadi kitchen should look like a community kitchen for the village children. In Kerala, the Balwadi kitchens run by Village Mahila Samajams are more involved and village-based. The whole purpose is to reduce the psyschology of free-kitchen, where food is not begged but cooked and shared. Children should not get the habit of begging food but of sharing the food cooked by their mothers and Anganwadi sisters. The present capacity of AW to mobilise such food resources is limited, because she has no time to do so. In fact the best AW is one who reduces her intake of government food and increases the intake of village offerings so that the Anganwadi kitchen gets a community commitment.

The AW has also to work as a teacher in her education-related tasks. Most of the pre-school learning is non-formal, nonstructured and her task becomes still difficult. Much of the pre-school learning takes place in the home situation and the efficacy of 3-hour morning learning is really not measurable. All that the children learn is to sing some songs in chorus when visitors visit the Anganwadis. The AWs are also involved in Functional Literacy for Adult Women (FLAW) which has remained a virtual flaw in all the Anganwadis. Here again we find that the National Adult Literacy Programme has not been linked with FLAW. If more women could be enrolled in the Adult Literacy classes, much ground could be covered to extend literacy of the functional type to them. There is need for horizontal linkage by the AW with the Adult Literacy classes.

The tasks of AW in book-keeping, growth monitoring of children, co-ordination with village and block level functionaries reporting to Mukhya Sevikas and Child Development Project Officers, are all time-consuming. She has been asked to keep accounts of how much grain and oil is consumed and all such trivial information is collected and reported round the year. Among the clerical tasks, the growth monitoring of children is more crucial and this should take precedence on other routine tasks like maintaining registers for food cooked and consumed. If the ultimate strategy is to make the mother to monitor the growth of her children, the AW has to train the mother and pass on the growth monitoring responsibility gradually to mothers.

Although the present training curriculum for AWs is quite comprehensive, spread over three months, the live experience of those non-governmental agencies engaged in running Balwadis/ pre-schools has not been absorbed by the AWs. In fact there is need for grouping the government ANMs, CHVs, VHGs and AWs and child workers with non-government organisers, for training purposes and provide them group training for child health care strategy. This involves multi-sector approach and each of the functionary would know his/her role in the context of what the other does for child care. This would lead to better performance of their tasks. The Training Institutes are mostly Home Science Colleges, Schools of Social Work and some local level educational institutes and health centres. In the wake of community development programmes, a number of Gramsevak Training Centres were established in all the states. Then there are government Basic Training Colleges, Food Crafts Institutes, and a number of others. These are languishing for want of work direction. All their past work experience could be harnessed for improving the content and quality of training of child care workers. Although these AWs are supposed to be village based honorary workers getting Rs. 150-175, they are getting unionised and like the PWD work-charged establishment, they would claim one day all the rights and privileges of government employees including pension benefits. One of the positive gains of recruiting local girls as AWs is that they get employment right in their village and they become forerunners in women's employment, rights of women, women's literacy and thus break the traditional barriers for women's development.

Management of services (or children and mothers has to be denationalised more and more if we believe in people's care by people. Although children need some critical services, their mothers could be trained to provide them so that both the cost of these services is minimised and their effectiveness enhanced. The ultimate objective has to be less dependence on formal care systems, including on paid government functionaries.

What Our Mothers in M.P. Eat? - Combating Maternal Malnutrition

In all societies, particularly women and children, have traditional beliefs and practices about food consumption - what to eat and what not to eat. These beliefs and practices are nothing to do with food availability or their prices. Even when abundant foods and fruits are available they are not consumed because of these food beliefs. Our nutritional experts, however, have not considered these beliefs and practices as important in designing nutritional intervention strategies for mothers and children particularly for those during pregnancy and early childhood stages. It is during these stages, any wrong food habits would get themselves reflected in growth stagnation and retardation and once the retardation due to malnutrition, sets in it is difficult to reverse the cycle of malnutrition, infection and subsequent stagnation.

What is the situation of our young mothers in M.P.? Several studies of National Nutrition Monitoring Bureau of ICMA and the National Family Health Surveys of Government of India have revealed not a happy picture of our mothers health in M.P. Our mothers are not even providing their own milk to their kids through exclusive brestfeeding. As compared with our neighbouring state of Rajasthan, the percentage of mothers doing exclusive brestfeeding in the first six months of the delivery is 31.4% as against 65.4% of Rajasthan. As compared with all India average of 51 % exclusive brestfed babies, the corresponding figure in M.P. is just around 31%. Mothers milk is the best milk and our grandmothers used to keep their kids on their breast milk sometimes for over a year in the early days. But now the commercial milkfoods are eroding those practices even in the semi-urban areas. This has partly led to the emergence of large number of low birth weight babies in M.P. In the first six months the percentage of low birth weight babies (Lbws) In M.P. is 21% but as the babies reach 12-23 months the percentage of underweight children reach as much as 65%. By the time they reach 36-47 months the number stabilizes at 64%. This means the stagnation stabilizes and no amount of Anganwadi or school level feeding can reverse the stagnation.

At aggregate level (all districts of M.P.) consumption of cereals and millets, the main staple foods of the people was above the level of 460 g/cu/day suggested in the low cost balanced diet recommended by ICMR, ranging from 470 to 600 g/cu/day. However, consumption of other foods like vegetables (particularly green leafy vegetables) was below the recommended level. Similarly the average dietary energy intake was above the recommended level of 2400 kal cu/day in M.P. but there are wide inter-district variations like 1800 kcal in Jabua and a high of 2700 kcal in Panna, Shajapur and Indore.

Maternal malnutrition reflects on child malnutrition. Children are categorized into four different grades of undernutrition, normal, mild, moderate and severe grades on the basis of weight for age deficit from the standards. Analysis of the available data suggests that a large proportion of children (about 60%) are malnourished and suffering from moderate (45%) and severe (16%) degree of growth retardation.

What can we do? Where to begin the attack on maternal and childhood malnutrition? First and foremost is to tackle the pregnant mothers, young mothers to be and very young girls who have been married off unfortunately at a very young age. *(The mean age of marriage of girls in MP is 13.)* They do not know what they are eating and what they should be eating. M.P. is not poor in fruits or cereal foods. Look at Narmada bank, tonnes of Karbhuj, Guava, lemons are sold in city markets. The families who grow these fruits - cheap ones like papaya, guava, water melons sell them for cash incomes and the young mothers are denied the nutritional advantage of eating them although they grow them because nobody has told them about the rich vitamins they contain. Soyabeen dal is not cooked and eaten despite bumper soyabeen harvest in Malwa belt of M.P. Food habits and beliefs are holding our mothers from eating rich vitamin foods. There are what are called "cold" foods and "hot" foods. In India some village communities which perceive food items as hot food are believed to be harmful. For pregnant women and those perceived as cold believed to be beneficial. In some communities all animal foods (eggs, fish and meat) are considered as hot food and is believed to be harmful in pregnancy because they are believed to make babies large and become a problem in delivery! But in U.P. ghee is perceived as hot and beneficial for pregnant women because it produces blood and strength. Each State has its own set of food beliefs and practices.

In M.P. there is no scientific data on food beliefs and we do not know the regional variations and patterns of belief. The forests of M.P. produce tonnes of mangoes in the season and many other fruits/nuts and flowers like mahua. Many villagers adjoining the forests do not know what all vitamins contain in the fruits they eat.

The fruit that is most widely believed to be harmful in India is papaya. Next in order of the reported harmfulness are banana, jackfruit, pineapple, custard apple, dates, groundnuts, guava, jambu fruit, mango, melon, nuts and palmyra fruits. What is left out then? What will the women eat and how will their nutritional anaemia be mitigated? The nutritional experts in India should go back to the rural mothers and do the extension education for changing people's harmful food habits, instead of crying hoarse against Multinational Vitamin A manufacturers and the Vitamin A supplementation programme. Rural mothers are not eating such fruits because of their own beliefs and fears and our nutritional experts are against vitamin A supplementation. Where will we therefore go from here? Mangoes in districts of Bastar, Sarguja and many parts of M.P. are in abundance in at least 4 months of the year. Mangoes contain richest vitamin A. Why we are not able to boost the consumption of mangoes among our pregnant mothers? Who is to do this - Department handling ICDS or Health Department or Horticulture Department?

Improving the Vitamin A status *of* our young mothers and children through low or high dose vitamin A supplementation in countries where vitamin A deficiency is a known public health problem can be expected to reduce mortality by about 23 per cent. If the mothers cannot take Vitamin A through a spoon they can eat mangoes at least in the season. The available scientific evidence suggests that vitamin A is transferred from the pregnant mother to the newborn very easily. "Vitamin A is tranferred in two ways from the mother to the offspring via the placenta during gestation, and via the mammary gland (breast milk) during lactation. Adequate transfer of Vitamin A is essential during both of these periods of development. Animal models of severe vitamin A deficiency have shown that maternal vitamin A deficiency during pregnancy results in placental dysfunction, stillbirths and congenital malformations. Maternal vitamin A deficiency during lactation rapidly disposes the nurseling to severe Vitamin A deficiency" (Stolzfus 1994). Colostrum is particularly rich in Vitamin A and thus provides an excellent dietary source of the vitamin A during the infants' first days of life. The mature milk of well nourished women contains about 2.3 umol/L vitamin A, ample to meet the infants metabolic requirement and to accumulate safe and adequate store of the Vit. A. Cases have been reported of congenital ocular defects in infants born to mothers who were very vitamin A deficient. Even when breast milk vitamin A content is less than optimal, mothers milk is the best dietary source of Vitamin A for the young infant and very likely continue to be the best source into the second half of life. Overall the typical breast milk vitamin A content in vitamin A deficient areas is about one half of the content of the milk from well-nourished mothers. Infants of well nourished mothers increase their vitamin A stores about 20 fold from birth to one year of life. In contrast if there is no or low vitamin A, the infant will accumulate no storage of vitamin A, a state considered to be sub-clinical vitamin A deficiency, a bout of anorexia, illness or a temporary shortage of vitamin A containing foods/fruits may bring about clinical deficiency.

There is also the prevalence of nightblindness among women and as per some ethnographic studies, women in India perceive this to be an important health problem. Among pregnant women nightblindness coupled with their beliefs on foods would have disastrous effect on their nutritional status. Women experiencing nightblindness are to be treated with a course of daily low doses of vitamin A (e.g. 10,000 IU) or advised to eat vitamin A rich foods/ fruits like papaya.

We, therefore, have to think of multipronged strategy for tackling malnutrition problems in M.P. The following steps, undertaken by sectors of governmental machinery, would help in combating maternal and childhood malnutrition.

1. Care during pregnancy, helping the mothers to eat proper foods (Health department to advise her during the antenatal care, during TT vaccination).
2. Care after delivery, importance of feeding the colostrum and exclusive breastfeeding for at least first six months (Hospital nursing staff and Dais in the villages who handle deliveries at home).
3. Initiating complementary foods to the kids gradually by the mothers and increasing the weight (Anganwadi workers and village Pancheyat Members. Weight is the index of good health of children and launching Bachon ki Wajan Bhadao Abhiyan in village Panchayats can be easily launched by Village Sarpanchas).
4. Mothers must know what food must be given to kids when and how much. This knowledge is not imparted by anybody at the village level. (Home Science colleges, Food and Nutrition Board Staff and Anganwadi Workers, Village Mahila Mandals).
5. Importance of green leafy vegetables in daily diets of poor mothers and children. In all villages of M.P. at least 4-5 Hand Pumps are installed and a large quantity of water is wasted down the Hand Pump Platform. Our Panchayats can fence

the water drainage area and grow vegetables round the year and feed the green leafy vegatables to the village Anganwadi kids. Some village Mahila Mandals have done this in Tamil Nadu villages. Our panchayats in M.P. are much stronger and they have only to be told to do this. All these little steps would improve the nutritional scenario of M.P. Now is the time to act.

References

1. Rebacca J. Stoltzfus, Vitamin A deficiency in the Mother - Infant dyad, School of Hygiene and Public Health, Johns Hopkins University, Baltimore, USA, Published in Administrative Committee on Coordination, Sub-committe on Nutrition, UN, No Mid-1994, New York, p. 25.
2. Government of India, The National Nutrition Policy, department of Women and Child Development, New Delhi, 1993.
3. National Nutrition Monitoring Board Report Surveys, 1991.
4. National Family Health Surveys, Govt. of India, 1993.

Why we should Universalise Iodised Salt, and How

The decision of the Government of India to re-introduce the sale of iodised salt in the country has been received by mixed reactions from public health experts and concerned citizens. The NDA government had imposed the ban on the sale of iodised salt owing mainly to the pressure of the salt lobby in Gujarat, which is the leading producer of common salt in the country. Many of the salt producers do not want to install salt iodisation plants at the salt heads. Both Gujarat and Rajasthan are the leading producers of common edible salt and the salt lobby is strong in these states.

The whole issue of universalising salt iodisation is more beset by the fear of the unknown than motivated by the urgency of tackling the public health menace of iodine-deficit diseases like the goitre. But the more invisible ones are low intelligence and the cognitive impairment of affected children. Iron, iodine and vitamins have to be consumed by all citizens. There is what is called an ecology of iodine deficiency. We have to understand how iodine deficiency takes place first in the soil, because it is through soil that water, food vegetables and fruits are produced and consumed. In India, the hilly regions like Himachal Pradesh, Jammu & Kashmir and parts of Assam face acute iodine deficiency disorders like the goitre, which has no cure except to consume iodised salt in a sustained manner.

Iodine occurs in the soil and in the sea as iodide. Large amounts of iodine are washed out from the surface of soil by rain and snow and are carried in the sea through rivers and floods. The iodine in the atmosphere is returned to the soil by rain and the cycle is completed. However, the return of iodine in the soil is slow and small compared to the original loss. Subsequent repeated flooding and soil erosion further aggravates iodine deficiency in the soil and food crops from such soil become iodine deficient. Animals also suffer from iodine deficiency and meat dairy products also suffer from iodine deficieny as revealed by several researches conducted in Australia.

Today, many public health activists have started a 'satyagraha' against iodised salt, using Mahatma Gandhi's salt satyagraha strategy. These activists argue that in the coastal belts and in south India, there is no iodine deficiency, and so there is no need to impose the unnecessary iodised salt on them.

Some companies sell salt only in the iodised form and have been doing so for some decades now. People consuming this salt have not suffered.

According to the World Health Organisation (WHO), normal people exposed to excess iodine, through adaptive mechanisms remain euthyroid and free of goitre. In Japan, where dietary iodine intakes are high, it has been shown that normal people who are not Iodine deficient can maintain a normal thyroid function status even with several milligrams of dietary iodine intake.

The incidence of non-toxic diffuse goitre and toxic nodular decreased by a high dietary iodine intake. The incidence of Grave's disease and Hashimoto disease does not: appear to be affected by a high intake of dietary iodine. Current estimates of daily iodine intakes in Canada and the United States are substantially above the physiological need -the range of 460 mg/day among 9-16-year-old children to greater than 1 mg among as many as 10-20 per cent of adults.

We cannot put iodine in drinking water or in foods or vegetables, etc, as these methods have been tried in several countries of the world and have failed. Salt iodisation at the salt heads is the only cost-effective method and hence India has to accept this universalisation of salt iodisation as a public health measure. Except industrial salt, all edible salt has to be iodised for both humans and animals. Iodisation plants are not expensive and the salt commissioner should force salt producers to install them. Loans can be given at concessional rates to install these plants and recover the costs through the sale of iodised salt.

Iodine evaporates and hence there is need for a proper packing of iodised salt, which of course adds to the retail price. The majority of private salt manufacturers in Gujarat and Rajasthan pack the salt in gunny bags and sell it as crude crystal salt in the name of helping the poor:

Even the poorest consumer wants good, clean and edible iodised salt. After all, a typical family needs a maximum of 2-4 kg of salt intake per month, and a price difference of only Rs. 2 to 3 for iodised salt does not really cut into the poor family's budget.

It is high time we tackled public health problems like iodine, vitamin and iron deficiencies, by adopting fortification technologies, so that our growing young population does not suffer from these micro-nutrient deficiencies.

Food for Thought

18 August 2003, 8.30 am, Hubli (North Karnataka)

LH Bajantri, headmistress of the girls' section of Government Primary School in Moorsavira Math campus welcomed us (volunteers of Hope Foundation, Bangalore). When we asked her to show us how the *akshara dasoha* programme is managed, she agreed immediately. She first showed us the kitchen and then explained the innumerable administrative problems of running a large kitchen to provide daily *beesi oota* to nearly 300 boys and girls of her school. She escorted us then to the one-room-kitchen stacked with rice, salt and vegetables. Of the three lady cooks, one was very angry as she showed us the big vessel which is heavy even if five men were to lift it. She spoke of how it has to be heated long enough for the rice to cook, thus consuming a lot of cooking energy, how the gas cylinder is getting exhausted every week, etc. As we listened to her, the cooking-gas in the cylinder actually finished with the rice only half-cooked. Even after a week of booking a gas-cylinder, it had not been delivered. There was a flurry of activities. The rice was to be ready at 12 noon when the children line up, and the women cooks started emptying the half-boiled rice to a spare vessel borrowed from the neighbouring house. They virtually pleaded with the house-lady to kindly allow the rice to be cooked in their kitchen. There were arguments and the house lady reluctantly allowed the cook of the school to boil the rice.

We returned at 12 noon and the headmaster of the boys' section, Dhalayat (a state level winner of the 'best teacher' award) began his sorry tale of the *akshara dasoha.* He was frank enough to admit that these non-teaching duties of running a kitchen is taking away a lot of the teachers' time. There are eight forms and registers prescribed to keep track of how much rice, condiments, etc. were used, how many kids attended and consumed it, disbursement of salary to the three cooks, etc. We talked to the kids who appeared to enjoy what they were eating but forgot all about it as soon as they had finished.

Adargunchi village in Hubli *taluk* is 20 kilometres from Hubli city. At 1.30 in the afternoon, the headmaster of Model Primary School, MV Javali, welcomed us and showed us the ready cooked food, the kitchen and introduced us to the three lady cooks, one of whom is from the Dalit community. They complained about how they are underpaid (Rs. 650 for the head cook and Rs. 450 and Rs. 250 for the assistant cooks). This is not even the minimum wage prescribed by the government of Karnataka! If we go to the field, they argued, they can earn Rs. 50 per day at least. The big vessel is too heavy to lift and empty the cooked rice from, they said. As we spoke, children formed a long queue, some with empty tiffin boxes and plates given from home and others holding newspaper sheets given by the teacher. The government has supplied no plates or mugs. Javali tasted the food before feeding the kids to comply with the government order that the teacher should certify the food is fit for eating. He also gave us some cooked rice. Children sat on the playground and ate their rice.

We moved on to Noolvi village just two kilometres away where *akshara dasoha* is not implemented in any of the four schools we visited. Siddangoudar, *sarpanch* of Noolvi *panchayat,* says that even the poorest' parents want better teaching in schools than cooked food. Earlier, the parents were given two to three kilograms of rice, which was consumed in the family kitchen, including the children.

This has been stopped with the arrival of *akshara dasoha*: Noolvi has lost out, *akshara dasoha* and rice in kind. Siddangoudar says, 'there is no *akshara* (education) - it is all *anna* (food). Kids want *akshara* and not *anna,* which, they can have easily in their house.

This small eyewitness account of *akshara dasoha* does not represent the situation in the entire state. It has some lessons for planners and managers of primary education in the state though. Tamil Nadu was the first state to launch the school meal programme (SMP) almost twenty years ago, thanks to late MG Ramachandran, who was believed to have starved in childhood and could not go to school. He launched SMP with the triple objective of increasing attendance, retention and learning. Several evaluations done in the state did not reveal any marked gains in all the three areas despite SMP. But it did achieve social recognition for Ramachandran and for subsequent governments, and some degree of malnutrition among school going kids was reduced. This was indeed a positive gain. This may as well happen in Karnataka.

Children attend schools in most states not because of cooked food but because of better teaching and joyful learning. Both Rabindranath Tagore and Mahatma Gandhi, in their basic education models, never thought of feeding in schools to promote learning. Kids have diverse tastes and eating habits, and to make a dent in their malnutrition levels menus have to keep changing. Our teachers are trained neither for catering nor for nutritional services. Our *panchayats* in Karnataka have remained spectators in all village development programmes. If the village *panchayats* are entrusted with the task of serving hot food to both *anganwadi* centres and primary schools with the help of women self-help groups, they can do a good job. What type of cooking vessels to be used, how many cooks and whom to appoint as cooks, what kind of rice and *dal,* etc. are all left to the wisdom of *panchayat* members.

Unfortunately, education bureaucrats sitting in Bangalore, without knowledge of village politics and economics, run *akshara dasoha.* A number of issues have been raised in the context of school meals all over the country and not just in Karnataka. There are several dimensions to the debate. First and foremost is the issue of the health of kids who are in school. What will improve their health? Is bad health a primary reason for dropouts and bad learning? Several studies have shown that SMP does help in promoting good health, provided it is linked to the provision of deworming and micronutrient supplementation like Vitamin A given as a package and not piece-meal. Cooking the food with iodised salt would add to the reduction of iodine deficiency among kids as well. The SMP in Gujarat has shown some gains in this respect (See Tara Gopaldas, *Nutriview 2003/2* Oxford).

Secondly, is there a link between learning levels and SMP? There are no micro-level studies to show that learning levels have gone up because of SMP. There are many unfounded claims by state education ministers on SMP directly contributing to better learning. Even in Tamil Nadu, which has run its SMP for more than two decades, there are no authentic studies to prove that learning levels have gone up as a result of SMP. Learning depends on several factors like the teachers ability to make learning joyful, the efficient use of pedagogy, textbooks, cognitive ability of kids and so on. It is argued that a hungry child cannot learn. It is also true that once the child's mind goes in search of learning, the teachers' skill becomes critical. SMP cannot substitute a good teacher for promoting good learning.

The third issue is that of catering. Cooking food daily, finding its taste, its nutrient value and content, timeliness of cooking operations, certification on its safety, cooks not reporting to duty and the alternate arrangements to be made, etc. are all management issues which cannot be burdened on teachers who are not trained to manage these services. We have created a constitutional body of the *panchayat* at the village level. Besides, there are hundreds of self-help groups in all the states. But school authorities in many state capitals still want to control the SMP by deciding the size of the vessel where rice and *dal* is cooked, the ingredients, the type of vegetables to be used and how much salt and condiments to be added, etc. Karnataka *Panchayat* Raj Act 1993 Section 58 Schedule I provides a list of functions to be entrusted to village *panchayats.* Sub-sections XIII, XX, XXI proclaim that *panchayats* have to promote school health and nutrltion programmes, participate in the implementation of women and child welfare programmes, ensure full enrolment and attendance in primary schools and promote public awareness and participation in primary and secondary education. In Karnataka's *akshara dasoha* programme, the *panchayats* have no role in managing the SMP except that the *panchayat* secretary is made to sign the appointment letter of cooks. The selection of cooks is made by a committee presided over by the sub-divisional officer in which the village falls. Karnataka has always claimed that it is very progressive in the matter of providing funds, functionaries and functions to the village *panchayats.* Karnataka has an imaginative minister in charge of *panchayats* and has gone on record to say that the government has delegated 29 functions as enshrined in the 73rd Constitutional amendments. The above situation continues to prevail in the context of SMP in the state.

Community Water Supply Programme: A Setting

Betul District is one of the forward-looking districts of Madhya Pradesh, where NGO innovations and partnership programmes with the District administration have always been in the forefront of development actions. The District is the centre of Evangelical Luthern Church activities like Hospital Care Schools and Water Development Activities. A Hand Pump demonstration project was initiated in late 1987 by Government of M.P. and UNICEF to assess the reliability and maintainability of India Mark III (VLOM) and improved India Mark II. Twenty Five handpumps of each type were installed and monitored and was found that India Mark III(VLOM) has a meantime failure of 18 months and almost 90 per cent of the repairs could be carried out by a village level mechanic. This was the prompting factor for taking up large scale awareness and training for VLOM and sanitation interventions with communities spearheading the programme since early 1992. Betul was one of the 10 development Blocks of Betul District which was selected for this experiment. "Successful Community Water Supply Programmes (CWS) involve a combination of hardware and software technology and institutional/organizational support elements matched in such a way that each community recognizes the benefits of improved supply and can afford at least the costs of operating and maintaining it and has the skills, spare parts, materials and tools available to sustain it. To maximise health benefits, parallel investments in health education and sanitation programmes should be planned alongside CWS improvements" (World Bank, 1987). As one of the activities in support of International Drinking Water Supply and Sanitation decade, VLOM was promoted as means of overcoming some of the major obstacles to sustainable water supply systems. Many past failures of CWS systems can be blamed on the inadequacies of central maintenance in which a Water authority despatches teams of skilled mechanics with motor vehicles from a base camp, often serving a large District, to respond to requests.

Response to Handpump Breakdowns

In Betul District there were about 5000 India Mark II Handpumps and about 120 Mark III. Each Block level mechanic is servicing about 400 Handpumps and it is physically not possible to attend to their breakdowns. The present system of informing the breakdown by the villagers is also not efficient. Any villager can inform the Block level mechanic by writing the complaint in the Register kept in the Block.

In some Districts of M.P. some villagers telephone the Executive Engineers about the breakdown. The Block level mechanic keep looking at the register of complaints and decide to "attend" to them. In some places the weekly markets are used by the villagers to inform the break-downs, where complaints are collected by the PHED. Thus there are different ways of informing the breakdowns by the villagers. This haphazard information system does not ensure quick and efficient response.

Villagers who are ignorant of the nature of the breakdown simply magnify the breakdown, even if the breakdown is minor. This is where the peoples knowledge of the Handpump becomes important. Given this present situation of Hand Pump functioning in Betul the process of building community awareness on the entire range of Water and Sanitation Issues assumed urgency. Thus emerged the WESA (Water and Environmental Sanitation Awareness) concept in this experiment.

Demand Generation Through WESA

WESA was spearheaded by the NGO in Betul with the objective of:

(a) Building community awareness on water and environmental sanitation.

(b) Forming WATSAN committees in each of the 160 Project villages, involving 120,000 population.

(c) Selecting by the people of the village their own Hand Pump User Representatives, who will select village handpump mechanic team with two women and a man.

(d) Train the selected Hand Pump Mechanics in the operation, repair and maintenance of India Mark II and III (VLOM) pumps and help the Public Health Engineering Department in the conversion of Mark II pumps to Mark III and their subsequent maintenance.

(e) Building the village WATSAN fund for upkeep of Pumps and sanitation facilities like toilets, soakage pits,drainage, cattle troughs etc.

(f) Ensure the safe custody of Handpump spares and tool kits.

WESA process has created in the past months a tremendous sense of community participation for WATSAN programme. (Village WATSAN Committees formed 172: Orientation of WATSAN Committee members - 1215: Orientation of HP Users Representatives - 536, Women' mechanics trained - 116, men mechanics trained - 44). The process has helped to evolve women as the principal actors in this whole experiment. The Village elderly men have come to believe that Water and Women go together because women's life is linked to water lifting, hauling, storing and using efficiently or inefficiently. One Village head man described such women as "Chaturis" (Intelligent). On the other hand village youth, though smart, cannot stick on to the village and even if trained, they would demand service charges.

Hence the selection of married women of the village for Hand Pump training emerged, married because they do not leave the village and go away and are available all 24 hours and at least part of the whole year! This helps the repair and maintenance of VLOM pump better.

WESA process highlighted in their awareness camps, use of Water, better handling of Hand Pumps, better drainage around the pump and platform use of soakage pits, cattle troughs, use of toilets, and better disposal of waste. In some Camps women asked questions on use of bio-gas, improved chulas (stoves). The training was participatory and village men sat behind and enjoyed their women folk asking questions. The whole village had a festival look and the flirting banners on safe water, posters on Hand Pump. wall paintings, videos and audios - all contributed to the effective communication of WATSAN messages. The video - Stree Shakti - (Women power) depicting how women can repair Hand Pumps was screened and many women got inspired to try their hands.

Focus on Women as Pump Mechanics

Early experiments in India on selection of Hand Pump mistries (mostly young boys repairing cycles, electric motors etc.) as Hand Pump repairers and mechanics did not involve women in the entire range of W ATSAN activities but confined only to repair of hand pumps. "Tilonia started experimenting to find out if it was possible for semi literate boys to repair the 300 handpumps the SWRC had installed. We trained them initially for a month. We found it just required some manual labour and common sense (Sanjit Roy, 1989)".

WESA's approach has been therefore different and took into account the "parallel investments" in health education and sanitation programs along side CWS improvements. As the WESA covered more villages, more requests came in for providing help to build pour flush toilets and improve the village drains. They found just in $ 80 dry pit pour flush latrines can be built and the repair of the pumps does not need 'secret knowledge' and the villagers who were exposed to WESA orientation came forward with money to demand more knowledge and action to build toilets. Some villagers collected anything between $10 to $ 412 from the interested villagers to defray the cost of building individual toilets and the cost of repair to Hand Pumps. They were not clear about the cost but their 'enthusiasm' was reflected in their contribution. Some villagers did not keep the W A TSAN fund in Banks but loaned the amount to the needy on interest but with the assurance that when the money is needed they will return it to the treasurer, who was in some villages, a barber! Why a Barber because the barber would always have cash and will not run away from the village.

VLOM Training

As the demand generation on WATSAN caught up there were more requests from Village WATSAN committees to organise the training on Hand Pumps. Each Village WATSAN Committee nominated two village women and a man, to undergo VLOM Training. When this training was launched two problems were faced (a) The existing Block mechanics of the PHED were little sceptical of such a training for village women. How can these semi literate women handle such a pump? Without the cooperation of Block mechanics such a training cannot sustain because they have to cooperate with these women and the women have to cooperate with Block mechanics to ensure functioning of purnps in the villages. There was also the fear of the unknown - these women would replace us, where will we go? Hence joint consultations were held with the Block mechanics under the leadership of the dynamic Executive Engineer of PHED of Betul District.

The NGO had already surveyed the Mark II Pumps which were not functioning and the Mark III (VLOM) pumps which were to be installed (converted from Mark II). The PHED had furnished the list of both types of Pump. The plan is to convert all Mark II pumps into VLOM (Mark III). The training was hands-on. As the training progressed the women demystified the English names of the parts of the pump. The following local names were given by these women to several parts of the Mark III pumps.

1. Plunger Rod = Chotu Chad.
2. Plunger Yoke body = Pinjara (Cage)
3. Upper Valve = Mendki (Frog)
4. Washer = Bucket
5. Spacer = Katori

6. Follower = Glassi (Like a glass)
7. Check Valve body = Badi Pinjara
8. Check Valve = Badi Mendki (Big Frog)
9. Push Rod = Choti kila kanta.
10. Cylinder Body = Pyle (measuring grain)
11. Inspection Cover bolt = Tala
12. Inspection Cover = Dhakan
13. Double end spanner= 19 & 17 Chawi
14. Head = Peti.

The aim of VLOM concept has been:

Pumps are easily maintained by a village care taker, requiring minimum skills and few tool.

- Manufactured in-country, primarily to ensure the availability of spare parts.
- Community choice of when to service pumps.
- Community choice of who will service pumps.
- Direct payment to the repairers by the community (World Bank, 1987, Page 13).

In the extended VLOM concept M means management of maintenance.

The VLOM training in Betul recognised this M factor from the beginning and the training style was oriented to drive home the M factor all the time with the trainees. In Betul District the PHED through their Block Mechanics had adopted the breakdown repair as the most common form of maintenance. As a result of this training large number of Hand pump mechanics nominated by the village WATSAN committees, came to know about the preventive maintenance like simple greasing of the chain, tightening of nuts and bolts, which has helped to spot the problem in good time.

Assessment of the VLOM Training

How do we assess the knowledge of these women/men trainees in VLOM pump? The NGO in consultation with the PHED Executive Engineer decided to provide the Spares and tool boxes in joint custody of the village Panchayat and Village WATSAN Committee, and these were to be used by the trained mechanics of that village.

We adopted a simple test. We spread all the parts of India Mark III pump on a table. We called each of the trained team (Two women and a man). We picked some part of the VLOM and asked the women to join them in 3 minutes. They did it with perfection. On one occasion we mixed up the parts of Mark II and Mark III (VLOM) and asked them to join. They could tell us they are separate and cannot be joined! Such was their knowledge of VLOM parts and the whole.

The Future

There are some constraints in the whole experiment. The conversion of Mark II into Mark III cannot be done in all cases since the Inside Diameter of bore well/tube well fitted with M II pumps do not match with the Mark III pumps. Spare parts and tool kits have to be properly distributed to all the trainees so that they feel that they are empowered. The partnership between State PHED, NGO and UNICEF has to be strengthened in order to sustain the future VLOM strategy in the remaining blocks of Betul District. Parallel investments in sanitation activities have to be stepped up to have better mileage for the communities in WATSAN tasks.

References

(A) Charles Kerr, Community Water Development, Intermediate Technology Publications, 1989. See Sanjit Roy, p. 179.

(B) Saul Arlosoroff et al, Community Water Supply, The Handpump Option, World Bank - 1987.

the author is *thankful* to *Mr. S.* A. *Wahid, Mr. Mansoor Ali and Mr. V. R.P. Nair* of *UNICEF, Mr.* Satish *Raghu, WESA Bewl, Mr. Tawani, Executive Engineer of PHED - for their valuable suggestions in the preparation of this paper. However, the author alone is responsible for any omissions.*

Trapping the Raindrops : Re-engineering by the people

What follows is the analysis of what happened when villagers, farmers, school children, women and ordinary folks responded and reacted and participated in the people's movement for rainwater conservation cutting across barriers of caste, class and creed.

Water, health and education are the three pillars of human development initiatives and these have been converted for achieving ground results into either technology missions or people's movement in MP. Political powers are now impatient to convert the dry and brown MP into a blue heaven with abundant water bodies. The state faced worst type of drought successively in the years 2000 and 2001. This disaster was converted into an opportunity by launching what was called *Pani Roko* (PR) campaign. The call was simple *Khet Ka Pani Khet Mein* (rainwater of the field to remain in the field) *Gaon Ka Pani Gaon Mein* (rainwater in the village to remain in the village) and *Ghar Ka Pani Ghar Mein* (rainwater in the house to remain in the house). These slogans are now a part of the vocabulary of thousands of farmers, school children, young and the old alike in MP. Since March 2001 through the *Pani Roko* (PR) campaign, by trapping the raindrops, people have re-engineered the hydrology of groundwater recharge and surface water harvesting technology all by do it yourself (DIY) methods.

Hydrology is concerned with the study of water in the air, lakes and streams or below the ground and its interactions with landforms, minerals and the biosphere. Although the people of MP have not followed this approach to hydrology, they have however shown their native wisdom in making hydrology more as an art and culture than a science. A total of 7,06,334 rainwater harvesting structures in five months in nearly 51,000 villages of the state is a record by any construction engineering standards. Figures are mind boggling: 11,690 new tanks, 16,213 old tanks repaired, 14,385 new dugwells, 79,671 dugwells renovated, 1,14,035 dugwells and 50,698 tubewells recharged, 1,70,777 soak pits made, 9,744 rooftop rain water harvesting structures created and 32,403 farm ponds constructed. Before the PR was launched, the Rajiv Gandhi Watershed Mission had initiated the watershed in just around 7,000 villages and it was more of a project approach for water conservation. But the PR turned it around to make it a sort of time bound mission fired and propelled by the farmers and the rural and urban folks of the state. PR thus moved watershed activities from a technocratic project to people's movement.

I was not convinced while glancing at the statistics on water harvesting structures and the amount spent and mobilised by the people and widely circulated by the department of water resources and Rajiv Gandhi Missions. According to MP government, out of Rs. 415 crore spent on *Pani Roko* campaign, Rs. 99.35 crore were mobilised by the people. Government pooled for this campaign, funds of drought relief, watershed, Employment Assurance Scheme, *Jawahar Gram Swarozgar Yojana,* (JGSY) state finance commission award funds, 10th and 11th finance commission award funds, and Department for International Development (DFID) funds through UNICCF. At the state level, such a pooling appears easy but when it reaches the district, block and the village level, "pooling" turns into "leaking" and we want to know how the pooled resources have reached the grassroots. Knowing the MP hinterland fairly well, I left on a field trip from August 16 to 26, 2001 to the three randomly selected districts by me viz. Mandsaur and Ujjain in the Malwa belt known for the worst type of groundwater depletion and Sagar in the Bundelkhand region known for lawless and gun wielding farmers who never believed in community participation. What follows in this note is the analysis of what happened when villagers, farmers, school children, women and ordinary folks responded and reacted and partIcipated in the people's movement for rainwater conservation cutting across barriers of caste, class and creed.

Baloda Lakkha - People as Checkdams

It was a cloudy morning when I reached Baloda Lakkha in Ujjain - a small village of 4,000 people and 200 households with several hectares of soyabean and maize sown in between. The first water tank to greet me on the outskirts of the village was Mukti Sagar, named so because on the bank of the tank is the village cremation ground and the tank is supposed to provide *mukti* to the departed! Kishore Singh Chauhan of the village proudly says that the tank was dry for several years and as part of PR, villagers desilted and removed 100 tractor loads of silt which was put on the banks and the rest was given to farmers free of charge. People willingly brought tractors for removing the silt. The relatives of those cremated are now paying Rs. 100 to the tank management body. Similarly four tanks were restored in this village and named as Ganga Sagar, Mataji Talab, Krishi Sagar, Shanti Sagar. The naming of these *talabs* in different parts of Indian villages is linked to village history, traditions, culture and anthropology of that particular village. *Sagar, Sarovar* and *Sar* are the suffixes of tanks. *Sar* is a Sanskrit word and *Saras* is a cultural trait of all village tanks and in many parts of India tanks are also named both as she/he like *Johad* and *Johadi* or *Bandh* / *Bandhia* or *Tal/Tallaiya.*

A small village like Baloda Lakkha has built 75 structures of all types - farm ponds, village tanks, run off management structures, *nala* checkdams and rooftop water traps, etc. The green flags were fixed on all these 75 structures and the heli-hopping chief minister was asked to make a helicopter survey to convince himself! I was taken on a transact walk and Bhagwansingh explained to me the various stone masonry works done by them while building a checkdam over a fast flowing *nala.* He showed me first the head wall, then the top wall and the key wall and then the apron - all structures to check the speed of water and subsequent soil loss. These cascading structures are in a way re-engineered based on the local wisdom and not on civil contractor's blueprints. The whole village approach road of three km is lined with *neem* saplings and according to Kishore Singh Chavan, this village would help the MP to emerge as a *"neem* state". When I asked why *neem* prompt came the reply that cattle will not graze them! The villagers have already used *neem* manure as pesticide. When I showed interest to see the roofwater trapping, I was taken to a small family where the water flowing from zinc sheet roof of the house was collected inside the house and through the funnel stitched from a fertiliser bag, water was made to enter the tubewell which had dried up earlier. By trapping this rainwater, he showed how the dry tubewell was recharged. When I asked him the proof of recharge I was promptly informed that the pump is on for two-three hours and the water comes out! Earlier the pump could not be kept on for more than half an hour.

Narayan Singh is the owner of 250 tubewells in nearly 1,000 *bighas* of black soil sown with soyabean. Only three pumps were operational and the rest had all dried up. Thus the groundwater regulation in Malwa was conspicuous by its absence. His field touches the big *nala* where as a result of checkdams, water was stored like a stagnant river. He had also dug some open wells which were all dry earlier. To capture the seepage water of the *nala,* he laid underground pipes to connect his dried open well. When I asked him the proof of recharge, he took me to his open well and showed the water dripping from all the four sides of the well! While walking through the field *bunds,* an elderly farmer stopped me and showed me the *"mitrakeet"* or the friendly worms coming out from the field to show that the water level is coming up. In Malwi dialect they are called *"Telan".* This incidently helped me to know the proof of water recharge.

The most interesting part of this *PR* campaign in this village is the gesture of the employees of the state agriculture department to restore an abandoned tank in the village with their own financial contribution of Rs. 40,000 and thus lending support to water solidarity of the people of the village. Different state departments played the nodal agency role in different blocks and villages in the state and in Baloda Lakkha, the SDO of agriculture department played a key role in the campaign and this was conspicuous by the way in which farmers talked about providing three and four waterings to the summer crops and taking more cash crops in the summer. The village has also uniquely adopted the NADEP compost pits as part of the PR - another proof of the agriculture department's influence. The inventor of NADEP, Pandharipande popularly called as NADEP *Kaka* has recently complimented MP in popularising his branded compost pits. The back-breaking journey started when I was made to mount a tractor to see another huge checkdam built to store 10,000 cubic feet of water. There was land dispute in building this checkdam and villagers resolved to forgo their rights on the land to build this checkdam which is now providing perennial water in the recharged wells in the lower reaches. In Baloda lakkha farmers kept asserting that "people are the checkdams" and not the cement structures and it looked as though they are rewriting theories on water conservation and recharge.

Tank Restoration - A Divine Intervention

The Mandsaur district is known for poppy crop, soyabean and oranges and the groundwater level in the district had reached its lowest levels of 100' and down below because of indiscriminate rigging of borewells. A crowd of villagers welcomed me on the bank of the river Shivana which is now cleaned to propitiate Lord Pashupatinath. The district *panchayat* booklet on PR reels out impressive statistics on hundreds of structures created across the length and breadth of the district! (old wells recharged 1,877; farm ponds built 3,447, handpumps recharged 1,412; tubewells recharged 227; field channels to trap rainwater 1,90,465; restoration of old tanks 166; new tanks built 23; five stop dams and the total people's contribution Rs. 272.31 lakh). People contribute not out of patriotism as in a war but out of the felt need for oneself or for the villagers. Water is the greatest need for everybody. The story of Ristal *talab,* in Ristal village of Seetamaoo *tahsil* of Mandsaur district, which was abandoned and silted for nearly 1,400 years, is fascinating. Sentiments ran high when the collector went to the village as part of PR campaign. Hari Singh Shaktawat donated Rs. 50,000 to start desilting the 1,400 year old Ristal *talab* about which a reference is made in the stone carvings of the district museum. Some farmers who were loosing land due to submergence voluntarily surrendered their land rights. These farmers resolved that if water is recharged then the loss of land would be compensated by increased value added crops like vegetables and fruits. The farmers showed their sense of cost - benefit analysis as well.

In our rural culture, building tanks is linked to divine salvation. Anupam Mishra (Gandhi Peace Foundation, New Delhi) narrates countless incidents from all parts of the country where kings and queens were great builders of tanks and ponds and river checkdams to store and impound water. In Lakhisarai region of Bihar, one queen was fond of taking bath every day in different tanks and the king built 365 tanks in one stroke to fulfill her bathing wish. Even today everywhere the tanks have been able to keep the groundwater level high. The PR campaign gave vent to the unfulfilled desire of many villagers to show their divine cravings by building tanks. The members of parliament and legislative assembly in Mandsaur did not lag behind in donating from their constituency development funds as their contribution to tank works.

Shivana river is an interstate river which provides water to both Rajasthan and Mandsaur villages and on a stretch of 15 km, 16 new stopdams have been built with the contribution of villagers on both sides and providing irrigation to about 506 ha. The water is impounded magnificently and the Rajasthan villagers have enough electricity to lift the water to the upper reaches of their fields. The farmers in Mandsaur side have acute power shortage and despite multiple electric and diesel pumps, the farmers of Mandsaur are not sure of lifting this impounded water in the coming summer L.K. Joshi, principle secretary of department of water resources of MP government says that the whole idea of impounding water in the dried rivers is not to encourage lift irrigation, but to recharge the river side open wells or borewells. When the summer comes, there may be clashes between Rajasthan and Mandsaur villagers for lift irrigation possibilities. One farmer echoed the fears when he said, "We have helped to impound water but the villagers of the Rajasthan side are getting the benefits of lifting water since they have no power shortage." This is going to be an important policy choice - whether we want only recharging through impounding or we should encourage lift irrigation societies to harvest impounded water.

Bhanpur ard Gharot blocks in Mandsaur have a different PH experience to share. The most articulate PR campaigner is Subhas Sojatia, MP minister for public relations and Nivesh Tiwari, member of Mandsaur district planning committee. When I reached Navali, a small village with its own *panchayat* I was struck by the earthern *bund* of the tank and Tiwari was quick to relate his re-engineering knowledge of stone pitching the earthen embankment. He was proud to inform the cement like qualities of Navali soil and the villagers decided to make earthen *bund* rather than stone *bund.* Navali village *panchayat* took the lead in this restoration work. Out of the total cost of Rs. 5.13 lakh incurred on the tank, the *panchayat* spent Rs. 0.58 lakh and another Rs. 0.5 lakh was spent from the MLA's constituency fund. The Navali villagers were not interested in lift irrigation of nearly 24,000 cubic feet of water, but in recharge of the downfield wells The land prices have already shot up and the farmers are unwilling to sell their lands at any rate. Oranges are now the choice of crops because of good subsoil water. Tiwari has a grand vision for all the tanks built and restored in Bhanpur-Gharot belt of Mandsaur.

Machhali Palo

To protect the water tanks, the best way would be to encourage co-operative fishing in these tanks because the fishing activities would keep away the farmers lifting water and provide the fishing families income source.

The nearby Gandhi Sagar has already provided livelihood opportunities from fishing and its famous *Katha* fish is exported to Kolkata and Chennai. Along with *Pani Roko* we have to start what he called *Machhali Palo Abhiyan* (Fisheries Missions) in all the water bodies of the state. Unfortunately the Fisheries Mission in MP has not clicked and now is the chance to revive it with revised strategy of forming co-operatives in all major tanks of 10 ha and above and the *panchayats* should be authorised to auction the fishing rights every year to the fishing co-operative federation of the district. These fishing activities would create a chain of employment opportunities in inland fishing, cold storage activities and transportation.

Kunal Sagar in Osran near Bhanpura is a legendary tank in itself. The tank has a storage capacity of 72 lakh cubic feet of water and a length of 360 metres and water depth of eight metres and has cost only Rs. Four lakh. After Gandhi Sagar, many tanks are now named after Indira Gandhi and Rajeev Gandhi in Hamirgarh. I left Mandsaur with full of stories of people treating water with divine love and tales of people trying to reach heaven by preserving water on the earth. The Dharma Guru Swami Satya Mitranand Swamiji in Mhow near Indore took up the tank work costing Rs. three lakh in Nanded village near Mhow and called it Satya Mitra Sagar. Why can't Viswa Hindu Parishad take a clue from this Swamiji and build or renovate all tanks in UP instead of wasting scarce resources on Ram temple?

Trapping Raindrops in Towns

What about the urban folk and their efforts to trap raindrops? Dewas town has some interesting rooftop water harvesting stories. Dewas district has witnessed phenomenal increase in tubewells from 3,887 in 1990 to 14,172 in 1998. The industrial units and individual households drilled new boreholes from 350 to 1,486 in the same period. The public health engineering department (PHED) of the state drilled tubewells in the district, from 2,338 to 5,416. No wonder, the central groundwater board, government of India has identified Dewas district as one of the 71 districts in 12 states as the fastest groundwater depleting pockets in the country. On April 25, 1990 a train with 50 water tankers of Narmada river reached Dewas from Indore and was welcomed with music and the local minister as a guest of honour. Every day these tankers are paid Rs. 40,000 as rail charges. Anupam Mishra says that if we add the pumping charges of these tankers, the cost of water in Dewas would be higher than milk. Hence the district collector Mohan Rao campaigned for the Dewas city water harvesting along with the rural water harvesting. The Dewas rooftop water harvesting filters developed by the collector and his team are now famous and 1,000 such filters have been installed. The Dewas municipal authorities are now insisting upon the assurance of installing rooftop water harvesting filters before approving building plans to new buildings. If rooftop water harvesting is patented, it can be sold to several urban dwellers in all cities of MP. Why this has not been patented and taken up on a bigger scale by a smart entrepreneur is still not clear.

Sagar into *Mahasagar*

Mandsaur to Dewas and then when I moved on to Sagar in Bundelkhand, I had already covered a distance of 2,000 km in the hinterland of MP and saw a scenic panorama of water tanks filled everywhere. The rains of July-August 2001 were almost sure to show the farmers and villagers that whatever earth digging they did was rewarded in terms of rain trapped in all these structures and the efforts were not in vain. The collector of Sagar, SR Naidu with his rustic *kisan* looks reels out figures of water bodies created in his district as part of PR campaign. Virtually each of 753 *panchayats* in Sagar district has dug a pond (1,235) turning into reality the slogan of *Ek Panch Ek Talab* given by the chief campaigner Digvijay Singh, chief minister, MP. Out of 1,235 tanks constructed, 891 are constructed on government land while 343 have been constructed on private land creating water holding capacity of 590,60,572 cubic metres

The Rajiv Gandhi Watershed Mission has a manual of Dos and Don'ts in constructing several structures on the ground as part of PR campaign. Sagar district trained thousands of *Jal Sainiks* and the rule of thumb was ponds should be constructed in such a manner that it should have greater depth and lesser surface area. Naidu sent out more than 1.5 lakh letters and appeals to students, farmers, young and the old alike to join the PR *abhiyan*. A unique method was created by the collector to get people's contribution for desilting Sagar lake, one of the biggest urban water bodies in the state. The rates for digging and desilting by earthmoving equipments was done in consultation with earthmovers based on per hour cost at the rate of Rs. 12,000 per 400 cubic metres. Those who are old but rich enough to pay opted for this option and paid the earthmover to desilt the portion of their paying capacity. By this process, the state administration was not involved in receiving cash and paying to the earthmover and the cash donation by the donors got instant results.

The state is the nodal agency for installing UNICEF patented India Mark-II handpumps in the state and as many as 2.50 lakh handpumps have been installed in the state in the last decade. In the wake of continuous groundwater depletion, majority of these pumps had lost their capacity to draw water and Sagar district had designed a colour coded system of indicating handpumps which can pump water for some months of the year with yellow, green where it can pump the whole year and red which is dead. The SDO of Sagar says now all these colours would have to be repainted with green, thanks to the PR campaign. PHED is always reluctant to hand over the maintenance of these handpumps to the village *panchayats*. The state government is oscillating between entrusting and not entrusting the maintenance to the village *panchayats*. PR campaign has proved that *panchayats* can maintain all structures of water bodies including handpumps, the state can thus at best hand over all the maintenance of handpumps once for all.

The India Mark-II handpumps installed in the villages of MP have been provided just a round platform to keep the buckets or utensils for storing water but the drained and spilled water created enormous sludge and in some places they turned out to be mosquitoe breeding places. This drained water is now trapped into cattle troughs in Sagar through as many as 3,549 cattle troughs. I saw in several villages of Sagar, cattle enjoying drinking water from these cattle troughs which have been built by *panchayats* roughly at a cost.of Rs. 2,500 each. What the PHED could not do in 25 years of its stewardship of rural water supply programme, the *panchayats* did it in few months of the PR campaign. When the cattle troughs are overfilled, the excess water of the handpump is again recharged by digging one metre trench around the handpump platform so that the excess water is recycled back into the water aquifer of the handpump. This again is re-engineering the India Mark - II handpumps by the villagers to protect the drinking needs of the cattle and the humans alike.

Need a *Pani Roko* Authority

The biggest outcome of the PR campaign is the hope of assured drinking water to the four lakh people of Sagar city. At present, the city supplies tap water once in four or five days. The drinking water requirement of Sagar city is 63 MLD but due to the non-availability of storage capacity, it is getting only 10 MLD against the established capacity of 13.5 MLD. The project to supply drinking water from Bebus river near the city was prepared in 1988 at a cost of Rs. 3,709 lakh by the PHED but was never implemented. In 1994, the project cost was revised to Rs. 6,763 lakh and the city municipal body was given the task of implementing this huge project without the technical capacity to do so. As part of the PR campaign, the collector mobilised both the funds and the technical expertise from HUDCO and PHED. 718.40 ha of private land was to be submerged in the proposed dam structure and the farmers were persuaded to accept *charnoi* (grazing) land in exchange for the submerged land instead of cash compensation under the ubiquitous Land Acquisition Act of 1894. This led to the speedier construction of the dam on Bebus river to a level of 516 metres and has been successful in holding sorne rainwater in this monsoon. Why is this not done in the normal course by the collectors is still a mystery for the public and for the members of the Indian Administrative Service. Who has stopped them from doing good work for the people? We do not need a disaster or a calamity or a campaign to do such development works.

The above snapshot field trip to see the various structures of rainwater harvesting created in some pockets of MP and listening to the people on how they responded to the water crisis, brings into sharp focus some pointers for evolving Water Resources Policy in the state:

- Re-engineering by people based on their traditional wisdom of the area and the various structures built for water harvesting, are far more cost effective and efficient than structures created by the irrigation bureaucracy based on the engineering skill of contractors. Water is a great leveler of people of all castes and creeds and people can face the crisis if the state and the local institutions of all types join the movement for water trapping as they showed in PR campaign.
- *Panchayats,* local water users, politicians and the pooled resources of the schemes of the state and the centre can collectively help the water conservation in both the urban and the rural areas than those water harvesting schemes which are executed in isolation or as stand alone schemes by the district collectors or the *zilla panchayats.*
- MP has at present no effective groundwater regulation. The state has to decide the policy options like groundwater recharge vis-a-vis lifting water through pumping, impounding flow water for recharging the aquifer or allow the owners of adjoining fields to tap the flowing water, community ownership of water resources vis-a-vis individual ownership through dugwells and tubewells. All options have their own costs, benefits and outcomes. In the country as a whole, the share of tanks in total irrigation has declined from 18.5 per cent in 1960-61 to about seven per cent in 1990-91. All these

water holding structures including tanks are in majority of villages. Wherever command areas under tank beds have been using the impounded tank water, the tank performance has been badly affected. The tank performance concept has generally been used to assess the actual area irrigated by the tank to the total command area.

- This concept is not useful if we want to promote recharging groundwater under the command area of the tanks in MP. In many parts of Tamil Nadu, the excessive growth of wells has contributed to the decline in the real performance of tanks. Comparing the performance of tanks without accounting for the impact of the wells would be misleading. If we want the tanks restored and renovated and built in MP as part of *Pani Roko* campaign wells are to be used exclusively for recharging the groundwater aquifer in both the command and non-command areas of the tanks, then the policy of the government has to be clear from the beginning and people must be told about it. Recharging is definitely more rewarding for the farmers and the urban dwellers in the long run than using tank water for crop irrigation.
- The village *panchayats* have shown that they can mobilise resources and manpower to restore water bodies in their area and continue to maintain the several structures created in the campaign provided the state entrusts the responsibilities to them by providing resources and technical manpower. Down to Earth (August 15, 2001) reported that it takes anywhere between 10-15 years to stabilise the water impounding and recharging processes to produce any sustainable impact on people and farming. The state water resources department would do well to move beyond PR campaign in the coming years and create sustainable institutional mechanisms through the *panchayats* and *nagarpalikas* (municipal authorities) to keep these renovated water bodies not to fall into disuse again. The present capacity of departments like PHED which looks after the drinking water provisions in the state and the irrigation department which looks after the construction and design, leaves much to be desired. The best option would be to

Pani Roko : Structures in Mandsaur District of MP

Development Blocks	*Mandsaur*	*Sithamhavu*	*Mallargad*	*Garota*	*Banpur*	*Total*
Wells recharged	599	428	570	175	105	1877
Pokhar construction	607	1787	726	239	88	3447
Handpump recharged	318	533	167	299	95	1412
Farm ponds	115	53	4	52	3	227
Bore well recharged	61540	115545	2150	8970	2260	190465
People's distribution (in lakhs)	10.74	19.03	7.27	3.90	1.46	42.40
New tanks	07	10	06	-	-	23
Renovation of old tanks	25	44	19	53	25	166
Checkdams	05	-	-	-	-	05
People's contribution (% total expenditure)	51.31	49.02	33.81	43.40	53.37	230.91
Total people's contribution	62.05	68.05	41.08	47.30	54.83	273.31

merge the two departments and create a dynamic agency like the *Pani Roko* authority presided over by the chief minister to oversee the sustainable use of these thousands of *Pani Roko* structures. The MP government spends more money on Narmada Development Authority without much results. The proposed *Pani Roko* authority not only can sustain the momentum created for water harvesting but also contribute to the conservation of water resources.

- There is need for central groundwater board to scientifically assess the rate of recharge that has taken place as a result of these various structures created in the rural and urban areas of the state as part of the PR campaign than just go by the anecdotal and anthropological evidences although they are extremely important for the people at their level.

Top Down

Of the three farm water conservation programmes in 2002 undertaken in Karnataka, the Jal Samvardhana Yojana (JSY) stands a unique. The programme's stated objective is to demonstrate the viability of community based approaches to tank rehabilitation. For this purpose an Integrated Tank Development Plan has been developed for each tank that is to be rehabilitated. These plans have to be prepared by tank user groups (TUG) with the assistance of cluster facilitation teams (CFTs) comprising local non-governmental organisations (NGOs). The programmes also has lofty aims to provide adequate representation to tribals and other vulnerable groups in its areas of operation.

The problem is: after a year, it is amply clear that there is no place for the village *panchayats* in the process. This is typical of all World Bank aided water — projects in Karnataka.

This author made an impromptu visit to one of the areas under JSY: Hangal taluk in Haveri district. Three CFTS comprising three NGOS - Taralabalu Rural Development Foundation (TRDF), Navodaya Educational and Environment Development Service (NEEDS) and Jana Para Vigyan Sansthe - are responsible for mobilising people into forming TUGs. These NGOs are still in the process of rallying people into forming user groups. And this looks to be a tough job.

For one, the village *panchayats* were not involved in the project. Secondly, the landless villagers are unlikely to cooperate unless they see some benefit. On a positive note, however, the TRDF team has been successful in forming women's user groups in Hangal. The women I met exuded excitement at the prospect of making savings once the tanks are revived. Many of them were landless and unlikely to have direct benefits from the revival of the tanks.

Tanks are not just water bodies; they are village institutions around which are attached the sentiments of local people. For example the Kalashnath tank - which the TRDF is trying to revive - is associated in people's mind with the submerged *kalash* (small urn) of a local deity. It is these sentiments that the NGOs have to work upon - reactivate this effective form of social fencing - in order to elicit the cooperation of villagers in resuscitating the tanks.

Then there are obstacles from powerful politicians and rigid technocrats. NEEDS, which is working to rehabilitate the Dashrathkoppa tank, is faced with such impediments. A powerful politician has encroached upon a substantial area of the tank and the users are engagcd in a legal battle to have the encroachment removed.

Second Obstacle

The second obstacle is from the assistant engineer of the JSY in charge of Hangal taluk. He wants the desilting of the tank to be upto its waste weir outlet and not go below to provide the much needed dead storage (the water that is left unused). The tank users told me with one voice that the dead storage would be enormously beneficial in recharging the dricd wells and handpumps in the village. It will also help the villagers to farm fish. Water stored upto the waste weir, on the other hand, will only help agriculture of the tank beneficiaries. The latest instructions of this assistant engineer to all tank users in Haveri is to allow dead storage up to 10 per cent of the tank's—capacity. Why 10 per cent and not the entire area is, however, left unexplained.

The assistant engineer's attitude is typical of the minor irrigation bureaucracy in Karnataka. It has always thought its engineering skills to be superior to the traditiona wisdom of the villagers. They never maintained the sluice gates and did not provide any support to the villagers. And now, their attitude has held up the rehabilitation of the Dashrathkoppa tank. Consequently disillusionment with the JSY is setting in among the villagers. The tank users committee (TUC) does not want to approach the legislative assembly members and ministers since they feel that "tank water is beyond politics". But the TUCs have not been mandated to draw on the resources of the *panchayats* - human and financial. What will happen when the NGOs withdraw and the TUCs have to "stand alone"? Who will maintain the tank structures, sluice gates and silt clearance works etc?

It is unfortunate that despite the 73rd Constitutional amendments Schedule I and the Karnataka Panchayat Raj Act 1993, Section 58 (VIII) - which specifically entrusts the construction, repairs and maintenance of drinking water wells, tanks and ponds to panchayats - JSY excluded village *panchayats* right from the beginning by forming TUGs and TUCs. Even the NGOs think that the *panchayats* are corrupt and politicised. There is no use asking these local bodies to maintain these tanks after the project period since they were never involved in the planning stage.

We moved on to Byagawadi village in Hangal taluk where the Jana Para Vigyan Sansthe is the CFT. On reaching the village we were delighted to see almost the entire village around the tank. Fresh desilted soil was being taken out in a tractor for distribution to farmers at a nominal fee of Rs. 30 per trailer load. But, because of the drought, villagers were reluctant to pay even this small amount. Mahadevappa Bullaannavar, the chairman of the TUC of Byagawadi, showed me written instructions of the assistant engineer to not go in for dead storage in this tank. Again the villagers repeated the same arguments of good water recharge in the village tubewells and open wells if this dead storage is achieved. Traditional wisdom has always showed the way in water conservation either through tanks, or water harvesting structures or field bunding. In the worst drought of 2000-2002, Madhya Pradesh was able to withstand water scarcity in farming by farmers re-engineering the hydrology of groundwater recharge and surface water harvesting technology. The figures were mindboggling. In the entire state 11,690 new tanks were built 16,213 old tanks desilted 14,385 wells dug and 17,671 wells renovated. All this without World Bank assistance!

After the visit was over, it became clear to me that the Jal Savardhan Yojana should get rid of the false mantle of technocratic superiority and engineering knowledge and skills it wears, and allow TUCS to find the best local solutions from its stakeholders. The Karnataka Irrigation Act of 1965 does not envisage any role for the *panchayats.* It is time the TUGs and TUCs are linked right in the planning stage with the concerned village *panchayats* so that they all work together. Their combined force would have a powerful effect on water conservation activities of the village. NGOs that work as CFTs *must facilitate* this *leveraging* work with the village *panchayats* right in the beginning.

Lessons

What are the lessons to be learnt after an year of JSY's operations? The major lesson is to leverage with the resources and the legal powers of the village *panchayats* and link the TUCs and the TUGs with the village *panellayat* sub-commitee on water and sanitation. In the words of Lennart Nilsson, advisor of the DANIDA water and sanitation project in Tamil Nadu, "India is fortunate to have a *Panchayat raj* system which provides a sound and democratic basis for development at the local level. But its potential to provide amenities in rural areas is largely untapped." In a similar spirit, the JSY should therefore rope in the village *panchayats* into the tank rehabilitation project.

Then there are questions related to the sustainability of the tanks and their maintenance. To ensure this, all the waterbodies of the village, and handpumps, should be maintained by the village *panchayat.* They have to levy water charges, user charges, and all other statutory levies, recover costs and invest them back for the well being of the villagers. This is what makes good governance possible. How long would the NGOs guide the TUCs and the TUGs. Why not involve the village *panchayats* right from the beginning.

Finally, the irrigation bureaucracy should work under the leadership of the village *panchayats.* Their role should be to render technical advice to the panchayat sub-committee on water and sanitation.The Amul experiment in India has shown that the so-called illiterate farmers are willing to accept technical advice only if it helps them, and not otherwise. Tanks are not just waterbodies but are living and vital village institutions where politics, economics, culture and caste are all mixed up. They are just not cold engineering structures to be used for water storage and distribution. The sooner we understand this, the better is for our bureaucracy.

References

1. Wilby, Robert L. (1997), Contemporary Hydrology, John Willy, New York.
2. Rajiv Gandhi Watershed Management Mission, *Pano Roko* Abhiyan, 2001. Government of MP, Bhopal.
3. See for an interesting account of Tanks in North India, Anupam Mishra, *Aaj bhi Khare Hain Talab* (in Hindi), Gandhi Peace Foundation, New Delhi and reprinted by MP Directorate of Public Relations, Bhopal, July 2001.
4. Wastelands News, May-July 2001, SPWD, New Delhi.
5. Palanisami K. & RB Balasubramaniam, July 2001. “Reconciling the Private Well with the Community Tank” in Making Water Everybody’s Business, Centre for Science and Environment, New Delhi, p. 309

6

Civil society and the Private sector

Selling Success

It was Saturday 5 PM in a primary school compound of Gadag town. Hundreds of women, all members of self help groups (SHGs) from different villages of Gadag district, had set up their stalls comprising eco-friendly vegetables, condiments, all types of powdered chutneys, crisp *jawar-ragi-sajji rottis* and papads, and fast food items. It was the usual Saturday bazaar at Gadag, meant exclusively for the SHG women of Gadag district. Jayashree Benni from Harti Village has been participating in this bazaar for the last 18 months and she has now become market savvy, selling all types of *rottis.* When I asked her whether she could sell *rottis* to me at Bangalore she promptly nodded to indicate 'yes' and pulled out her visiting card indicating her telephone number at Harti village. She asked me to place my order on the phone! She has already supplied her special rottis to many customers in Bangalore. The Saturday bazaar at Gadag is now a niche market where hoteliers make bulk purchases of her *rottis,* and special powdered chutneys and pickles. Her average income from these sales is around Rs. 2000-3000 per month.

The Saturday bazaar is organised by K H Patti Krishi Vigyan Kendra (KHPKVK) in Hulkoti, Gadag district. In the last one and half years, the bazaar has caught the attention of the people of Gadag town. Many homemakers I interviewed revealed that every

Saturday they stock up fresh rottis, vegetables and powders of all types. The average sales are around Rs. 20,000 on a single day and as many as 100 women members of SHGs bring their organic products for sale in this bazaar.

There are 301 villages in Gadag district, out of which KHPKVK has organised 1,233 SHGs in 93 villages covering 13,933 members in Gadag taluk alone. Out of these 1,233 SHGs, 1110 are crop based groups, 83 animal based and the rest belong to other product enterprises. There is a constant effort by KHPKVK to add quality and value to the wonderful work they have undertaken. For instance, by preparing masala chilli powder, the returns per hectare of the SHG members have gone up from Rs. 650 to Rs.1350.

Gadag District is a drought prone area, and most of crops are dry land crops. As many as 900 SHGs are centered around crops like chilli, groundnut, Bengal gram, and the rest around sericulture, vermiculture, sheep, poultry, goat and bakery items. The SHGs members have been trained in all aspects of vegetable crop production, including supply of quality seeds and technology advice and links with Banks for production loans.

Thus because of both forward and backward linkages they have emerged as economically viable enterprises. A total of 240 SHGs with 3232 members have been linked with various financial institutions for availing Rs 170.47 lakhs of credit.

The Saturday bazaar is just one instance to show how self-help groups in Gadag are emerging as model groups, with village women turning fully market savvy.

The retail traders and vegetable vendors of Gadag Town fought a vain battle against the SHG members because these women had made inroads into their business and posed a major threat to these traders and vendors. In the initial stages, these women were threatened by wholesale and retail vegetable merchants with dire consequences if they continued to sell their products.

In a consumer survey conducted by KHPKVK many consumers felt that the food stuff sold by these women were not only fresh but are also on par with the retail prices prevailing in Gadag town. Most of the buyers are homemakers and they feel at home, buying from these SHG women. Over the months, the SHG women in this Saturday bazaar have established a sort of "relationship marketing".

SHGs in Gadag are emerging as model groups because they are getting triple bottom line strength — sound credit, production and marketing. In many parts of Karnataka SHGs or Stree Shakti groups have remained mostly as thrift and savings groups, and even when they are engaged in production activities, for want of marketing support they soon fold up.

Credit and thrift alone cannot sustain these SHGs. They have to function as enterprise units, which alone can lift the SHG women from poverty. The SHGs in Gadag have these market virtues to offer.

Right to Defecate

Ashok Vihar jhuggi dwellers in Delhi had converged on the north-west district police commissioner's office and protested against the ban on their right to defecate in the open These jhuggi dwellers have no other place to defecate except the space around the park surrounding the DDA colonies. The stench for those living in the DDA flats adjoining the park prompted them to complain to the DDA which constructed a 1-km long wall to keep them away. However, the wall was breached a number of times over the months. The police were called, some arrests were made but to no avail. The problem persisted and ultimately the residents went to the court which ruled that the jhuggi dwellers be prevented from defecating in the open. "Where should we defecate? Nobody is interested to answer this question. Courts cannot unfortunately adjudicate on where to defecate. Courts can at best stop them for a day. But next morning they have to answer the call of nature somewhere in some space ! There cannot be any contempt of court if the ban orders of the court are disobeyed." This is just not an environmental problem but a biological and physical problem too and it is unfortunate that no serious efforts are made by the policy makers to address these environmental sanitation issues. The agony of Ashok Vihar jhuggi dwellers is just a symbolic manifestation of the acute problem of environmental sanitation in the country.

Hundreds of men, women and children in the country keep defecating in the open - all along the highways, railway lines, airport routes, open grounds/spaces. Women are the worst sufferers. They have to wait all the time to defecate either after sunset or before sunrise. In the villages during the rains the situation gets worse. When crops are standing and fields are muddy, people come out to defecate on the road side. Women getting up when vehicles pass is a familiar sight in the countryside. Once, when Prince Charles visited Madhya Pradesh, he was escorted by a young collector and by the time he reached his rest house it was dark. All along the route he saw women getting up when his car passed through. He asked the collector why they were getting up. The collector replied, "Sir, they were all waiting to see you since morning and when they saw your car they got up to get a glimpse of you." The Prince replied, "I am so sorry I kept them waiting. Please convey my apologies."

This is how we are fooling others and ourselves. How long do we have to wait to provide a leach pit toilet to every family in the country? The task is daunting and difficult both in rural and urban slums. The total rural population in 1991 census was 627.1 million. Just 10% of the rural families have what are called safe sanitation facilities. This would mean that 112.9 million rural households are yet to be provided with basic sanitation facilities. That means they are defecating out somewhere! Even at a modest cost of Rs. 2500 for a leach pit latrine, which does not need flush of water, but just pour flush, we need a gigantic investment of Rs. 28,255 crores. According to the National Seminar on Rural Sanitation, 16-18 September, 1992, Ministry of Rural Development, Government of India, New Delhi: "If a contribution of 20% of the cost by the beneficiaries is assumed, the investment on the part of the government would be about Rs. 22,580 crore. Such a huge investment will be obviously beyond the means of the centre and state governments in the foreseeable future." Only 250 of the 3500 cities and small towns of India are equipped with adequate drainage facilities. Consequently insanitary conditions prevail. Normal urban toilets require an average of thirty gallons of water, which is just not possible to provide given the acute shortage of even drinking water. How can we, then, solve this problem of human waste disposal?

One relatively inexpensive and effective solution is the marketing of the leach pit or pour flush (PF) toilet technology, which consumes just 1.5 to 2 litres of water. The government of India has popularised these PF latrines but they have not marketed them aggressively. In states like Gujarat with the efforts of the legendary Ishwarbhai Patel who is popularly known as Mr.Toilet, these PF toilets have been aggressively marketed. I am emphasizing the marketing approach because the government building of toilets through contractors involves subsidy to the beneficiary, which mostly ends up on paper and not on the ground. Marketing a PF toilet can be done easily. It is a convenient product and has to be marketed as a user-friendly toilet. If Gujarat can do it why not other states? The most important components of a PF toilet are the trap, the squatting pan, the foot-rest, the leaching pit or the honey-combed pit and the superstructure. In the minds of a poor family, a toilet means a luxury and our public health engineers have kept the PF toilet technology as a mystery. That is why it has to be marketed by a street-smart salesperson. If our jhuggi dwellers can install a colour television, they would definitely love to have their 'own' PF toilets. Mr. Ishwarbhai has built toilets in slums, where one tailor has a PF toilet in the sitting room where he works on his tailoring machine. When he wants to defecate, he puts his tailoring machine a side, completes his shitting and puts back the machine on the top to start the stitching!

Over the last few years many have started manufacturing traps and pans - Gwalior Potteries in Gwalior, Shital Sanitary Sales in Ahmedabad, a ceramic factory in Morvi and a fibre glass factory in Rajasthan and Saniplast in Delhi. The pioneering work done by Ramakrishna Mission in Midnapur in West Bengal for popularising PF latrines is noteworthy. There are many such experiments, but the aggressive marketing is missing in many of these. The main culprit in poor marketing is the state housing agencies. Look at all rural houses built under Indira Awas Yojana. They never planned a leach pit latrine along with the house. They presumed that the poor occupant does not need a toilet and all the Indira Awas Yojana occupants were forced to go out and defecate! Many of these houses are now crumbling and the people are taking out the doors and window frames to make money. Similarly look at our schools and health centres. Urinals and toilets are never designed and provided when they are built.

PF toilets need little masonry skill. We do not need architects and engineers to build them. In Uttar Pradesh, Haryana, West Bengal, Madhya Pradesh, thousands of village *mistris* have heen trained to build PF toilets. Some women *mistris* have also taken up the work of building PF latrines. The best salesmen would be the village mason. In our Indian villages any villager who wants to build a house, repair a house or a cattleshed or a house roof, the first to be called is the village mason.

Any company interested in the toilet business can appoint these village masons as their sales force. The business can fetch high returns since only systematic marketing can sell good sanitation practices and not government sponsored latrine programmes. Unfortunately private entrepreneurs are not getting into the business on a big scale. It is high time sanitation business gets the attention of young entrepreneurs and village youth.

Several experiments in social and community forestry in India have focussed attention broadly (a) on involving school children in programmes for raising nurseries and planting saplings in school compounds (b) in raising plantations on government waste land with the help of villagers and (c) in raising consciousness of villagers for the protection and care of trees.

Taralabalu Seedlings (TS) is a social forestry project of Taralabalu Rural Development Foundation (TRDF)-a development wing of Taralabalu Brihanmath, Sirigre, in Chitradurga district of Karnataka. The math is managing a conglomerate of 157 primary schools, high schools, residential schools, free student hostels, an engineering college, spread over in different rural areas of Karnataka. Some of these schools are more than 50 years old. This conglomerate has a total student and teacher population of 20,000 and 2,000, respectively. The schools and colleges together own more than 15,000 acres of land used mostly as school gardens playgrounds and some kept as vacant strips. In addition the then maharaja of Mysore granted nearly 1000 acres of degraded forest land to grow fuelwood to feed the free kitchens run in 25 hostels catering to the food needs of 10,000 students, irrespective caste and creed.

These schools were established to respond to the felt need of villagers to get their children educated and as such many villagers offered land and cash donations to build them. The Brihanmath played a catalytic role under the dynamic leadership of the older Shivakumar Swamiji in transforming the villagers' response into a movement for rural education in Karnataka. The Brihanmath and TRDF is now headed by Shivamurthy Mahaswamiji - a post doctoral fellow in indology from the University of Vienna - and the motive force behind many development initiatives of TRDF.

These schools and institutions together constitute a "development resource" for social action. The Taralabalu Seedlings project was launched in early 1985 with the help of Society for Promotion of Westeland Development, New Delhi, and the social forestry department of the government of Karnataka. The objective were (a) to raise experimental nurseries in 60 schools involving school children and teachers and impart technical knowledge to children on seed selection, seedling production, germination, polybag care, transplanting saplings in home gardens and distributing saplings to farmers for care, protection and growth in their farm land (b) to take up scientific afforestation of degraded forest species. This involved surveying the land, preparing contour maps, trenching, surveying the present vegetative growth of degraded species, assessing rain and moisture conservation in the land - all involving students, teachers and villagers. (c) To develop five village gomal (pasture) lands by TRDF by involving deprived families of the village where gomal lands are located (d) To initiate a movement by the Brihanmath in social forestry by providing "fruit seed" packets to devotees who come to the math for the blessings.

In the current monsoon nearly seven lakh saplings were raised and distributed to farmers and school children for planting. However, the months March-June were found unsuitable for proper care because of holidays in May. The ideal months to plant seedling were found to be October-April, so that saplings would be fairly developed to withstands summer of May and the survival rate in polybags would be higher. The important issues is that saplings should survive in polybags and the learning value that accrues to students should be high.

Seed collection was done by craft teachers but in some schools the percentage of germination was poor and in some excellent, reflecting the efficiency of craft teachers. The Swedforest handbook on "village nurseries" was extensively used to teach students and craft teachers the various aspects of nursery raising. While the educational aspects of nursery raising is progressing well, the survival rate of saplings distributed to farmers is causing worry. How many saplings and what type are to be raised by each school? How many months or years do saplings have to be kept in the schools before distribution to school children and villagers? These are the questions to which firm answers are not available as yet. Side by side Kissan nurseries are also developed by the social forestry department of Kamataka and the villagers in TS project area have now a choice of taking saplings from Taralabalu schools and Kissan nurseries. Taralabalu saplings have been accepted because school children have raised them and villagers feel like encouraging the school nursery because their children have grown them.

The saplings raised are papaya, bamboo, jamun, custard apple, jack, neem, cassia, casurina, glaricidia etc. The poorest *of* the poor villagers prefer coconuts and cash saplings because they want income saplings and not social saplings. While survival rates of saplings grown in children's homes are better (80% survival) those planted in villagers' field are not surviving well (40% survival). Paradoxically despite fuel wood and fodder shortage in rural Karnataka, landless families do not show any preference for planting fuelwood and fodder in their small courtyards. If the schools have to continue raising saplings every year, then demand and supply of saplings have to balance. While supply can increase demand cannot increase quickly. Assuming that every year Taralabalu school children plant a few saplings in their homes and the entire vacant land of the school is also covered in a few years, and assuming most of the villagers also plant Taralabalu,saplings, then in the next five years the other problem would be one of protection of saplings planted with production of fresh saplings every year. The schools would have to reduce large-scale production of saplings and set up instead, school Herbariums for understanding plants and their botanical characteristics and the ecological balance of land and plants.

The implications are clear. What begins as a social forestry programme, will gradually become non-social once supply of saplings outstrip demand and raising saplings every year would be counter-productive. All those who plan massive nursery raising programme through schools would do well to remember the demand problem for the school saplings and accordingly switch over from fuelwood and fodder species to cash species like tomatoes, pulses and nuts. These have high consumption/nutritive/ price value. Social forestry, through schools, has to become, therefore, at some stage, a profitable forestry if it is to sustain itself and not just remain social. Thus there has to be trade off between social and profitable forestry as far as schools are concerned.

TRDF efforts in developing degraded forests alloted to it by the government have brought out a few interesting issues. The government claims that NREP and RLEGP works could be taken up on forest lands so as to generate employment through trenching and planting activities.

Tree pattas could also be given to landless families to enjoy the usefruct. In 1985 the TRDF aproached the DRDA project authorities of Chitradurga district in Karnataka, and pleaded with them to take up RLEGP works in TRDF land. TRDF even requested the DRDA not to hand over cash to TRDF but entrust only supervision work and hand over the responsibility of wage payment to the concerned BDO. In 1986 TRDF again made a request for taking up RLEGP works in TRDF land. The BDO said when RLEGP works are sanctioned in the area, preference would be given to take up works in TRDF land. In reality nothing came of these requests. TRDF is the biggest NGO in Karnataka, in terms of its infrastructure and land resources, and mobilised 1000 students and voluntary labour to dig trenches and plant saplings. An area of 100 acres has been brought under plantations in the monsoon of 1987. The contour mapping was done by the faculty of Taralabalu Engineering College. Two implications emerge. While students can be involved in trenching and planting, the time spent by them has to be monetised and paid. If rural landless labourers are paid when they work on RLEGP works, why should not students get paid at the same rate or less?

If social forestry has to become social, it must take roots in the minds of the people - boys, girls and adults - and not just in the minds of foresters and bureaucrats. The TRDF experiment would continue in years to come to consolidate its gains in at least 100 villages and provide guidelines for effective management of social forestry programme.

Role of Tanks in Water Conservation

Noted Journalist P Sainath in his book *Everbody Loves a Good Drought* (Penguin, 1996) says, "drought relief is rural India's biggest growth industry. There is little relation between drought and relief. Relief can go to areas/regions that get lots of rainfall. Even where it goes to scarcity areas, those most in need seldom benefit from it. That is why the poor farmers call drought relief teesra fasal - third crop. Only they are not the ones who harvest it!" There are reports from all parts of Karnataka that this year's rainfall is short by 30 per cent and our MLAs are clamouring for more relief works. But farmers are looking for rains, not works.

Over the years, according to the data provided by Indian Meteorological Department, rainfall has not ditched us but we have ditched rainfall by wasting water and by silting and encroaching our tanks and water bodies. Karnataka, with World Bank aid, has now launched Jala Samvardhane Yojana (JSY) to rehabilitate 37,000 tanks in nine districts of the State. The objective is "to demostrate the viability of community based approaches to tank improvements and management by returning the main responsibility of tank development to Tank Users' Group (TUGs) on a select basis. For each Tank and Integrated Tank Development Plan (ITDP) will be prepared by the TUGs with the assistance of Cluster Facilitation Team (CFTs). ITDP is tank specific and contains safeguard mitigation plans (Resettlement Action Plans and Tribal Development Plans)."

The JSY further states that "the project does not involve any major adverse effects particularly physical dislocation of population and new acquisition of land, house and other assets. Similarly, the project recognises the need to evolve adequate representation in decision making to tribal and other vulnerable groups for securing meaningful participation and fair share in the benefits of the project by making safeguard plans."

Dying Wisdom

Rain water harvesting is not just a hydrology and civil engineering work but a mixture of the art, science and culture of conserving rainwater wherever it falls - in the farms, on roof tops, in forests, on roads and mountain tops. Unfortunately, the ancient wisdom of water harvesting is now a "dying wisdom", thanks to World Bank experts advising State governments on rainwater harvesting through their "blue prints".

Karnataka has a long history of tank culture but over the years most of the village tanks have either been silted up or encroached upon. Hirekerur, a Taluk town in Haveri district of the State, was known after the Hire Keri (Big tank) of the town. Its nearly 10,000 hectares of storage space is silted and encroached upon by farmers. Hire Keri of Hirekerur is only one example of the deplorable condition of water bodies in Karnataka.

Krishna Deva Raya, the greatest of Vijayanagar Kings, believed that tank restoration was a divine work. An inscription of 1413 states, "A ruined family, a breached tank or pond, a fallen kingdom, whosoever restores or repairs a damaged temple, acquires a merit four fold of that which accrued from them first". The majority of our temple priests and Veerashaiva Maths have built over the years many institutions of higher learning but have not bothered to take care of the water bodies in their area.

Karnataka had been a forerunner in managing water harvesting structures. Apart from tanks there were a range of traditional water harvesting structures like arakere, volakere, devikere, katte, kutte and kola. Some tanks were named after wives of rulers and deities (Devekere) and others.

Success Story

Bangalore has always depended heavily on lakes and tanks, Kempegowda built tanks like Sampangi tank and Dharmabudhi tank. Sir Lewing Bentham Bowring, Commissioner of Bangalore in 1866, laid out an intricate system of harvesting rain water and very little water was allowd to go waste. A systematic survey of tanks in Bangalore was made in 1985 by the committee headed by N Laxman Rau. Of the 127 tanks in Bangalore city, 46 were classified as defunct and in the words of N Laxman Rau, "Most of the tanks were freely encroached, polluted and silted."

Agencies like BMC and BDA are the biggest enemies of lakes and tanks in Bangalore. Part of the Sampangi tank has been turned into Kanteerava Stadium. Pollution is also killing tanks. The

Domlur tank was polluted by sewerage canal as early as 1875. There are three major valleys - the Challeghatta valley, Hebbal Valley and Vrishibhavati valley - where sewerage is dumped after the so-called treatment.

Karnataka has to go beyond the tunnel vision of the JSY which is more concerned with forming user groups and Tank Development Plans. It has to think about trapping raindrops in farmers fields, on roof tops and in all "spaces" which contribute to the conservation and efficient use of rain water. Madhya Pradesh had the worst drought in 2000 and 2001 when it launched 'Pani Rokho' campaign, a massive social mobilisation, for trapping raindrops in village tanks, farmer's field and roof tops. The slogan was simple: Khet Ka Pani Khat Mein (rain water in the field to remain in the field) Gaon Ka Pani Gaon Mein (rain water in the village to remain in the village) and Ghar Ka Pani Ghar Mein (rainwater in the house to remain in the house).

Thus, Madhya Pradesh was able to re-engineer the hydrology of ground water recharge and surface water harvesting technology all by Do It By Yourself (DIY) methods. The figures were mind boggling. In the whole of the State, 11,690 new tanks were built, 16,213 old tanks desilted, 14,385 wells dug and 79, 671 wells renovated. Again, as many as 50,698 tube wells were recharged, 9,7444 roof top rain water harvesting structures were created and 32,403 farm ponds were constructed.

Today, Madhya Pradesh is able to withstand the shock of drought and missed rainfall.

Demystifying Water Issues

The Jala Samvardhana Yojana (JSY) in Karnataka has to go beyond the World Bank blue print of Tank User Groups, Tank Development Plans, Cluster Facilitation Teams and so on and so forth. Let us face the fact that struggle for water resources in the State operates in many complex ways between villages, between hamlets within a village, between caste and class groups, between lower-end users and upper catchment level users and between owners of ground water recharging bore wells and open wells at different geographical zones. Water is politics and sharing rain water is super politics. JSY is silent on how it will tackle tank encroachments, how it will involve or not involve the village, taluk and zilla panchayats, how it will remove legal hurdles in the complicated ownership of minor and major tanks, the pricing of water for different water users etc.

JSY is also silent on its relationship with Minor Irrigation Department. It is not just a question of spending World Bank money as per their advice. Building sustainable water harvesting policies for the benefit of the people of the State has to be the guiding principle. According to Prof. C H Hanumanth Rao, "As much as 80 per cent of usable water resources in the country are now allocated for irrigation, where water-use-efficiency is very low and this sector offers major avenue for water savings." There is no penalty for those who waste water.

Karnataka has to evolve a long-term water harvesting and recharge policy covering all the districts. JSY has to get out of its tunnel vision of implementing the wishes of the World Bank in the matter of water resources conservation and development. Karnataka has seen enough of World Bank aided projects in health, water and sanitation and unless we involve villagers/farmers and the village panchayats in water harvesting, tank restoration, caring and sharing of water equitably we will continue to depend on "cash" for drought relief.

Encroachment

The following action points are crucial for the State in evolving and implementing a sound water harvesting policy in the days to come: First, the Rural Devlopment and Panchayati Raj Department has to study the legal ownership of all the minor and major tanks in the State and divest them from the ownership of departments of the State. Article 243 G of the Constitution read with 11th schedule provides for devolution of powers with regard to minor irrigation, water management and watershed development.

The Karnataka Irrigation Act 1965 defines "Irrigation work" but does not distinguish a major irrigation work from minor irrigation work (rules define a minor irrigation work). The powers under the Act are exercised by the Irrigation Officer, the Chief Engineer for Irrigation, the Tahsildar, the Deputy Commissioner and finally the State government. No role is envisaged under this Irrigation Act for the panchayats. The gram panchayats are capable of desilting the village tanks but they have to be legally empowered to do so.

This means that encroachments can be removed by the panchayats by law. Our bureaucrats and water engineers are in the habit of mystifying the water issues. Villagers know why tanks are silted and they also know how to desilt them!

Let us empower them to act with guts and authority. In the entire policy documents of JSY there is not a single word on how to involve panchayats in tank restoration work. By using confusing words like 'community ownership', 'community managed', 'user groups' and 'user charges' we are bypassing legally constituted bodies like village panchayats from the domain of managing all village level water bodies and not just tanks.

Re-orientation

Let us not be confused. The message of the 73rd Constitutional amendment is clear - village panchayats shall manage all development works in the village. The tendency of the State to go on forming World Bank aided special societies like Jal Samradhi Yojana Sangha and bypassing the Constitutional bodies like village panchayats has to be stopped. NGOs are roped in to form user groups and mobilise communities and the panchayats remain mere spectators. This would force panchayat members to scuttle all user groups and tank restoration plans of JSY.

Second, taluk panchayats and zilla panchayats can handle bigger water bodies and structures like major check dams cutting across several villages. In the early days we had Soil Conservation Departments which were doing soil conservation work and recovering the conservation charges form the farmers. It is high time such departments are renamed as Water Conservation Departments and the funds are handed over to the panchayats.

Third, the powers and functions of the Irrigation Officers have to be transferred to the respective panchayats at different levels and they should be empowered to price and recover user charges from time to time. Fourth, the chief minister should urgently spearhead a sort of Neeru Nillisi campaign all over the State to drive home the importance of trapping in drops. Fifth, major and minor irrigation departments have to be reoriented to make water harvesting as their mandate and not building concrete structures by inviting "tenders" and keeping people away in the name of accountability.

Finally, in most of the urban areas like Bangalore and other fast growing cities in Karnataka rain water harvesting has to be made mandatory before giving building permission for the new construction. Also state-of-the-art advice on capturing rainwater should be given to the owners of the older buildings. Most of the buildings in Bangalore city are fitted with solar water heating systems and now is the time to propagate rain water harvesting systems as well. Chennai is leading in this effort. The Urban Affairs Department in Karnataka should wake up to the call without any delay.

From Darkness to Light, it's been a Long Way

Covered in darkness till recently, this village in Uttara Kannada district is churning electricity through a simple technique.

It was getting dark in the evening and we had to rush to reach Asolli village in Ankola taluk, Uttara Kannada district. Asolli is a sleepy village in the valley of Western Ghats. Ganesh Shetty of Hill Tribes Development Society in Kuntagani was urging the jeep driver to reach the Pico Hydro power-house before the lights came on. He was keen that we see how the meandering spring water is harnessed to reach the powerhouse, where 3 KW electricity is generated through a hand operated turbine.

A Glow, at Last

Asolli village is a remote hamlet with about ten households and they had never seen an electric bulb till recently. The KEB power never reached that village and for a few houses they could not lay down poles and wire the village and electrify the houses. The villagers were tired of approaching the KEB and had stopped worrying about electricity anymore.

Thanks to Indo Norwegian Environment Programme and the Technology Informatics Design Endeavour (TIDE), villagers of Asolli could see how an electric bulb gives light as they moved into the 21st century. Incidentally, there are many hamlets in Western Ghats which have not seen electricity even today!

Pico Hydro projects convert the energy in the water flowing down a gradient into electrical energy. All that is to be done is to direct the natural stream flowing down from a gradient at higher elevation, pass through a water conducting system and let it into a turbine which drives an electrical generator to produce electricity. It was just getting dark and the two brothers of Asolli village. Venkat Lingegowda and Vidyadhar opened the powerhouse and with a spanner started the turbine and the powerhouse bulb was on.

Then the brothers took me outside the powerhouse to show how the water moves and enters their areca garden and goes down the Western Ghats to join the rivulet.

It was time to listen to their success story. The brothers narrated how they had to bring bricks and cement from Ankola to build the water tank and powerhouse and lay down the underground cables. As per the deal of the Pico Hydro project, the community has to contribute 40 per cent of the cost. The Asolli villagers have spent Rs. 5 lakhs to get this Pico Hydro and they are happy because there is no billing from KEB, no meter, no fuse, no shut down and no power fluctuation!

Just a Switch Away

Whenever they want electricity they put on the turbine switch and when they do not want they put off.

When I asked them whether they could use fans, refrigerators and threshing machines, one of the brothers took me inside their house and showed me the electric iron box they were using to press their clothes!

Pico Hydro technology is aggressively marketed by TIDE Technocrats Pvt Ltd, Bangalore and in the districts falling in the purview of Western Ghats like Dakshina Kannada, parts of Chickmagalur, and Shimoga they have appointed selling agents to promote and get villagers to go in for this eco-friendly hydro power.

Spreading Hope

In 2002 at least 42,221 Small Hydropower Stations (SHPs) were operating in China, supplying adequate power to more than 300 million people. The slogan in China is who invests and who owns, benefits.

Likewise in Asolli village too, the villagers have invested in Pica Hydro project and now are not only owning it but also benefiting from it.

Large hydro projects are costly to operate in a state like Karnataka and these SHPs have to be promoted. In the Western Ghats especially, where many hamlets have not seen electricity as yet, there will be several takers for this project.

Biotech Ventures and Ethics

Writing in the latest issue of The Bulletin of the Institute for Business, Technology and Ethics, USA (March-April 2003) Prof. David W Gill of New College Berkeley, argues that "violating a legal regulation and violating an ethical principle are not the same thing. Ethics and law are related of course or at least we hope they are. But confusing them, not seeing the difference, or worst of all reducing an ethics programme to a compliance programme (usually staffed by attorneys rather than ethicists) is a big mistake. In fact, reducing ethics to little more than compliance may lead to more non-compliance and more regulatory infractions than if ethics (the real thing) were allowed to share the corporate agenda with compliance. Compliance means operating in conformity with. Compliance is not ethics."

Drug Trials

This is precisely what is happening in the case of The Millennium Biotechnology Policy in Karnataka announced in 2000. Every year the Bio events are held with fanfare and the Government claims that almost every month a biotech venture is coming to Karnataka. If we examine the ethical side of each venture it leaves much to be desired. The objectives of the Millennium Biotech Policy in Karnataka, among others, are (1) to spread awareness about investment opportunities in biotechnology, genomics, bioinformatics, biofuels, contract research etc to the entrepreneurial community, (2) to outline a set of incentives and concessions for the biotechnology industry to attract investments in the State, (3) to provide specific infrastructure as well as enhance human re-sources for the development of biotechnology and (4) to provide appropriate institutional framework to achieve the objectives. It is also mentioned that each Biotech company shall constitute a bioethics committee to consider ethical and legal issues in the area of their work. The public is not aware of how many bioethics committees have been formed in which companies and with what consequences. Particularly in contract research for undertaking drug trials human ethics assumes critical importance.

Since the announcement of the Millennium Biotech Policy in 2000 many biotech events and processes in the field of agriculture and medicine are emerging in Karnataka and one does not know the regulatory and ethics monitoring processes established in the Department of Biotechnology.

There is total ignorance and non-involvement of the Department of Agriculture either in promotion or in regulating or in benchmarking ethics in GM cotton crop technology. More GM crops like GM tomato,GM rice, GM potato are all in the pipeline and nobody knows who, how and when they will be regulated. The cost of mismanaged and mis-regulated technology is going to be high. In the case of GM cotton crop it was all the way Monsanto/ Mahyco driven BT Cotton technology that was pushed right in the farmers field. Right from the sale of BT Cotton seeds to the cultivation and the subsequent harvest there was neither regulation nor any ethical assessment of the BT cotton cultivation by the farmers.

More and more new drugs will be released in the market and the Government of Karnataka and the contract research companies have to declare their ethical practices to research subjects/individuals who are subjected to drug trials.

Roche Global Development which is trying their new drugs has this to say on confidentiality of records and patient privacy and concerns: "The patient who is consented to subject himself or herself for drug trial has a right to privacy and all information that is collected in the context of the particular drug trial is kept confidential that is possible by law. The Roche Global Development will not voluntarily disclose the concerned person's medical record such as the information of the person's health, how the person has responded to treatment, any side effects, and the result of tests earned out during the trial period. Data will be analysed to determine how the drug has worked on the person.

Sensitive area

"Occasionally at any time during or after the study the Roche Staff and FDA health authorities will be granted direct access to the person's medical records so that they confirm that the information collected during the study is accurate. In these circumstances alone the person's identity would be disclosed..."

Biotech affects animals, human beings and their livelihood. It is not like regulating Electricity generation and distribution. Regulating new and emerging biotech products and processes are highly people-sensitive. It is very easy to benchmark financial and product standards but most difficult to benchmark ethics in biotech products. It is hoped that the Vision Group of Karnataka, headed by Kiran Muzumdar, would benchmark ethics in the biotech ventures more stringently and share it with the public.

Politics and Policy of Ending Hunger

With Prof. Amartya Sen, getting Nobel Prize in Economics the interest of every policy maker in hunger issues has been revived. The same bureaucrats years ago dubbed the issues of malnutrition, hunger, child mortality and morbidity as non-issues. The hot ones like bridges, buildings and mega plans for hightech hospitals caught the fancy of young bureaucrats in developing countries. Thanks to the collapse of Capitalism among Asian Tigers and the collapse of Communism in Russia the hunger and malnutrition issues have come to the fore once again. People in Russia are not able to get their food rations and shadow on many poor rice farmers in Indonesia is looming large. Other countries in Africa are no better. In India if onion and common salt prices can skyrocket, we do not know what will happen to rice, wheat and pulses in the days to come. Green revolution will soon evaporate and the food basket, and "family pot" of the poor households in States like MP, Bihar, Orissa and UP - the heartland of India may turn out to be empty. None of the political manifestoes of the parties which are going to the polls are concerned with hunger issues.

Against this background one day workshop of the NGOs of MP at Bhopal on 30th October, on fighting hunger and malnutrition organised by the Hunger Project an international advocacy NGO on hunger has gone unnoticed by the press and the media which are busy in chasing election politics and not the politics of the hunger. Issues such as - can the government alone end hunger and malnutrition? What constitutes public action for ending huriger? Who are the critical players in this game of ending hunger? Is food availability enough to end hunger? If not what else is needed? What is the fate of public distribution system in MP? Are two meals enough to end hunger? What is the entitlement of kids and pregnant women to the food and who ensures that entitlement? What is the culture of food? What are those cold and hot food habits which make women and children more malnourished even when food is available? These and many more were the endless questions that were brainstormed in this workshop by the NGOs. At the end of the workshop many agreed to prepare Janpad level hunger free plans in selected Janpads/Blocks by the select NGOs and implement and monitor them for ending hunger over a period of time.

The first and foremost issue in any programme connected with hunger and malnutrition is the one related to the ability of the family to buy food (purchasing power) or the ability to produce food on its own land or the land of the others. The poorest households or the ultra poor more often do not have any of these' strengths and ability. So what do we do? Give them purchasing power (employment) or give them land. Unfortunately with the failure of land reforms and demographic explosion land is just not available, and the proportion of landless labour families is increasing. How much employment we can generate in drought and rainfed areas is still not clear despite community watershed land/soil conservation programmes.

Hunger is not just a question of providing meals to members of.a household. It is just not availability but also the ability of the family in buying it (purchasing power) or procuring it and have access to the source of food (PDS) on a sustained basis so that starvation is avoided. Thus both income and access to food become important strategies in fight against hunger and malnutrition at the family/household level.

Health protection and care-giving within the family is the second strategy to fight hunger in a household. Very often hunger follows malnourishment. Malnourished children and mothers in a household are susceptible for infection and anemia and despite availability of food in the absence of health protection and anemia control maternal mortality and infant mortality will increase. Thus what started as a fight against hunger will become a fight against anemia and mortality. All hunger projects have to be concerned with the twin worries of anemia and mortality particularly of women and kids.

Empowerment of women/mothers both in terms of economic and healthy living is an essential strategy of hunger free projects. Mere economic empowerment is just not enough. A better off woman/mother in terms of income if not also a healthy woman/ mother will not be able to sustain her income. Hence her health and income should go hand in hand. Mothers, not only earn well, but also live well so that her kids and other family members can also live well. Linked to her health and income empowerment is her overall status in the family, in the civil society and in the larger world outside her household and family unit. Her status depends thus on her, education and her ability to negotiate for herself and her family out in the community which has subjugated her. Hunger free projects should have strong elements of empowerment process built into them.One of the problems of managing hunger free projects at the micro-level i.e. level village and block (district is too big an area in MP) is its manageability by an NGO. The ideal area for hunger free activities should be a Block at least not just a few villages. With the emergence of a strong Panchayati Raj in MP we have now a workable structure at all the three levels viz., Village Block and District. Village Panchayat has its own resources, stricter and powers and the Gramsabha is now emerging as a strong body of assembly of adult men and women where people can question the deeds and misdeeds of the panchayat members. Hunger issues can be a subject of great importance in the Gram Sabha meeting. We can pose some relevant issues - how many deaths took place due to hunger, sickness and malnutrition since the last Gramsabha took place, how many pregnant women died due to complications in the delivery and so on. If these questions are repeatedly asked then hunger issues will become part of the agenda of the Gramsabha and that of the people of the Gram/village.

Similarly at the Block level we have now a strong Janpad Body where all the village panchayats are represented and at this level resources reach whether it is JRY money, or EAS money or whatever. Janpad president wants to show some results in his/her tenure. NGO working for the hunger project should work at this level with this body. Working in a few cluster of villages would not spread the hunger free message fast and to a scale where it should make a dent. The selected NGO should liaise with all the woman focused groups at the Janpad level like Self-Help Groups (SHGs) Mahila Mandals mother groups formed under Anganwadis etc.

At the Block Level services like Primary Health Care Services, water and sanitation services, primary education all can be strengthened by working constantly with PHC medical officer, block education officer, sub-engineer of Water Supply (PHED).

Hunger fighting cannot be done without improving the services particularly the Health Services for women/mothers because maternal anemia is linked with hunger/malnutrition.

The sixth element in Hunger free strategy is to improve the information and knowledge of particularly the women groups for self action. Access to information on schemes and programmes particularly the beneficiary oriented ones are crucial for women and vulnerable groups. Who gets what and when should be known to all the families. The NGO working for the hunger project at the Block Level should have the skill and ability to access, both legal and economic information for themselves and to the families with which the NGO works.

The final element in the hunger free project is the' assessment of impact of what we do. There are now clearly accepted impact variables like reduction in anaemia among women, reduction of infant morality, increase in the age of marriage of girls and so on. If this is not documented then the hunger project would not be able to substantiate the successes achieved, and those who give money would not be able to know what is happening to their money! Documentation and constant assessment is the basic requirement of a hunger free project activity.

A final word is on the food security and how nutritional security is often forgotten by those who provide grain (food) security to the families in both rural and urban settlements. The Mission on Food Security which was launched in MP with a fan fare has remained on paper only and there is an urgent need to link up that mission beyond food and to include food+care+health which together can fight not just hunger but, the consequent malnutrition, morbidity and mortality. In the words of Prof. Amartya Sen "We have to take morbidity and mortality issues more seriously in economic planning and planning for growth. Income is only one variable among many that affect our chances of enjoying life and some of the other variables are also influenceable by economic policy".

Availability of health care and other services like education are the important influences on life and death. Let us make the lives of the poor before they die a little enjoyable. Politicians and Bureaucrats are you listening?

7

Emerging Technologies for Whom?

Asia Technology Future

'Charkha vs chip, penicillin vs pentium, sorghum vs software, house vs mouse' these were the choice of words and thoughts heard from the world technology leaders in Bangalore in the recently concluded 12th annual corporate leaders conference of Asia Society in New York. This was jointly organised by Asia Society, CII, government of Karnataka and Dowjones and many other corporate tech companies who exhibited their brand names on the podium. The last annual gathering of Asia Society was held in Shanghai and according to Frank Wisner, vice-chairman, American International Group Inc, US, India and Asia were the three pillars of global modernisation process who have to be watched carefully in the days to come. The Bangalore conclave was inaugurated by the prime minister Atal Behari Vajpayee and in the words of Dowjone's CEO and trustee of Asia Society Peter Kann, it has been the tradition in Asia Society that these conferences be inaugurated by Heads of State to know the policy environment of the countries where technology and business leaders have to work for achieving their business objectives. In his characteristic style the prime minister urged "the Asian leaders in business and technology not to forget that the future of technology and business is only a subset of the future of humanity. Scientific and technological knowledge is the common heritage of human race and its true value lies not so much in profits of individual businesses but in its ability to improve the quality of life of all the children of mother earth. Can we produce affordable vaccines and medicines for all the needy people in Asia? Can we devise new and low cost means of providing drinking water and housing for all?"

The range of topics covered and the thought-leaders who spoke were of great significance for the future Asian economies. Unfortunately after hearing nearly 60 outstanding speakers and moderators spread over in two days in the hi-tech ambience of the Taj West End one left with the feeling that transforming business through technological innovations in Asian region was far more important for these leaders than ensuring a better quality of life to the people through harnessing emerging technologies of the 21st century although every one felt concerned with the digitally divided lot. Except some leaders every one spoke of an either or type of strategy that was unable to provide both penicillin and pentium for the vast majority of the Asian population.

Future Focus

The broad themes discussed were (i) Asia: innovator or follower in the global tech area. Will the digital revolution create a new wave of Asian tigers? What will its impact be on the original tigers? Which business models and practices have succeeded in the region?; (ii) Information Technology: services and software. Does the government really have a role to play in this sector? Is the growth in the Asian and Indian IT sector industry sustainable? How can Asian companies better collaborate among themselves - why does it seem that they just compete amongst each other?; (iii) The 'Tel Me Net' (i.e., Telecom, Media and the Internet); convergence problem. Given the convergence of telecom, media and the internet, how can Asian countries create the right regulatory environment? Will there be reliable nationwide networks offering broadband services? Will broadband ever become a commodity or will it remain a dream? How can government (which largely controls the infrastructure) and the private sector (which drives technology and application) come together for common good? Who will pay for wiring up rural Asia?; (iv) Where are the skill shortages going to occur - both technical and domain? What are some innovative ways to overcome this people problem, off-shoring, etc.? How can one ensure that this does not lead to brain drain?; (v) What are the fast emerging technology hubs and how do they compare against each other? What are the key infrastructure requirements (global parity) and who should build them? How do you market destinations as technology hub? How do we ensure availability of trained qualified manpower for the hubs? (vi) What can we do to ensure 100 per cent access to the benefits of the IT revolution in Asia. Who will be responsible for promoting access to rural Asia?; (vii) Social impact of digital revolution and what are the issues leading to the digital divide? What strategies have emerged to extend the benefits of the internet to those at the bottom of the market? How are the public and private sectors joining forces to share the risks of market development on behalf of the poor? and finally would the old brick and mortar economy survive or die? What old economy reforms are necessary to enable the new economy to succeed? How interdependent are the old and new economies?

Innovations are the hallmark of IT and BT revolutions, though some IT zealots felt as if innovations were taking place for the first time in Asia. The Japanese were dubbed by Americans as copy masters or followers but not innovators forgetting the fact that Japan brought to the not so affluent world consumers the best electronic products. They were not just followers but top class innovators as well. Innovations need not be confined to IT and BT alone and Asia is a home for hundreds of indigenous knowledge (I-K) domains. The question remains how will we build the future in Asia on the existing level of I-K among the people and also carry the marginalised people along the way? No answers were forthcoming on this. When Infosys went to do business in the US in the eighties everyone said how can Indian software engineers do business because when the people in the US sleep Indians wake up! This was when the concept of Virtual Office or 24 hours Office or the Global delivery model was born.This was innovation costing nothing! Innovations are nothing but solutions provided all the time by all the people all the while and it is not a one time task. Innovations cannot thrive when the educational systems from the primary to the university level does not inculcate the value of problem solving and learning abilities among the learners. With half the population of south Asia still illiterate and malnourished how can the countries in the subcontinent become tigers in the digital age?

Yeo Cheow Tong, minister of communications and IT from Singapore spoke of 'public trust' on e-commerce and banking. Not long ago it was the banking system in Asia which brought on the financial crisis and the Asian tigers were overnight made into cats. There was total collapse of the banking system a few years ago. How can we overnight create a supply of e-talent to handle not just innovations but also efficiently operate day to day transactions? It is here where Tong underlined the cultural understanding for customising the software. India and China are now in the words of Jack Welch of GE the 'labour powers' and labour is going to play a crucial role in the days to come in India especially. Nobody threw light on how to convert India's huge unskilled labour into e-labour. Then only Asians can be Net-Users and would-be entrepreneurs.

How do we measure the innovations in Asia and what are the indicators for emerging innovational leadership? W Bowman Cutter, MD of Warburg Pincus suggested five indicators: (a) how many patent applications are filed from time to time (b) share of venture capital funding (c) market share of new technology firms (d) share of leading universities/think tanks in innovations and how they support and empower students with knowledge and finally (f) how much the civil society supported the innovations and how friendly civil society is to the market. The last is the most difficult to achieve as could be seen from the NGO's attack on GM foods and terminator seeds. If everybody innovates who will follow them? Someone echoed the proverb - early birds get worm and the followers get cheese! It was Vijay Mallya of UB group who said he wanted to be a follower than an innovator because he has been successful in doing so!

Working Towards Solutions

Anupam Puri of the Mckinsey group set the tone for discussions on IT-software developers and application service providers (ASPs). IT appears complex in contrast with electrical systems. The US recession will impact the Asian economies in a positive ways i. e., outsourcing will increase but it will be more complex as well. Cost alone will not be the consideration and China and India will dominate the software landscape and will share anywhere around one-fifth of the world software market share (around $ 5 billion). China, due to its poor English language skills, will outbeat India in hardware who will do better in software along with other Asian economies. But among Asian countries inter se there is little coordination. Indian software engineers are more lured by US market than, say, Hongkong or Thailand. Singapore's experiment of an e-passport arrangement with Malaysia makes sense. But it is too early to pass judgment on how it has worked. Asian countries have not done enough to capture the opportunities within Asia itself. The ASEAN summit has not done enough to boost IT revolution within the region.

The critical area of e-governance is linked to issues concerning 'Tel Me Net' convergence. Andres Bande CEO of FLAG Telecom had all praise for China in bringing about this convergence in the Asian region more than any country. Asia has too many regulators and too many walls between 'Tel Me Net' and as a result there are digital distortions and what Bande called dictatorship of the bandwidth and cartel of telecom providers! Telecom sector has a direct multiplier effect on GDP and growth. Telecom Monopolies act in collusion to thwart competition. In Philippines out of six million phone connections four million are idle all the time. In India itself telecom is not ready to go to market and broadcasting is still largely under government control. In China any telecom global player can meet key government functionaries like the prime minister or other ministers. In a time bound way things are done despite their poor democracy and human rights record which have nothing to do with rapid modernisation. China will no doubt emerge as IT superpower in the days to come because they know the value of 'time' and they mean business. All customers - rich or the poor need integrated services and a reliable broadband networks. Hence the need is to collaborate to leverage convergence. In the words of John Helleur, CEO of Mahindra-British Telecom Ltd, we need fibre and not multiple infrastructure. Convergence alone would bring the cost down to the consumer of these services. In the end customer need integrated services. First we set up separate entities and then try to integrate which would increase the integration cost as is happening in India. We have to avoid aggression in advocating an indigenous approach for the risk lies in not moving rather than moving. All foreign investment in telecom is not a security threat. US took 60 years to achieve 50 per cent of convergent services and we can imagine the hard road ahead for Asian economies. Instead of measuring per capita telephone connectivity in a country like India we have enough access by now to most of the habitations through our famous yellow brands called ISD/STD booths across the length and breadth of the country. This was done by one Indian visionary Sam Pitroda. Can we not have another visionary to connect PCs to all these booths and bring at least internet services within the reach of every Indian? We need tech-visionaries than tech-entrepreneurs alone.

As Asian economies move ahead in global and regional integration the biggest worry is about the people who will be left behind. Digital divide is not imaginary but real. How do we ensure inclusive e-learing so that kids get into the digital age. Indian schools in most of the Hindi heartland do not have even chalk and slates and enjoyable learning space. Unfortunately Bangalore is not India and India is not Bangalore or Hongkong or Singapore. Techies forget that any technology has to be people friendly if it is to be embraced by the literate and the illiterates alike. Unfortunately when software moghul N R Narayana Murthy, CEO of Infosys, was asked about the digital divide and what would happen to the rural and to those left ,behind the digital progress his answer was a typical urban Indian response. "There are two Indias - urban and the rural. Do not worry about rural India: once the urban India leaps forward the rural India will somehow catch up". He gave the example of a bright boy in a typical Indian middle class family. The bright boy gets all the support and he outshines and then others emulate him. To him rural India did not matter and it is for the government to take care! Contrast this with what James B Hunt Jr. governor, state of North Carolina in the US said about basic education. The only way to fight digital divide is to take care of basic education and not just higher technical education. He narrated how North Carolina had emerged as a Knowledge Hub.

North Carolina was an agrarian economy several years back. The political leaders consciously took up the task of building a research triangle around Duke University, North Carolina State University and the North Carolina University at Chapel Hill. A state which was known only for agriculture, textiles and furniture has now world's prestigious R and D centre for major pharmas and other hi-tech industries. It did not happen by accident. Eight million people of NC were involved and the basic education of kids and agricultural folks were not forgotten. Today the NC area has nearly 1,00,000 R and D workers. We cannot force scientists to locate themselves in particular areas. Young scientists need an enabling milieu not only for themselves but also for their wives and kids. Without good elementary schools the scientists would leave. Is Narayana Murthy, CEO of Infosys listening?

Another Indian public leader, Andhra Pradesh chief minister Chandrababu Naidu presented his political strategy for promoting technology hubs in AP. Naidu is fanatical about e-governance and IT as the harbinger of human happiness. He narrated how he was promoting IT enabled governance in AP which is by now well known. He believes that normal literacy is only half literacy and only if one is a netizen then one is truly literate, an argument difficult to believe at present when AP is still not 100 per cent literate in terms of 'the three Rs'. If there is any state in India which is using IT in state administration it is no doubt AP. Naidu presented how the state is using GIS for assessing not only the forest cover but also the performance of forest officers in Adilabad district of AP. How can AP become e-enabled if the constitutional bodies like village panchayats are not e-enabled and state controlled schemes like 'Janmabhoomi' programmes are hoisted on the panchayats? Decentralisation is the hallmark of e-governance and politicians like Naidu may do well by strengthening the constitutional bodies than weaken them. Naidu needs to democratise democracy in AP and he should use IT for doing that. In the absence of S M (Simply Marvellous - was the initial given to S M Krishna, Karnataka's CM, in the" conference) Krishna, Karnataka industries minister R V Deshpande narrated how Karnataka was now the preferred destination in IT and BT enterprises. Karnataka has a tradition of promoting R and D with as many as 103 scientific institutions and knowledge centres providing the support. Although Karnataka is mainstreaming IT through its Yuva.com and other IT programmes, a less known state like MP has hit the headlines by bagging the Stockholm Challenge award for its unique Gyan Doot project in Dhar district, which is now serving the farmers and villagers by providing much needed services like providing, at cost, land records, caste certificates, income certificates, etc.

It is nice to provide Technology Parks and Hubs and in the words of Jairam Ramesh build 'IT agrahars' (sacred temples where only some are admitted) but when will they be mainstreamed for the good of people?

In the past we have seen District Industrial Centres promoted by GOI with all their zeal. Now all of them are either closed or defunct but the budget is still spent on them. Why do the states not make use of them as IT hubs instead of targeting the big cities to set up IT agrahars with heavy cost to the state in terms of infrastructure? Scalability is the word used often by IT guys and Tech Parks are not the way to up scale IT activities among the people.

Bridging the Divide

The whole issue of scaling is linked to the problem of digital divide and people skills and how the new economy will move on with the old. Some like Srinivas Ramani Director of R and D of Silverline Technologies felt that digital divide is inevitable and he used the example of sorghum cultivation vs software development. In the ideal situation sorghum growers should move on to software business but it cannot happen on its own. Sorghum growers can live without software but software engineers cannot live without sorghum! There is a mistaken belief among some that in the new economy people can live without food and manufactured goods. The idea is to make the old economy embrace the new economy. Traditionally the economies have progressed from forest to agriculture to manufacturing to services. We cannot jump the levels all have to remain but the number of people dependent on each will keep reducing and services occupy a greater share in the end. It is not a zero sum game. The best example is BPL selling mobile phones to fishermen/women in Kerala and to grape growers in

Nashik. 60,000 villagers in Maharashtra are now using handset along with their kurpis. They are using them because they know the value of these technologies. It is the illiterate farmers of Tanjore and Ludhiana who pioneered the Green Revolution in the 1960s in India. Now the techies have to convince the farmers, small weavers, and manufacturers of tools, traders and the marginalised people to adopt IT to earn and prosper.

The best example of old economy is Ford which is now gearing up to the new economy. In the words of John Larson Director of Ford Asia Pacific, new assembly techniques were followed in Brazil and bids were invited on Internets. One can see the design of cars on the web. Old economy is all about people. One in four persons in South Africa are dying due to HIV / AIDS and the biggest problem faced by Ford is worker shortage. Hence state health care sector and the industries have to' work together in the interest of both. What is needed is what is called the productive diversity, more diverse means more productive people. The best example of old and new economies was shared by Jurn Makihara, chairman of Neoteny Co. Ltd., Japan who analysed the Japanese economy. He said he escaped from the house to catch the mouse! The old Japanese economy was a corporate big size economy and now he feels Japan is moving and should move towards entrepreneurial economy. Japan never believed in small and medium sized entrepreneurial adventures. They were happy with big sized companies which offered lifetime employment and 'also life-time protection.

IT is unpredictable and it cannot be centralised and Japanese are more inclined towards centralisation and that is the reason why Japan is slow in adjusting to new economy. Society has to reduce the risk of leaving the old economy and moving to the new. In the new economy options are fast moving - close or sell or spin off. It is changing the way of thinking itself. It is therefore not the old or the new but a mixture of both. The resources are no doubt critical for both the economies what is needed is efficiency, equity and productivity. That was the message that people like me got and perhaps it was precisely that message the corporate leaders could not, unfortunately, convey.

Bioinformatics and Genomics Bazaar

Bioinformatics and genomics is now emerging as a global business after the gloss on dot.com has started diminishing and concluded (January 15-17, 2001) the recently International Symposium on Bioinformatics and Genomics organised jointly by the government of Karnataka and the CII at the Indian Institute of Science bears testimony to the increasing interest of multinatiomal pharma companies like AstraZeneca, Biocon India and DSQ and others to wean young biotech students and venture capitalists to this emerging lucrative business. In this bazaar efforts were made by US firm like Viaken Systems, SurroMed, Spotfire. Proteome, Molecular Simulations and several others to wean the Indian professionals particularly in IT to switch to the bioinformatics and genomics business. The US in particular is facing an acute shortage of human power in this field and hence this bazaar. In the words of S M Krishna, the chief minister of Karnataka, who inaugurated this symposium there is need to use the emergirig biotechnology for ensuring gains in agriculture, pisciculture and sericulture so as to help the poor farmers. But the three day symposium never touched the topics like how biotech could help impoverished cotton farmers who are committing suicide because of cotton crop failure in Karnataka. how GM foods are good or bad for human health, how Monsanto cotton-seed trials currently conducted in Karnataka would help the cotton farmers, etc. Sadagopan of Indian Institute of Information Technology echoed the words of prime minister Atal Behari Vajpayee who said IT meant India of tomorrow when he said BT meant biotech of tomorrow.

With the arrival of the human genome project genome hunters worldwide are now trying to marry computer technology and biology (better known as computational biology) to transform medicine and life sciences. The IBM has built Blue Gene to help. biologists explore how proteins fold themselves up into their distinctive shapes. A typical protein contains thousands of atoms and the forces on every atom must be evaluated for each time-step. Hence there are global business opportunities for bioinformatics and genomics professionals and the Bangalore bazaar was organised to promote that business indeed.

In the words of Charles Cooney of MIT, USA, a world authority on biotech, who set the tone for the symposium the objectives were (1) to improye the health care by leveraging information technology to the growing needs of pharma companies to find better drugs; (2) Since it takes 8-10 years to find an effective drug before it comes to the market and costs anywhere between $ 300-600 million, how can advances' in bioinformatics and genomics cut short the cycle and bring fast the useful drugs to the market at less cost and more quickly? (3) How do we use the genomic data, the information on protein structure and functions? (4) How do we combine bioinformatics health information and clinical information? At present nearly 40 per cent of the time of a typical pharma company is spent on infarmation processing for effective drug discovery. Mining the data is becoming crucial. IT needs are therefore growing enormously and that is expressed in the' new science of computational biology which is going to hit the curriculum in technology institutes around the world. (5) How do we manage the information supply chain? How do we handle bioinformatics health informatics, and process informatics? (6) Finally, the goal is improved health care the problem is to reduce uncertainty, the approach is to improve information management like acquisition improving data mining and interpretation and the significance of the informatics is better therapeutics to improve the quality of health care.

But as we kept listening to outstanding speakers one after the other, the concern for health care was almost sidelined except by some who could demystify the science of informatics and genomics for the human well-being. The completion of the human, genome sequence and that of many other animals has led to the need to understand the function of all the proteins coded for by the genes. In the words of Tim Harris of the Structural Genomix. structural genomics uses genome information to speed up the process of obtaining the three dimensional structure of the encoded proteins.

Not only will this enable the prediction of the function of many more proteins but it will also allow the design and synthesis of many new drugs for those proteins which are targets for drug discovery which is described as functional genomics. According to Indra, Sanyal of Genome Science, USA total sequencing of the human genome has a tremendous impact on science would result in opening the foodgates of research to discover novel therapeutics to meet unmet medical needs. He claimed that in his Company they have established an efficient high-throughcut functional genomics process that enables the expediting of ciscovery and the clinical evaluation of new therapeutics. When he was asked whether lab work would be replaced by the emerging bioinformatics in the days to come Mathew Woodwork flatly said No, in fact only the nature of lab work would change.

The recurring theme was how we could leverage the bioinformatics for evolving what was called 'personalised medicine'. This sounded more like a designer medicine tailor-made to a particular care-seeking patient. It may or may not happen. This is where majority of the speakers avoided the questions on bioethics although they were very concerned with cross discipline and relationship network, using overlapping domains and what have you. Bio-ethics should also be seriously discussed by bioinformatics pundits because clinical trials are becoming more and more critical. There is so much epidemiological data that has been generated in the past decade by WHO-supported research agencies around the world on all types of diseases and unless that is all analysed it would be a waste of such valuable data for drug discovery. There was no discussion on how clinical trials are done on whom and with what consequences. Obtaining informed consent of the person subjected lo trials is a simple thing. What about trials or animals? What happens to them when something goes wrong or are never revealed? We still remember the horror stories of injectable contraceptive trials conducted in UP heartland some years ago. Very few drug companies reveal stories of failed drugs to the public. In the words of Charles Rockland of RIKEN Brain Science Institute, Japan, biology is not like engineering - precise and defined. Heterogeneity is the problem, and there are no clear cut boundaries piecing the heterogeneous elements is the big job in bioinformatics. In all this bioethical issues are generally forgotten.

At this point of the discussion Christopher Ahlberg, CEO of Spontfire talked about how decisions were taken in actual practice. He said that even now 80 per cent of the decisions are made based on intuition.In his characteristic style he said that there is a tornado of data and the clients need help to analyse the waves of data coming every second. A time has come when pharmas have to 'outsource innovations' and the challenges are basically to turn data into information, organise and relate information into cross domain interrelationships and finally turning those into good decisions. Skills are involved in presentation and the traditional presentation on Pie charts, etc. is dead now and does not work any longer in genomics science.

The entire biotech business is now in the range of some $80 billion and the issues on venture funding were debated hotly in the symposium. The most incisive and frontal attack was made by CII's chief economist Onkar Goswami who said that venture capitalists, have in their 'pockets as much as two and half billion dollars for India and they just do not invest in biotech ventures because they do not know what it is all about. This is primarily because scientists do not know how to communicate with the venture capitalists. Many bright science ideas are not converted into business products and services. Despite the outstanding science graduates turned out by Indian Institute of Science (IISc) none of their scientists know how to leverage science with business. Goswami asked what prohibits the IISc from forming a bioinformatics company with 51 per cent initial share capital. Basically our scientists do not know how to create wealth out of science and ways of corporatising without sacrificing science talent. In this context the interesting experience of transfer of technology unit of the California Institute of Technology (CALTECH) in the US was shared with the audience by Richmond Wolf, associate director of the unit. CALTECH, launched in 1995, has focused on entrepreneurial start-ups and has so far concluded 27 equity deeds. In such start-ups it is not just the technology that works but economics and the nature of relationship with the faculty. The academic bureaucracy does not help in such ventures and the spirit of CALTECH is to combine the three roles of a faculty in one-technologist, entrepreneur and manager. Today CALTECH has earned $ 20 million from this unit. Instead of endowment chairs now they want more such ventures and stock options for the faculty and the institute.

Linked to this whole business of venture capital was the vexed issue of patents and intellectual property regimes. Neil Philips, the senior patent authority of AstraZeneca, UK, who analysed some of the implications was quite evasive when I asked about the havoc created by patented antiretrovirals (ARVs) like AZT drugs in the treatment of HIV/AIDS by US drug companies. When half the population of Africa is being wiped out due to HIV/AIDS there is no sense in sticking to patents for more than say five years and any pharma willing to bring down the cost should be allowed to produce the drug. Patent protection is set at 20 years and governments including developing countries will have to allow the protection of products and process by 2006. TRIPS is supposed to safeguard public health but it is not doing that. In India compulsory licensing could enable our country to manufacture a drug in emergencies without the permission of the patent holder provided that "adequate remuneration is given to that company". CIPLA India has come forward to do this for US AZT manufacturer, but it has not succeeded yet.

The final theme was the human resource and people factor in the whole business of bioinformatics and genomics. The volume of data in public data repositories is growing rapidly. In May 1999 the public archives contained about 700 million bases of the human genome. In May 2000 the figure was more than 3 billion. So pharma companies are establishing their own databases of genomic and proteomic information. In Germany, rest of Europe and US, there is shortage of computational biologists which will continue for years. The tacit and evolving nature of bioinformatics requires the physical presence of individuals who can work in the area within the research environment. Software and models are often specific to the research agenda of the firm and thus cannot be purchased from outside. The Bangalore bazaar on bioinformatics left a ray of hope for the students and smart entrepreneurs who want to venture into these fortune-making ventures. Those like me wondered what would happen to people's health.

Bt Cotton in Karnataka

Suman Sahai's field visit to Wardha to understand the problems of cotton farmers who are opting for Bt seeds is a good beginning to unravel the mysteries of GM crops like Bt cotton in India ('Bt Cotton: Confusion Prevails EPW August 2002). The recently concluded flagship event Bangalore Bio 2002 has thrown several challenges for the Bt cotton crop and its performance in the farmer's field in Karnataka. Monsanto/Mahyco has been allowed by the Genetic Engineering Approval Committee (GEAC) of the government of India to sell commercial Bt cotton seeds MECH-12, MECH-162 and MECH-184 for three years from the current year's cotton sowing season. There is no price control on these Bt seeds and considering the monopoly of Mahyco, farmers would be paying through their nose to purchase them. This author posed several questions in the Bangalore Bio 2002 along with many others on the farmers' perception of Bt cotton and who is to answer their questions in their field situation. Crop scientists are all busy in laboratories and the farmers cannot come to them and seek answers for their cultivation decisions. Monsanto/Mahyco by its very nature of business, cannot do extension work for the benefit of farmers. Its job is to sell the seeds and be done with it. Pushpa M Bhargava, noted molecular scientist, has raised several questions on the trial conducted by Monsanto/Mahyco and the manner of approval accorded by the GEAC without doing a thorough risk assessment ('GMOs: Need for Appropriate Risk Assessment System', EPW April, 13, 2002) This author went to Haveri district in Karnataka and interviewed farmers who were part of the trial run by Mahyco before getting GEAC approval. The farmers were silent spectators on their own fields and the Mahyco plant managers did all the record keeping without involving the farmers, who were given a shawl and a watch for accepting the Bt cotton trials in a grand luncheon gathering held in Davangeri! Basically, the farmers have questions on 'refugium' , under which they have to grow non-Bt cotton within a distance of 20 metres of the Bt variety. This is to allow the bollworms to migrate to the non-Bt variety. In Bt variety the bollworms will not be completely eliminated, and their severity will be minimised at best, thus helping to reduce the cost on pesticides. Their holdings being small, they prefer to mix the crop with any other crop like sun hemp or vegetables to get a good return by mixed cropping. Scientists are divided on this 'refugium' and as the adage goes, if two doctors disagree the patient dies! In this case the farmer may die! Most of our farmers fall in the category of what is called low external input sustainable agriculture (LEISA) and high doses of external inputs like pesticides have already ruined the farmers. According to Kameshwar Rao, founder of the Bangalore-based Foundation for Biotechnology Awareness and Education, "If the refugium is a crop/ species different from GM crop it functions as a virtual pollen sink as no intercrossing is possible. Vegetation surrounding a crop acts as a screen and prevents pollen from drifting away from the field. This purpose is served by any species that grows dense and is taller than the crop like sun hemp. If the refugium and the main crop are the same there will be intercrossing at the interface of the two varieties in both directions and the intended benefits of a considerable part of the GM crop are diluted by the intercrossing. It is not necessary that the refuge belt be formed of only cotton around a Bt cotton field. Even green manure sources like gliricidia and sun hemp will serve the purpose of a pollen sink around a GM crop."

The farmers I interviewed are not convinced of this refugium business. GEAC has mandated that Mahyco should sell along with Bt cotton seeds some non-Bt seeds and farmers are supposed to cultivate them. This is an absurd condition, and who is going to monitor it? The village accountants of the revenue department doing the crop inspection in the villages are not competent to do this. We now have elected village panchayats, for whom agriculture is a major concern. It is unfortunate that GEAC, sitting in New Delhi, has not thought of involving these gram panchayats. The zilla panchayats have an agriculture sub-committee and they should have been involved. Today in all economic reforms and the threat of new technologies invading the countryside, these local bodies have been kept out. Adoption of new agricultural technologies will have serious repercussions and those immediately affected, like the panchayats, have to be involved whether we like it or not.

The second issue is the cost and impact of Bt cotton cultivation on the cultivation cycle. At different stages of the crop maturity from sowing to flowering to final harvest, farmers are exposed to several risks. There is no crop insurance and many cotton growing farmers in Andhra Pradesh and Karnataka have committed suicide by drinking the same pesticides they were spraying on the pests. Bt cotton has the promise of reducing the pesticide cost as much as 70 per cent and this cost saving is a boon to cotton growers. But what the other risks are, nobody knows. Many commercial seeds in the early days of the green revolution failed in germination. The poor farmer had to face the effects. The Seeds Act has many loopholes. According to Bhargava, there is at present no organisation in India which would test on a reliable commercial basis whether a seed is Bt or not. According to present indications, only the farmers who were under the Mahyco trial would be given the Bt seeds for sowing at Rs. 1,600 per packet, which would be sufficient for 1-2 acres. But what about other farmers who want to cultivate? They will buy smuggled Bt seeds as happened in Gujarat. Already there are reports that in Punjab - which was not taken up for Bt trials earlier - a seed company has promised to sell Bt seeds without the approval of GEAC. Thus the farmers will be exploited further and the GEAC is powerless to do anything to clear this imbroglio. The government of Karnataka has fixed April 15-17 every year to hold its bio-technology showcasing in the state. This is a good thing to do because every biotech enterprise can prepare its 'showcasing' events accordingly. Will the 'Vision Group on Biotechnology' of the government of Karnataka arrange to 'showcase' the performance of Bt crop next year and will the farmers be provided a 'platform' to air the problems they would have encountered in cultivating Bt cotton? Many so-called farm leaders in Karnataka want to "steal the show against the Bt seeds" and Monsanto/ Mahyco will tell its side of the story and the real farmers are left high and dry. It is time to act on Bt cotton and "listen" to the farmers' version. The practising farmer - not the absentee farmer - is the best person to do the risk assessment of not just Bt cotton but all genetically modified crops. Why can't our plant scientists train the farmers to record the complete "site" and "sequence" of every genetic change that has occurred in the GMO, and assess the impact on ecology in controlled field trials? Farmers understand well but they may not be able to communicate in scientific terms.

When I was evaluating the water recharging work under the 'pani rokho' programme in Madhya Pradesh, I asked one farmer to show me proof of water recharge. He took me to a corner of his field and showed me the worms called 'mitrakeet' surfacing up from the ground because the water was touching them! There are different ways of understanding ecological factors and our scientists have to work with farmers to learn their version. In the early days of green revolution, farmers were involved with several types of adaptive research trials on their farms. In Tanjore, several paddy varieties were tried first on the farmers' field and then released commercially. From the beginning the trials were in public domain, unlike the GM seeds, which are not known to the public. India has a well established network of ICAR research stations and network of home science colleges attached to agricultural universities. Sharat Chandra, a member of the Karnataka Vision Group of Biotechnology, bemoaned in the Bio 2002 Conference about the lack of public education on biotechnology. This public education has to be done through the existing network of institutions established over the decades, instead of creating new ones. There was this 'lab to land' programme of the ICAR and then we have Krishi Vigyan Kendras all over the country. Why not use them to spread the message of modern and globalised agriculture involving biotechnology? Our institutions are sitting idle and the best way is to use them and make biotech enterpries to leverage with them. Only then will the benefits of biotechnology penetrate in the countryside.

I happened to be in Hirekur *taluk* in Haveri district of Karnataka to attend an Independence Day flag hoisting function this year. Farmers dominated the gathering. Not surprisingly, all talk seemed centred around the Bt *(Bacillus thuringiensis)* cotton experiment in the state. Pleased with my evident interest in their talk, the farmers invited me to see their Bt cotton. I promptly took them up on their offer, and gathered my colleagues in Hope Foundation to tour these fields.

We were clear about how we wished to set about this study. We would tour the fields randomly, and work without bias. All we wanted to do was arrive at an understanding of how Bt cotton is faring in cultivation. But when my colleagues and I landed in Hirekur, we found farmers whispering worriedly among themselves. They seemed convinced that we were part of M D Nanjundaswamy's

Karnataka Rajya Ryota Sangha, and that we would uproot their Bt cotton crop at his behest! It took some convincing to reassure them that we had nothing to do with the Sangha, and that we were merely impartial observers.

The Genetic Engineering Action Committee (GEAC) had approved the release of Mahyco's Bt cotton MECH 12 and MECH 162 in June 2002. Mahyco lost no time in selling its seeds all over Karnataka. By and large, seed dealers have sold MECH 162 - at a cost of Rs. 1,600 for a 400 gram packet - to farmers in Hirekur. They have also given farmers 125 grams of non-Bt seeds to cover one acre of crop land.

We started with Danappa Muthur's cotton fields. In a one-acre plot, Muthur has planted four rows of non-Bt cotton. He informed us that Mahyco gives out an audio cassette with its seeds to guide farmers. He planted four rows of non-Bt cotton according to those guidelines. But he is not happy with the 'refuge plantation' stipulation, because he could have sown some pulses or cash crop in that space.

We examined the already maturing cotton buds. There were green bollworms on them. The farmers assembled explained that when a bollworm is born it is green, turns yellow during its cotton-eating phase, and then turns brown and dies. They also said they need to continue spraying the Mono pesticide, which costs Rs. 250 per litre to counter this threat. Mahyco's assurance that they will not need pesticides after an initial spray or two doesn't seem to have convinced them.

We asked the farmers how Bt cotton is better than hybrid seeds that were already available, like DCH 11. The unanimous opinion was that DCH 11 had lost all pest resistance. In terms of quality and yield, farmers are still anxious about whether Bt cotton will better or match DCH 11 or local varieties like Jayadhar and Laxmi. At any rate, they agreed, if they could save on pesticide, it would be a huge cost saving.

But there are many things farmers have been confused about. For instance, can delinted Bt cotton seed be fed to their cattle? One farmer informed us in all earnestness that some cattle did graze on Bt cotton plants and were still alive. Farmers are also unsure about the strength of Bt cotton. They have heard reports from Gujarat that Bt cotton shreds when spun into yarn. And after it was made into *khadi* cloth, those wearing it developed an itchy sensation. Farmers in Hirekur, however, are not convinced that these reports are true.

A number of farmers are worried about the prospects of the Bt cotton harvest. How and where will they sell this producc? Karnataka has introduced crop insurance for dry crops like *jowar,* maize and other minor crops, but not Bt cotton. This despite the obvious fact that farmers in Karnataka have taken a big risk in cultivating Bt seeds. As regulatory bodies, they promote GM crops but do not protect farmers from multiple risks.

The state government has organised large events discussing the merits and benefits of Bt cotton, but farmers are never invited to these events to present their experiences or doubts. But come October 2002, we will know exactly how Bt cotton has fared in the fields.

Unlike White Cotton, Coloured Lint is Not Tainted by Biotechnology. It also Yields More Per Hectare

BM Khadi is a shy - almost reclusive - cotton scientist at the Agricultural University, Dharwad, Karnataka. But even a stray remark on the need to find substitutes for environmentally-dangerous dyed fabrics is enough to break his reticence. "We have heard stories of chemical dyes playing havoc with our rivers and water systems. It is imperative that we find alternatives," he says. Since the last three years, Khadi and his team of scientists at the Agricultural University's Cotton Research Centre at Hebbali (near Dharwad) have turned their energies on developing brown coloured cotton - the Dharwad Desi Coloured Cotton (DDCC-1, *Gossypium arboreum).*

Studies conducted by this team has shown that DDCC-1 is best-suited for rain-fed areas in Karnataka, such as Dharwad. The crop matures in 170-180 days and yields 800-1,000 kilogrammes (kg) per hectare (ha). Conventional cotton, in contrast, yields about 600 kg per ha. DDCC-1 has a ginning output of 30-32 per cent, which is also higher than that of conventional cotton.

The coloured cotton was produced with painstaking effort. First, genes of the brown cotton were inserted into the white variety to create DDCC-1. Khadi and his team then washed the processed product twenty times - with a variety of soaps - in order to make sure that the lint retained its almond colour.

How has it fared?

Today DDCC-I is grown by 60 farmers in around 70 ha of land in Dharwad. The local Khadi Gramodyog buys back the crop from the farmers. This arrangement works well for the agriculturists, since they are paid about 25 per cent more than that is paid to farmers who grow conventional cotton. According to Khadi, DDCC-I fields have to be at a 50 metre distance from the white cotton farms in order to avoid contamination by the conventional variety. Before every sowing season, scientists of the agricultural university personally supervise that farmers keep this distance.

Khadi and his team are now developing blue cotton farm variety much in demand from maker of jeans. The Dharwad scientists draw much inspiration from the work of the entomologist-turned plant breeder, Sally Fox. Since 1982, this resident of Arizona, USA, has bred pink, yellow, reddish brown and bluish green varieties of cotton. These lints have been commercially marketed as Fox Fibre, registered by the Natural Cotton Colours, Inc, Arizona, USA.

Unlike their US counterparts, the Dharwad Agricultural University scientists have not got their product patented. Says Khadi, "The work of the Cotton Research Station is meant to guide cotton growers and not to get into the corporate agenda." But the fact remains that like the Council for Scientific and Industrial Research laboratories, the Agricultural University scientists must patent its products and plough back the profits into further research and development. The university should also not forget that it is up against multinational giants such as Monsanto. Patenting will, also help the Cotton Research Centre tide over it's resource crunch-the institute has not had much funding from the Indian Council for Agricultural Research or any other government agency.

Commercial potential

The prospects of coloured cotton appear bright because it is untainted by biotechnology. This is because the countrywise quotas on cotton imports, imposed by the US and UK, have ended. All this augers well for the natural cotton growers of Dharwad. But according to economist, Arvind Panagariya of the Colombia University, USA, "India has failed to become a part of the global production chain (of cotton)." This in spite of the fact that textiles and clothing account for nearly 40 per cent of our manufacturing output.

So, shouldn't cotton scientists such as Khadi pick up the gauntlet and link cotton growers to apparel manufactures and traders?

Drug Makers, Providers and Users

The Encyclopaedia Britannica describes therapeutics as the "treatment and care of a patient for the purpose of combating disease or injury, is concerned with the total management of the patient including the supervision of diet and fluid intake, the employment of symptomatic and supportive measures to relieve pain and ease discomfort; the administration of drugs, vaccines and antitoxins, and finally the application of human sympathy and understanding to cope with the disease and the hardship". Unfortunately, the word therapeutics is not frequently used when we hear and talk about drugs for the promotion of good health. Today, the drug industry is a booming business and, with new advances in genomics and genetic engineering and advances in personalised medicine, the industry is poised for exciting growth. But the human side of drug discovery is missing. Clinical trials are done more to comply with regulatory provisions than to 'find out the pain of the disease and what human side is telling'. Against this background, the recently concluded IBC Life Sciences 2nd Annual Asia Pacific Conference: Drug Discovery to Manufacturing held in Mumbai during October 18-20, 2004 was an eye-opener for those who are concerned with the health of the people. IBC Life Sciences, based in Boston, has been a pioneer in providing scientific information for the biomedical and pharma industries. The Mumbai conference drew over 200 global drug experts, biomedical scientists and market players in the drug industry, and shed light on the emerging drug scenario in the rich world more than the poor world, where people suffer for want of basic drugs and therapeutics. The main objectives of the conference were: (1) To take stock of the state-of-art and science of drug discovery and their manufacturing challenges, (2) To build alliances with the Asian and particularly Indian pharma industries and understand outsourcing problems and prospects, (3) To protect intellectual property of newly discovered drugs and the role of the regulatory bodies in India, (4) The readiness of Indian drug companies in conducting clinical trials before the drugs are released in the market, and (5) The prospects for China and India in the business of drug discovery, manufacturing and delivery in the Asian and world markets.

The demographic picture of the world is changing fast. The US and Europe and other G8 countries including Japan will have ageing populations. Fertility rates in the US are falling. In sub-Saharan Africa, the disease burden of HIV / AIDS, tuberculosis and malaria is increasing rapidly with falling purchasing power. But the discovery cost of a drug and the time to reach the market is also increasing. From discovery to delivery it takes 7-8 years and up to a few billion dollars. The Tuft centre for the study of drug development calculates that, taking into account failed products, it now costs $ 900 million to develop a new prescription drug.

According to the CEO of Pfizer, Henry McKinnel, "It commonly takes more than a decade and $800 million to turn a molecule into a pill that can be taken safely by a patient. Second, even with that effort the odds *of* success are long. Finding the right compound is like finding a needle in a Kansas cornfield. We get one profitable drug out of every 5,000 to 10,000 compounds we test. On average, the proceeds from only about three in 10 drugs exceed R and D costs. Who could afford this Herculean effort without incentive? Thus the incentive of patent is unavoidable about, which Abraham Lincoln said it is like adding the fuel *of* interest to the fire *of* genius,"

It is no wonder, therefore, that all multinational drug companies are eager to protect their patents, so that they can recover the costs and make profits. There is nothing unethical about it. What is unethical is, when half of the world's population is afflicted by diseases such as tuberculosis, malaria and HIV / AIDS, the best of brains in drug companies like Pfizer, Roche and Merck, are least interested in developing drugs to combat them. Astra Zeneca of Sweden has to be complimented for its efforts in discovering an effective drug for TB. The emerging target-drugs are all focused on liver, kidney, heart, brain and bone and not on infectious diseases like malaria, TB and HIV/AIDS (MTH), The MTH are considered as problems of the state and the state has no money. The private sector money is for profits and not for public well-being. How do we reconcile these conflicting objectives in drug discovery, manufacturing and delivery to users via physicians? The industrial west wages a war on cancer but not on MTH. With the increase in HIV / AIDS, TB has become more complicated. The well known directly observed therapy short course (DOTS) offers a ray of hope and Astra Zeneca's discovery of a short course combination drug lasting for four months, enters the market early, would be a relief for many developing countries. In the words of Balaganesh who presented the discovery-process of this drug, "Combination drugs are the preferred ones because they would prevent appearance of drug resistance mutants". In the context of HIV/AIDS, these combination drugs are welcome. Disease targeting is more difficult, and in the case of cancer it has been perfected. The same kind of genetically-based precision should be possible in treating other diseases as well with beneficial results. "Most drug firms concentrate on so-called 'blockbuster drugs' one-size-fits-all treatments for common conditions. These sell in huge quantities and are wonderful for profits. But in fact, many such drugs work only on some patients, even if all the patients appear to have the same symptoms. Worse, some patients suffer serious side-effects while others have none. In the worst case, this can lead to the withdrawal of a drug that clearly works, in order to protect that minority. Worries of this kind about Vioxx, a pain reliever given to people with arthritis, caused manufacturer Merck to withdraw it from the market recently two weeks ago".

Withdrawing drugs has more devastating effects on the users (patients). WHO has recently delisted five HIV/AIDS medicines of Cipla and Ranbaxy on the ground that they lacked bio-equivalence. Nobody knows whether they are still being consumed. Interruption of ARV treatment constitutes a serious risk for the individual and may have negative implications from a public health perspective.

WHO is not a supranational regulatory authority. Its list doesn't have any legal status and the Drug Controller of India has to take a decision on the banning of drugs which are found wanting by agencies like WHO. The standards used by WHO for prequalification are more stringent than those applied by national drug authorities. For example, not all countries legally require in vivo bio-equivalence studies (small clinical trails conducted on healthy volunteers) for generic drugs; nor do they have stringent requirements for the quality of active pharmaceutical ingredients (see www.who.int/mediacentre/news/releases/ 2004). Unfortunately, at the recent conference, WHO drug experts were not present, to explain how bio-equivalence studies were conducted and why they were important. However, the sessions on manufacturing were interesting in the sense that multinational drug conglomerates are now looking to Asia for outsourcing not only in manufacturing, but also for contract research work through contract research organisations (CROs). China will be a formidable competitor to India in this area. Although entrepreneurs like Kiran Mazumdar of Biocon and technologists like R Mashelkar made a passionate case for India as a destination for drug discovery and manufacturing (DDM), the fact remains that China is going to have a bigger slice of DDM. A more realistic picture was presented by Lars Walan, vice president of Astra Zeneca, who has worked both in China and India. He said "China's aggressive growth coupled with good health indicators and experienced medical staff has a better chance for DDM activities". There is as yet no data protection nor a good IPR regime in India. But China has already established a good patent regime. The only problem is China's English language capabilities; however, English is now spoken widely by the younger generation. The drawback is that all submissions have to be translated into Chinese, which add to the cost. But Hong Kong, Korea and Taiwan have compensated for the difficulties experienced in China.

Manufacturing Skill

India's manufacturing skills in drugs are yet to be proven. According to WHO, good manufacturing practice (GMP) is a "part of quality assurance which ensures that products are consistently produced and controlled to the quality standards appropriate to their intended use and as required by the marketing authorisation". GMP is also linked to alliance building in the pharma sector because a good partner would always bring in GMP. How to build alliances and sustain them were among the issues that were highlighted at the conference. Nailesh Bhat, compared alliance building to a successful marriage alliance and partnership, where both sides share risks, responsibilities, resources, competencies and benefits. Drugs manufacturing goes beyond GMPs and touches upon good patenting and good clinical practices as well (GCPs). GCPs in India are as yet not mandatory but they have been developed as per WHO standards based on the experience of many countries.

Compliance with GCPs ensures that the rights, safety and well-being of human participants are protected and that clinical trial data are credible. This leads to the issue of clinical trials (CTs), which were not deliberated upon in great detail at the conference, perhaps because the focus was on discovery and manufacture. Much of the controversy around clinical trials the world over either relates to data disclosure or involves patients who were poorly informed about risks. While the integrity of data is certainly an issue in India, a more worrying factor is the unethical recruitment of patient for trial.

According to a report in *(The Economic Times,* 'For Tough Regulation of Clinical Trials', October 29, 2004), "The very attractiveness of India as a clinical trials destination lies in its huge population and prevalence of a large number of diseases, which makes enrolment of trials relatively easy. Unfortunately much of this recruitable universe is also very poor and ignorant. In a country where a patient loses a kidney while going under the knife for appendicitis, there is a serious risk of the gullible and often hapless masses being exploited".

The ICMR and drug controller are poorly equipped to oversee these complex clinical trials. Then simple toxicology studies are not properly done in India, according to Dr. Rashmi Barbhaiya, an NRI and head of Dynametics in India who spoke passionately at the conference on the need for India to be an active player in DDM. The US has an office of human research protection (OHRP) under the department of health that looks into ethical issues in biomedical research. The US Food and Drug Administration (FDA) has a separate human object protection programme. Then there are institutional review boards in each research outfit, apart from a host of NGOs who keep highlighting the issue of failed drugs on humans. NGOs in India are sceptical of CTs. One case in point was the Horlicks study conducted by the National Institute of Nutrition, Hyderabad, in which micronutrient-fortified malted beverage were given to healthy children in some Hyderbad schools. "In the study report, researchers withheld the fact that the beverage in question was Horlicks. The conclusion was tailor-made: the micronutrient fortified malted beverage (a contrived camouflage for Horlicks makes healthy children healthier and NIN-ICMR have proved clinically that Horlicks improves growth of even healthy children!" (statement by Dr. C R Soman, chairman, Health Action by People, Kerala). These may be isolated cases but the Indian medical community has to gear itself for the entry of global pharmaceuticals and make CTs *least doubtful* in the minds of the public. The pharma industry has faced a dilemma - how much of the drug reactions they should reveal to the public? "The clear risk industry is that publication of negative/equivocal trial results could undermine the commercial status of a given product. Equally, failure to enter a study in registry/database initiatives may tarnish a company and its products to the extent that a given product may not be fully adopted into medical practice. Pharma analysts believe that registering a clinical trial could result in some loss of competitive edge and potential loss of commercial advantage." *(Chemical Weekly,* 'Pharma companies contemplate greater transparency in revealing clinical trial information', October 12, 2004, p. 159). In the interests of the pharma industry in India, the more they reveal better it is for the public and for themselves. At the conference not much discussion on CTs was attempted perhaps because the focus was more on discovery to delivery. Another missing issue was an analysis of the functional dynamics of all three partners in drugs, namely, makers, providers like doctors, and consumers like patients. This functional dynamics in the end determines how much the people are going to benefit from the drugs they consume.

Reference

McKinnel, Henry (2003): 'Patent Protection is Good for Patients Too'. Global Business Agenda, World Economic Forum Annual Meeting, Geneva.

Looking for Markets or Tackling Diseases?

The October 2005 concluded Seventh Asia-Pacific Economist Roundtable on Pharmaceuticals in Singapore discussed burning issues like phase III clinical trials, counterfeiting of drugs, cutting edge R&D for drug companies, balancing clinical and business challenges and managing expectations. The elite speakers were Ross Horsburgh, regional medical director of Astra Zeneca in Asia-Pacific region. Michael Richardson, executive medical director of Bristol-Myers Squibb, Ray Velez, corporate asset protection officer of Eli Lilly Asia as well as John Wong of Boston Consulting Group in Asia-Pacific, Vijay Shah, executive director of Nicholas Piramal and C N Potkar of Pfizer India. Shereen El Feki of the *Economist* - a molecular immunologist from Cambridge moderated the whole roundtable as a typical teacher!

The conference no doubt highlighted the business challenges of the pharma sector but the emerging disease scenario of the Asia-Pacific region was missing, as also the drug discovery and R& D challenges to address them. One left with the impression that the Asian pharma sector is worried about its bottom line more than the health of the Asia-Pacific population. The objectives of the roundtable were broadly: (a) to maximise the full potential of the pharma industry in the region; (b) to cope with the challenges of the growth in generic drugs; (c) take up increased clinical trials in Asia-Pacific region: and (d) to counteract the emergence of counterfeit drugs and extend the pharmaceuticals life cycle.

In the words of Michael Richardson, executive medical director, Asia-Pacific, Bristol-Myers Squibb:

> Asia Pacific is at the forefront of the current epidemic of diabetes. In 1998 it was estimated that globally, there were already 140 million people with diabetes. The World Health Organisation (WHO) predicts that this number will rise to 300 million by the year of 2025. Of these, more than 159 million will be in Asia. Although much heterogeneity exists,rising prevalence rates are being seen throughout the region and appear to be closely associated with a combination of genetic predisposition and environmental risk factors such as westernisation change in nutrition decreasing physical activity levels and central obesity.

There was neither any discussion nor presentation by public health experts from agencies like WHO on the HIV/AIDS scenario in the Asia-Pacific region. Of all the drugs approved in the US by FDA in the past two decades, only a fraction were for tropical diseases like HIV/AIDS, malaria and tuberculosis. These diseases are unfortunately present in countries in Africa and parts of Asia, where the poor cannot buy expensive drugs. There is a serious shortage of lifesaving drugs like anesthetics, antivenins for poisonous snake bites, steroids for premature infants, anti-clotting drug for hemophilia, an injectable drug used in cardiac resuscitation, antibiotics for sexually transmitted diseases, antiretrovirals for HIV/AIDS and most importantly, vaccines for preventing childhood diseases.[1]

The generic drug market is a very complicated field and there was not much discussion on when to licence patented drugs, how long patents have to be honoured and what the pros and cons of manufacturing generic drugs to meet the public health needs of poor countries in south Asia are. The generic market is expected to grow at almost 11 per cent pa in next five years and Asia-Pacific is a key growth driver according to Srini Srinivasan, country head and general manager. Sandoz Philippines, Malaysia and Singapore. The presentation on clinical trials in China by Anthony Bishop, associate director, business development. Quintiles Asia highlighted three pressing needs in conducting phase III trials, namely better trial design reducing time and cost by balancing increased productivity and representative data and simultaneous global registration in large markets. There was no discussion on setting standards for clinical trial registration. Whilst everyone seems to agree on the need for trial registration, there are differences of opinion about which trials should be registered, what information should be made publicly available at the onset of a trial, what information should be disclosed after a trial is completed, and where the trials are to be registered. Furthermore, registers exist for different purposes and contain different levels of detail, and it is fair to say that many existing registers are underused, not easily accessible and unwieldy.[2] Increasingly countries are moving towards setting up of national registers (e.g. Australia, Japan, India and South Africa) and national capacities to establish such registries has to be strengthened. South Asia affords a huge captive population for clinical trials in the years to come and we have to be careful with the various processes of clinical trials.

The generic and counterfeit drug markets almost coincide in a poor economy and according to Ray Velez. corporate asset protection officer. Asia-Pacific, Eli Lilly Asia, counterfeiting is a permanent thorn in the side for manufactures. Before the advent of the internet, the distribution of counterfeit was restricted to personal relationships and/or contacts. The internet has changed the playing field. Anyone with internet access can find a source of supply for any kind of counterfeit goods, including drugs, auction sites. B2B sites, message boards and search engines. The WHO has unveiled the world's first web-based system for tracking fake drugs: the Rapid Alert Systems (RAS), which allow members of the public to report discoveries of counterfeit medicines as fast as possible.[3] According to WHO up to 10 per cent of the medicines available on the global market are fake - representing the sales of over US$ 35 billion per year and that developing countries, particularly those in the Mekong region of south-east Asia, were most affected and the victims are very often the rural poor who cannot afford to buy drugs from legitimate outlets.[4] The type of drugs which are counterfeited are common antibiotics, pain killers and multi-vitamins, which are extremely popular or too expensive for the local markets. In Africa the counterfeit version of antiretrovirals for HIV/AIDS are beginning to appear. Public health centres in Africa and South Ssian countries have low stocks of essential drugs due to poor health budgets and this encourages a market for counterfeit drugs. In Philippines only 30 per cent of essential drugs are in stock.

The Economist roundtable did bring in distinguished pharma industry leaders to share their experiences but in the absence of users and consumers (Patients) it did not provide a well-rounded view of the drug situation in the Asia-Pacific region.

References

1. See for an interesting analysis of the drug companies, Marcia Angell. *The Truth About the Drug Companies.* Random House, New York, 2005.

2. See www.thelancet.com. Vol. 365, May 28, 2005.
3. RAS can be accessed online at http://218.11.249.28/ras.
4. See *Medical Tribune,* June 2005, p. 10.

Fighting Diseases or Drug Makers?

The world over diseases affecting humankind are being tackled by therapeutics, doctors and care givers. But in today's America the drug makers are deciding the health of the nation and not the doctors. This is evident from the spate of drug scandals that the country is witnessing now.

The most famous case is the latest award against the drug giant Merck which has been asked to pay by a Texas jury $ 250 million to the wife of a patient who died of heart attack after consuming Vioxx, a pain killer manufactured by Merck.

The drug has since been withdrawn from the market. Vioxx was used by more than 20 million patients before it was withdrawn on the basis of a clinical study that found; cardiovascular problems in some patients who used it longer than 18 months.

Merck is facing more than 4000 law suits and analysts estimate that it may ultimately have to pay tens of billions of dollars in liability awards to plaintiffs drawn from the huge pool of Vioxx users.

Big companies involved

In another case the Attorney General of California sued 39 drug companies recently accusing them of milking the State of California of millions of dollars by overcharging for medicines. Big global pharmas like Glaxo Smithkline and Bristol Meyers Squibb are involved in this.

Marcia Angel, a former editor of The New England Journal of Medicine, says in her bestseller *The Truth About Drug Companies* that the US drug companies are now promoting diseases to fit their drugs. Instead of promoting drugs to treat diseases!

As the population gets old, new types of ailments are coming to the fore. Some are in the nature of ageing and are part of the ageing process. New types of ailments are discovered by drug companies to bring out what Marcia Angel calls me-too drugs, some minor variations of the old drugs only to create markets and sell them with impunity.

Nearly everyone experiences heartburn from time to time. The remedy used to be a glass of milk or an over the counter antacid to relieve the symptoms.

But now heartburn is called acid reflex disease or gastroesophageal reflux disease (GERD) and the disease itself is marketed along with drugs to treat it.

GlaxoSmithKline's Paxil, for instance, was approved to treat something called social anxiety disorder, said to be a debilitating form of shyness! The best way to sell drugs in the US is to sell psychiatric illness.

Similarly the normal sexual life cycle has been distorted and a new phenomenon has been invented called erectile dysfunction and a drug called Viagra is being sold like anything.

Tropical Diseases

Of all the drugs approved in the US by FDA in the past two decades, only a fraction were for tropical diseases like HIV / AIDS, malaria and tuberculosis. These diseases are unfortunately present in countries in Africa and parts of Asia, where the poor cannot buy expensive drugs.

According to some doctors in the field of public health, both in the US and in developing countries, there is serious shortage of life saving drugs like anesthetics, antivenins for poisonous snake bites, steroids for premature infants, anticlotting drug for hemophilia, an injectable drug used in cardiac resuscitation antibiotic for sexually transmitted diseases and antiretrovirals for HIV/AIDS and most importantly vaccines for preventing childhood diseases.

It is a shame that a country like the US, which is worried about weapons of mass destruction (WMDs) in other countries, is not able to produce harmless humanitarian vaccines against childhood diseases affecting its own children, let alone children of other countries.

According to the World Health Organisation, the supply of combined DPT vaccine was so short in the US in 2000 that the premier health agency, the Centre for Disease Control (CDC), was forced to recommend that infants receive only the first three of the five recommended doses, eliminating the booster doses.

The CDC also recommended the deferral of the second dose of the measles, mumps, and German measles vaccine and the chicken pox vaccine.

As globalisation goes on, new markets like South Asian markets for drugs become attractive for the US drug makers and they would shift their marketing strategies to capture the young baby boomers in countries like India, Pakistan and Bangladesh.

New diseases would be discovered by these drug giants. To do this clinical trials would be manipulated to prove the efficacy of these drugs.

This is where countries like India have to watch carefully so that our healthy citizens are not treated as guinea pigs for the clinical trials conducted by US drug companies. Will our Health Ministry and the drug inspectorates in different states be able to face such a situation and take preventive action much before the drugs damage our healthy population?

To Outsource or not: The US Dilemma

Ever since the telecast of the documentary on Business Process outsourcing from the US on the Discovery Channel by Thomas Friedman of the *New York Times,* the debate on outsourcing has intensified in the US. John Kerry the Presidential candidate has gone on record to say that "wanting to export more of our jobs overseas" is not going to help the US economy. But President Bush's Head of Council of Economic Advisors N Gregory Mankiw says "outsouring is just a new way of doing international trade and that makes it a sound thing". Many US reseachers on International trade and gobalisation have been writing in full force to argue for more outsourcing and not less to get the benefits of booming educated manpower at "cheap rates" in countries like India.

Writing in the Foreign Affairs (June, 2004) Daniel Drezner, a researcher from California says politicians want to be popular among voters when this issue is debated and he says, "Scapegoating foreigners for domestics business cycles is smart politics and protecting domestic markets give leaders the appearance of taking direct and decisive action on the economy." Drezner adds that "when forced to choose between statistical evidence showing that trade is good for the economy and anecdotal evidence of job losses due to imports and competition, American go with the anecdotes."

American Outcry

Just as we have in India the Swadeshi Jagran Manch, conservative Americans are also floating forums like Resue American Jobs, Save US Jobs, Coalition for National Sovereignty and Economic Patriotism, etc. In February 2004 Senate Democrates announced their intentions to introduce Jobs for America Act requiring US companies to give public notice of three months of any plan to outsource 15 or more jobs. In the past two years more than 20 State Legislatures in the US have introduced Bills designed to make various forms of offshore outsourcing illegal.

McKinsey Global Institute estimates that the volume of offshore outsourcing; will increase by 30 to 40 per cent every year for the next five years. McKinsey predicts that for every dollar spent on outsourcing to India US gains $ 1.12 to $ 1.14. There is no wonder why the US companies are so eager to set up shop in India. Thomas Friedman's documentary vividly portrayed how the Bangalore middle class English-speaking girls are monitoring the American accents, in the several call centre set up in and around Bangalore and how they are getting rich. When the US argues for increased globalisation it has also to accept the free trade principles which it is not doing. Few support the cause of free trade for its own sake out of principles and certainly not the US corporate leaders.

Outsourcing by US companies is not happening just now. It started ten years back quietly when the American Express set up back office operations in India. Nobody cared about it because the number of jobs leaving US was lower than jobs created in the US economy. Delta Airlines outsourced 1000 call centre jobs to India in 2003 but the $ 25 million in savings allowed the firm to add 1200 reservation and sales positions in the US. Very few know that 90 per cent of jobs in the US require geographic proximity like high technology oriented innovations, high technology Labs and knowledge centres like the US Universities and such jobs are not shifted.

Fluid Situation

Certain manufacturing jobs are being shifted and that too involving unskilled labour. But here again the situation is fluid. Prof. Uday Karmarkar of UCLA, writing in the June issue of Harvard Business Review, say that "between 2000 to 2003 more than two million US manufacturing jobs were lost to outsourcing. About 10 million service jobs could be lost to all causes. As technology turns information services into industrialised components on assembly line, jobs will become ripe for the plucking by offshore outsourcing. Manufacturing work has tended to migrate from countries with high labour costs to those with low cost regardless of culture/language. Information trade like call centres will follow culture and language."

Basically three languages predominate in the world of business, English, Spanish and Chinese. India has a lead on English and it will have advantages over other contries in grabbing call centres. Manufacturing jobs are likely to shift more to India than to China provided Indian labour becomes more skilled and aggressive than follow the public sector culture of strikes and hartals.

The message is loud and clear that outsourcing has come to stay in the world. Unfortunately the political leadership in the US is still not prepared to accept it. The problem of offshoring is team one of economics than psychology - people feel that their is jobs are threatened. Politicans have to deal with people's psychology everywhere. Hence the US politicians are dealing with this psychology and are doing everything possible to "show" the ordinary American folks by bringing in all types of laws which are ineffective.

Emerging National Biotech Policy

The stakeholders meeting hold in June 2005 to finalise the National Biotechnology Policy, jointly organised by Prof. M S Swaminathan and Dr. M K Bhan, Secretary of the Department of Biotechnology at the MSS Research Foundation in Chennai, augurs well for the country. Just as war is too serious a matter to be left to generals, public policy-making, which affects millions of ordinary folks, is too serious a matter to be left to scientists, bureaucrats and ministers.

It was therefore heartening to see a cross-section of civil society activists, scientists and biotech corporate executives sharing their ideas and concerns in the meeting held to finalise a National Biotechnology Policy. For the first time, we see a concern for evolving a biotech policy that would serve the needs of a large number of farmers who are craving for new crop technologies and patients who are in need of fighting, deadly diseases like HIV/AIDS, malaria and tuberculosis which are killing thousands.

At the same time, it also aims trying to attract investments in high investment areas like the pharmaceuticals and education sectors, which would have to supply technical manpower for the growing biotech industries in the country in the days to come.

Balancing interests

How do we balance these interests? What are the regulatory and monitoring mechanisms that we need to establish at different levels in the country so that proper care and caution is ensured in the sharing of the benefits of the emerging biotechnologies? How do we ensure that established ministries like those of agriculture, health and environment both at the Centre and in the states, take up these challenging tasks, and not instead depend on a nascent Department of Biotechnology of the Centre, for ideas and actions?

How do we find resources to establish competent and effective regulatory bodies in India? How do we promote excellence in research in the emerging biotechnology\fields, like the development of genetically-engineered crops for semi-arid areas? How do we promote and establish educational institutions which would adequately cater to the manpower needs of the biotech industries?

These were some of the policy issues that were articulated, and there was a broad consensus on some of the major issues like the need for a Strong Regulatory Framework for the effective monitoring of biotech products released from time to time, and for compensatory support for those who consume biotech products like drugs and the farmers who grow GM crops. As Dr Bhan said, why cannot we have a regulatory body for the Biotechnology sector, like the Election Commission of India that has stood the test of time for holding fair elections? We need to invest lot of time and money to build such a regulatory body in the country and to train its staff in the complex issues of biotechnology regulation. Ministries like agriculture, health and environment must lose some of their "egos" and work at evolving this regulatory body for the biotechnology sector because in the final analysis, it is these parent ministries that must bring about change.

These ministries should act not only at the Central level but also at the state level. The Ministry of Agriculture and the state-level agricultural universities must all act "together" for monitoring GM crops. They cannot do this sitting in the Krishi Bhavan of New Delhi or in the state university campuses. Unfortunately, some organisations monitor these GM crops and publish sensational news to the detriment of the farmers. Many GM crops like golden rice, GM tomatoes, etc. are in the pipeline and they should not be, released unless their effectiveness on the farmer's field is tested for at least three years.

Area of concern

Another area of concern is the manpower and the talent pool for the biotech sector: It is not like the BPO sector or the manpower needs of the call centres. We are dealing with "human lives", and all biotech companies have to be subjected to 'bioethics', which is never taught. Biotech colleges/institutes are now mushrooming without any standards, and churning out half -baked graduates to man these difficult biotech enterprises, which is dangerous. The All India Council for Technical Education (AICTE) is incapable of regulating these mushrooming educational institutes.

Even the universities and the Indian Institutes of Technology (IITs) have no capacity for undertaking frontier biotech research. Recently, the NIH (National Institute of Health) in the US banned its employees from consulting for biotech and pharmaceutical companies and even from owning shares in such campanies. According to the principles of scientific ethics, there is more danger to science and technology in India from the unholy trinity of fabrication, falsification and plagiarism. We hope that Indians would get the best from the emerging biotechnology policy.

Biotechnology : Policing or Regulating ?

The report presented by M S Swaminathan (hereafter MSSR) to the union minister for agriculture in October 2004, on bio-technology regulation, particularly agribiotech, needs to be discussed among a cross-section of farmers, environmental activists, policy-makers and agricultural scientists. We need to establish, in this country of farmers, a faith and willingness to take up transgenic crops without fear and with concern for the safety of consumers in mind. The world over, attitudes on farming are divided. On one side are cost-conscious cultivators who use chemical fertilisers and often grow genetically modified crops, which are considered to be harsh on the environment and are supposed to produce residue-tainted food. On the other side are organic farmers who use methods that are less harmful on the environment and that produce healthy food but they are criticised for not generating high yields to feed the growing population. In India, the perception on GM foods is sharply divided and if we can establish the rules of the game for both GM seed sellers and environmental groups, and most importantly for growers/farmers who are the real stakeholders, then we can hope to accept transgenic foods and fibre for our growing needs without any fear. The terms of reference of the MSSR were: (I) formulate a draft long-term policy on the application of biotechnology in agriculture; (2) suggest modifications in the existing administrative and procedural arrangements in order to streamline and harmonise decision-making under various ministries/organisations; (3) suggest a future role for the ministry of agriculture view of the developments taking place the field of agriculture biotechnology; and (4) generate awareness on matters relating to agriculture biotechnology.

On all these counts the report leaves much to be desired. Maybe this is because the government wanted a quick report but, unfortunately, implementing the suggestions of such reports cannot be quick since many players and stakeholders are involved. The MSSR makes out a case or an apex National Biotechnology Regulatory Authority (NBRA) with two wings, one for agri and food biotech and another for medical and pharma biotech. The chairperson of this NBRA is supposed to provide leadership for both wings; so far so good. But when we come to the constitution or the agri-biotechnology regulatory wing we are disappointed to see that there is no representation for farmers. The report says, "It will have five part-time Members dealing with the following areas, viz. Member (agriculture, animal husbandry, fisheries and forests). Member (health and food safety), Member (Environment). Members (Social and Gender Audit) and Member (IPR and legal affairs)." There will be a state level Regulatory Advisory Board and a Risk Assessment and Communication Committee at the district level. At all the three levels, viz, national, state and district, there is no representation for farmers of GM crops.

The report stresses the importance of awareness building on genetic literacy among schools, colleges, panchayats and Krishi Vigyan Kendras (KVKs) but does not spell out how the risk assessment of GM crops at the village level should be carried out, who must be involved and what steps they must follow. There are more than 460 KVKs to cover the 460 districts of India and they have scientific staff to carry out risk assessments of all GM crops in cooperation with zilla panchayats, taluka panchayats and village panchayats. Today, in AP and Karnataka, more than 20,000 acres of Bt cotton is grown and neither the state agriculture department or the agricultural universities nor the KVKs have done any risk assessment of Bt cotton. Farmers are not sure of the quality of Bt seeds and neither is market support for Bt cotton is assured by the state. Farmers have sold Bt cotton mixing it with DCH and other commercial variety of cotton. The report is silent on how and who will test the GM seeds and who will prosecute dubious GM seed sellers under the provisions of Seeds Act. Risk assessment of GM is a complex process. In US where GM crops like maize and cotton have already made strides, risk assessment of GM crops is still not perfected. When Bt cotton seeds were sown Mahyco kept telling farmers to keep refugium around the Bt cotton to capture bollworms and disable them. In the words of GM crop scientist Mark L Winston (2003), "The farmers do not want any pests to thrive and providing areas in which to deliberately grow pests on crops is not an agronoMic practice that intuitively appeals to farmers. Consequently, the refuges actually set out in their fields tended to occupy their least productive land, were often not irrigated and were frequently sprayed with insecticides..." (I) Many small farmers in Karnataka cannot afford space for the refuge and they have grown chillies along with Bt cotton as a mixed crop with good results. If we want farmers to grow GM crops they need to understand the best scientific advice on refuge crops, on insect resistance management and so on. Unfortunately our agricultural universities and state agriculture departments have failed to guide farmers and today farmers have nowhere to go for advice on these emerging crop technologies. MSSR makes out a case for, "an integrated GM Seed-cum-Crop insurance system to promote desirable new technologies and confer benefits to resource poor small farmer families". The crop insurance scheme that Karnataka had developed for normal crops has been a disaster in the last three crop seasons. Farmers ended up paying more premium than getting any compensation for the loss of crops. Rather than GM crop insurance, the government should spend more money to provide farmers with assured quality inputs and markets.

MSSR has also made a pointed reference to the "linkages between organic farming and GM crop technologies and the need for protecting organic and traditional farming zones from potential cross pollination by GM crops". Worldwide there is a fear that wind blown or bee carried pollen from GM crops contaminate organically grown crops and whether consumers will tolerate the infiltration of GM genes into organic produce. Organic agriculture has now become an Industry in the US and if India has to retain its traditional and organic agriculture more thought has to be given to make it really organic. The question is how organic is our organic agriculture? Organic food sales grew at a rate of 20 to 25 per cent and sales in US reached US $ 6.6 billion in 2000, making up slightly more than 2 per cent of the food market. The report has not spelt out how to stop such GM infiltration into organic farms but they are perhaps difficult to specify in such a brief report.

In the past the release of GM seeds in the market by Monsanto/Mahyco was clouded in mystery and nobody knew where the trials were carried out, on whose farms and with what consequences. The report has streamlined the procedure of testing and release of GM seeds by entrusting the job to All India Coordinated Research Projects, the sole body for the testing of GM crop varieties under the supervision of ICAR. Already there are a plethora of agencies in the field like the state agricultural universities, crop research stations of the state governments, ICAR managed research stations, the district level KVKs, etc. and clear-cut responsibilities have to be laid down for them. These agencies continue doing crop research in isolation on 'elite crops' rather than on 'orphan crops'. There has to be proper coordination between all of them so that the GM farmer gets a broad picture of GM crop technologies. In addition, many environmental NGOs raise alarm bells about GM crops and the farmer is totally confused with the multiple opinions that are expressed through a sensational media.

We still have large pockets of open and hidden hunger in the country and malnourished mothers and children often hit the headlines in the media. The claim is that GM crops can tackle malnutrition and hunger issues. In the words of the MSSR, "A food based and not drug based approach is needed to overcome hidden hunger caused by deficiency in the diet of micronutrients such as iron, iodine and vitamin A". Linked to this issue of hunger and malnutrition is the issue of labelling and safety of GM foods. In the US, the FDA has refused to label GM foods on the following grounds, "Foods developed through GM processes [do not] present any different or greater safety concern than foods developed by traditional plant breeding methods. The 'potential' harm were mainly expressions of concern of the unknown." In India we need to build, over long periods of time, the proof of food allergens in GM food crops and we need to build labs to do this first —and then think of labelling. The rice that our poor children and mothers eat has no vitamin A or beta-carotene, which is metabolically converted into vitamin A. The Rocketfeller Foundation has spent a staggering amount to carry out research for GM rice to yield beta-carotene, through its International Rice Biotechnology Programme started in 1984 and since then, it has invested over US $ 10 million in rice biotechnology research. ICAR has to invest huge money to carry out research before we conclusively assert how good golden rice would be for our population.

The MSSR makes a suggestion to allocate Rs. 150 crore to establish agri-biotech parks in every state, but makes no mention of the huge resources needed to evolve our own golden rice to meet the fast growing needs of the population. We do not need any such agri-biotech parks and, if the performance of IT parks are any indication, they have mostly remained show-pieces to tempt overseas companies. Many software firms have set up their ventures outside these IT parks. The money earmarked for parks must be spent for GM technology transfer to farmers through KVKs instead. The ICAR and All India Coordinated Research project should announce a research agenda on GM crops that is relevant for our farmers. Indian farmers are badly in need of good crop technologies - high yielding but heavy input cost reducing- as the green revolution has already become history.

India's patchy policies on farming are neither satisfying agri-biotech companies who want to move ahead with new GM crops, nor consumers who want to know whether their food is genetically engineered. Environmentalists who fear that transgenic crops may be inflicting irrevocable harm on ecosystems already damaged by demographic pressure are also not satisfied. If the new body called the National Biotechnology Authority, as suggested by MSSR, can promote better understanding of biotechnology issues through autonomous science then Indian farmers would be a happier lot.

Reference

Winston, Mark L (2003): *Travels in the Genetically Modified Zone.* Universities Press (India). Hyderabad.

Epilogue

Where do we go from here after reading the past stories of development in the preceding pages ? What is the future of people, processes, politics and policies that shape the destiny of the most ordinary people of India and other developing countries? Will the Globalization impoverish the people without skills and those without access to markets? What is the structure of governance that would evolve in the years to come - will it be people friendly or market friendly ? What would be the interface between State, Market and the Civil Society which will impact the well-being of the people at large? Will the emerging technologies around the world make the lives of the poor and the neglected better of or worst off? Will they get better jobs? These simple issues pop up as we ponder over the future development scenario in this Millennium. The scenario depends on who is questioning and who is answering. If the respondent is an activist or a leftist we get an answer which would be against LPG (liberalization, privatization and globalization). If he/she is a tech-friendly and tech savvy entrepreneur we get a rosy picture of a world where poverty would end because of technologies and wealth generating entrepreneurship. If he/she is a Politician we get an answer eulogizing the virtues of equity conscious Leader who would end poverty. If he/she is a God man or woman one gets an answer that the best way to end poverty - is through God realization (though these God men and women themselves lead a Jet set life of luxury !) If he/she is a scientist or an academician we get an answer which will fix Knowledge.at the center of all change.

As the future catches us we get an unprecedented cascading effects of digital, genetic and knowledge revolutions in our everyday life (Juan Enriquez. "As the Future Catches you - How the Genomic and other forces are changing your life, work health and wealth" Random House, New York. 2000) But will it affect the last man or woman or the last child in countries where food, shelter, water are getting scarce. Consider, in the words of Juan Enriquez, what will happen, when your genetic code can be digitally imprinted on ad ID card and your insurance company and the employer see that you are genetically disposed to heart diseases. Pharmaceutical products are developed so that you can eat genetically modified broccoli to protect yourself from cancer. Cloning will be as common as in *vitro fertilization* and scientists can influence the genetic design not only of other species but of your own children. Creating wealth no longer requires many hands. Lone individuals are giving birth to entire new industries that rapidly become bigger than the economies of most countries on earth but create fewer jobs.

Contrast this future with the present as reported by Frontline Magazine of The Hindu dated March 24, 2006 "Villages for sale in Vidarbha. Debt ridden farmers announce that their villages and some of their kidneys are for sale" More than 300 farmers have committed suicide since June 2005 and distressed farmers have set up kidney sale Centers in many villages because they have nothing else to sell except their body parts. Agrarian crisis has reached its worst form in many parts of India with suicides of farmers emerging as the worst indicator of the crisis. Again compare P Sainath's lead stories in The Hindu for several months in the years 2005-2006 with Juan Enriquez's "As the Future Catches you". Boya Madhiletti - a Farmer in Andhra Pradesh - went to the Government "help line" for aid ended up in hospital and then in Jail. There is an Official Help line for Farmers in the most progressive State of Andhra Pradesh in India. This farmer out of deep frustration as a result of crop failure and subsequent indebtedness went to the "help line". Digital help line cannot solve the institutional crisis affecting the farmers. In the wake of rapid globalization the farm sector has been affected not because globalization is bad but because of the inability of the State to foresee the future and take advance steps to support the farmers with better technologies market and price support and enable the farmer to compete in local and global markets. The agrarian crisis is one example in India which demonstrates the failure of the State to empower the farmers not just with market or price support but with the overall support of the State to the farm sector like transfer of farm technologies through extension education, input regulation and standardization of farm practices etc. When 70% of India's population is still pursuing farming the best of global technologies and farm practices should reach the farmers. We see a reversal *of* Gandhian principle which said "Greatest good of the greatest number. Now in the wake of globalization we see a greatest good of the smallest number in India. We have to reverse this trend if we want equity at the Center of development.

As these Thoughts from the Dust settle (they are not going to settle anyway) we keep asking very many questions on the future and the prospects for tomorrow. This author is not a Futurist but many eminent Thinkers on the world of Tomorrow have predicted that the future is going to be rather unpredictable. According *to* W Warren Wagar "humankind would make transition from techno liberal capitalism to social democracy in a peaceful manner without armed violence and without the kind of injustice that violence almost breeds. But such a peaceful transition it seems unlikely or at least unlikely in every country and in every part of the world". He further predicts that "as long as the world is governed by a Central Guidance system, in which day-to-day decision making is vested in huge bureaucratic apparatus - no matter what its historical origins, official world view, or initially pious intentions - the danger remains that the apparatus willlearn how to disempower the people it was created" (See Yorick Blumenfeld" Prospects for Tomorrow - Scanning the Future - 20 Eminent Thinkers on the world of Tomorrow, Thames and Hudson, London, 1999)

As the future approaches we have to think of broken boundaries and the global greed - local and the global collide and merge. The most ordinary, the unskilled and the marginalized have to compete for "spaces" and this space is going to be grabbed by the more smart and the knowledgeable. Knowledge is going to be a critical factor for survival in the years to come and poor societies can hope to become rich first through literacy, education and finally through knowledge acquisition. The next Century would really be knowledge-driven.

As these Thoughts from the Dust settle we hope that our Institutions which Govern us at all levels are repaired or drastically reformed so that if they are to support a pattern of cultivation rather than one of exploitation we must put in them in the hands of good and visionary leaders so that they lead those Institutions for the good of all and not for a few. These Institutions are not just national ones but also the global ones like the UN bodies and the super power Institutions.

Finally as these Thoughts from the Dust settle, there would be storm as well, storm of ideas, of actions, of disappointments and despondency, of joys and sorrows of ordinary folks of India that is Bharat, this author would continue to capture them and thus the journey is never ending. As the woods are lively and dark we have miles to go and miles to go !

Index

E

F

G

R

V

W

Y

Z